Your All-in-One Resource

On the CD that accompanies this book, you'll find additional resources to extend your learning.

The reference library includes the following fully searchable titles:

- *Microsoft Computer Dictionary*, 5th ed.
- *First Look 2007 Microsoft Office System* by Katherine Murray
- Windows Vista Product Guide

Also provided are a sample chapter and poster from *Look Both Ways: Help Protect Your Family on the Internet* by Linda Criddle

The CD interface has a new look. You can use the tabs for an assortment of tasks:

- Check for book updates (if you have Internet access)
- Install the book's practice file
- Go online for product support or CD support
- Send us feedback

The following screen shot gives you a glimpse of the new interface.

Windows
Vista Step by Step

Microsoft

Welcome	Additional eBooks

Welcome to the Windows Vista Step by Step companion CD. Here you will find invaluable resources, including eBooks, practice files, and resources for Vista.

- MS Press Online
- Product Support
- CD Support
- Feedback
- Author Connection

View the eBook

View the entire book on your desktop as a pdf. You will need the Adobe Reader download from Adobe.com.

⊙ Check for Book Updates

Search

Need to locate something in Windows Vista Step by Step eBook? Enter keywords for a full text search.

[_____] (Go ›)

⊙ Browse CD Contents

Sample Files

You can practice with files referenced in Windows Vista Step by Step by installing them on your computer.

[Install Sample Files]

© 2007 Microsoft Corporation. All rights reserved. Terms of Use.

Microsoft

Microsoft® Office Word 2007 Step by Step

Joyce Cox and Joan Preppernau

Published by
Microsoft Press
A Division of Microsoft Corporation
One Microsoft Way
Redmond, Washington 98052-6399

Library of Congress Control Number: 2006937018

Printed and bound in the United States of America.

2 3 4 5 6 7 8 9   QWT   2 1 0 9 8 7

Distributed in Canada by H.B. Fenn and Company Ltd.

A CIP catalogue record for this book is available from the British Library.

Microsoft Press books are available through booksellers and distributors worldwide. For further information about international editions, contact your local Microsoft Corporation office or contact Microsoft Press International directly at fax (425) 936-7329. Visit our Web site at www.microsoft.com/mspress. Send comments to mspinput@microsoft.com.

Acquisitions Editor: Juliana Aldous Atkinson
Project Editor: Sandra Haynes

Body Part No. X12-48764

Contents

What do you think of this book? We want to hear from you!

Microsoft is interested in hearing your feedback so we can continually improve our books and learning resources for you. To participate in a brief online survey, please visit:

www.microsoft.com/learning/booksurvey/

11 Creating Documents for Use Outside of Word   305

12 Customizing Word   329

What do you think of this book? We want to hear from you!

Microsoft is interested in hearing your feedback so we can continually improve our books and learning resources for you. To participate in a brief online survey, please visit:

www.microsoft.com/learning/booksurvey/

About the Authors

Joyce Cox

Joyce has 25 years' experience in the development of training materials about technical subjects for non-technical audiences, and is the author of dozens of books about Office and Windows technologies. She is the Vice President of Online Training Solutions, Inc. (OTSI). She was President of and principal author for Online Press, where she developed the *Quick Course* series of computer training books for beginning and intermediate adult learners. She was also the first managing editor of Microsoft Press, an editor for Sybex, and an editor for the University of California. Joyce and her husband Ted live in downtown Bellevue, Washington, and escape as often as they can to their tiny, offline cabin in the Cascade foothills.

Joan Preppernau

Joan is the author of more than a dozen books about Windows and Office, including the popular *Microsoft Windows XP Step by Step*. Having learned about computers literally at her father's knee, Joan's wide-ranging experiences in various facets of the computer industry contribute to her enthusiasm for producing interesting, useful, and reader-friendly training materials. Joan is the President of Online Training Solutions, Inc. (OTSI) and an avid telecommuter. The power of the Internet and an obsession with technology have made it possible for Joan to live and work in New Zealand, Sweden, Denmark, and various locations in the U.S. during the past 15 years. Having finally discovered the delights of a daily dose of sunshine, Joan has recently settled in San Diego, California, with her husband Barry and their daughter Trinity.

The Team

Without the support of the hard-working members of the OTSI publishing team, this book would not exist. Susie Bayers and Marlene Lambert guided the editorial process, and Robert (RJ) Cadranell guided the production process. Jaime Odell copyedited the book, and Jan Bednarczuk created its index. Lisa Van Every laid out the book using Adobe InDesign, and Jeanne Craver processed the graphics. Another important member of our team, Microsoft Press Series Editor Sandra Haynes, provided invaluable support throughout the writing and production processes.

Online Training Solutions, Inc. (OTSI)

OTSI specializes in the design, creation, and production of Office and Windows training products for information workers and home computer users. For more information about OTSI, visit

www.otsi.com

Introducing Word 2007

Microsoft Office Word 2007 is a sophisticated word processing program that helps you quickly and efficiently author and format all the business and personal documents you are ever likely to need. You can use Word to:

- Create professional-looking documents that incorporate impressive graphics such as charts and diagrams.

- Give documents a consistent look by applying styles and themes that control the font, size, color, and effects of text and the page background.

- Store and reuse ready-made content and formatted elements such as cover pages and sidebars.

- Create personalized e-mail messages and mailings to multiple recipients without repetitive typing.

- Make information in long documents accessible by compiling tables of contents, indexes, and bibliographies.

- Safeguard your documents by controlling who can make changes and the types of changes that may be made, removing personal information, and applying a digital signature.

The 2007 release of Word represents an extensive overhaul and update from previous versions. You'll notice some obvious changes as soon as you start the program, because the top of the program window has a completely new look, described in Chapter 1, "Exploring Word 2007." But the improvements go way beyond changes in appearance. Throughout this book, we include discussions of each new feature that is likely to be useful to you and how and when to use it.

> **Tip** Included in the back of this book is a four-color poster provided for your reference. This convenient guide points out some of the best new features of the redesigned Office user interface and includes tips to get you started. You will learn about these features and many more while working through this book.

New Features

Because there are so many new features in this version of Word, we don't identify them with a special margin icon as we did in previous versions of this book. We do, however, list them here. If you're upgrading to Word 2007 from a previous version, you're probably most interested in the differences between the old and new versions and how they will affect you, as well as how to find out about them in the quickest possible way. The sections below list new features you will want to be aware of, depending on the version of Word you are upgrading from. To quickly locate information about these features, see the Index at the back of this book.

If You Are Upgrading from Word 2003

If you have been using Word 2003, you will soon realize that Word 2007 is not just an incremental upgrade to what seemed like a pretty comprehensive set of features and tools. In addition to introducing a more efficient approach to working with documents, Word 2007 includes a long list of new and improved features, including the following:

- **The Ribbon.** No more hunting through menus, submenus, and dialog boxes. This new interface organizes all the commands most people use most often, making them quickly accessible from tabs at the top of the program window.

- **Live preview.** See the effect of a formatting option before you apply it.

- **Building blocks.** Think AutoText on steroids! Predefined building blocks include sets of matching cover pages, quote boxes, sidebars, and headers and footers.

- **Style sets and document themes.** Quickly change the look of a document by applying a different style set or theme, previewing its effect before making a selection.

- **SmartArt graphics.** Use this awesome new diagramming tool to create sophisticated diagrams with 3-D shapes, transparency, drop shadows, and other effects.

- **Improved charting.** Enter data in a linked Microsoft Office Excel worksheet and watch as your data is instantly plotted in the chart type of your choosing.

- **Document cleanup.** Have Word check for and remove comments, hidden text, and personal information stored as properties before you declare a document final.

- **New file format.** The new Microsoft Office Open XML Formats reduce file size and help avoid loss of data.

If You Are Upgrading from Word 2002

In addition to the features listed in the previous section, if you're upgrading from Word 2002 (part of the Microsoft Office XP system), you'll want to take note of the following new features that were introduced in Word 2003:

- **Reading Layout view.** View and easily read a document on the screen without needing to print it, and use buttons on the Reading Mode Markup toolbar to make comments, highlights, and revisions.
- **Thumbnails.** Get an overview of a document by displaying small images of its pages.
- **Smart Tags.** Flag items such as names and addresses, and then display a menu of options for performing common tasks with that type of information.
- **Research service.** Locate supporting information in references stored on your computer or on the Internet.
- **Handwriting support.** On a Tablet PC, write your comments in Word documents by hand.
- **Insertion and deletion colors.** When tracking changes and comments in a document, easily distinguish between insertions and deletions and between the changes made by different reviewers.
- **Balloon control.** Independently display or hide revision balloons and comment balloons.
- **Editing and formatting control.** Specify whether and how a document can be modified.
- **Shared workspaces.** Send a file as an attachment and automatically create a workspace on a collaboration site built with Microsoft SharePoint products and technologies.
- **XML capabilities.** Save a Word document as an XML file.
- **Document summaries.** Extract the key points of the document.
- **Readability statistics.** Display statistics that help you gauge the reading level of the document.

If You Are Upgrading from Word 2000

If you are upgrading from Word 2000, you've got a lot of catching up to do, but this upgrade will definitely be worth the effort. In addition to the features listed in the previous sections, the following features and tools, which were added in Word 2002, will be new to you:

- **Styles And Formatting task pane.** Work with paragraph styles and character formatting in an entire document from a single task pane. Create, view, select, apply, and clear formatting from text.

- **Reveal Formatting task pane.** Display the formatting attributes of a text selection.

- **Improved collaboration.** Use the improved Reviewing toolbar when collaborating on documents with colleagues.

- **Improved table and list formatting.** Easily copy, format, and sort tables, and create lists with complex paragraph structures.

- **Improved security interface.** Access security options on a single tab in the Options dialog box.

- **Information protection.** Remove personal information stored as file properties and names associated with comments or tracked changes.

Let's Get Started!

We've been working with Word since its debut, and each version has offered something that made daily document creation a little easier. But this is the first version in a while that has actually had us smiling and even elicited the occasional "Wow!" We look forward to showing you around Microsoft Office Word 2007.

Information for Readers Running Windows XP

The graphics and the operating system–related instructions in this book reflect the Windows Vista user interface. However, Windows Vista is not required; you can also use a computer running Microsoft Windows XP.

Most of the differences you will encounter when working through the exercises in this book on a computer running Windows XP center around appearance rather than functionality. For example, the Windows Vista Start button is round rather than rectangular and is not labeled with the word *Start*; window frames and window-management buttons look different; and if your system supports Windows Aero, the window frames might be transparent.

In this section, we provide steps for navigating to or through menus and dialog boxes in Windows XP that differ from those provided in the exercises in this book. For the most part, these differences are small enough that you will have no difficulty in completing the exercises.

Managing the Practice Files

The instructions given in the "Using the Book's CD" section are specific to Windows Vista. The only differences when installing, using, uninstalling, and removing the practice files supplied on the companion CD are the default installation location and the uninstall process.

On a computer running Windows Vista, the default installation location of the practice files is *Documents\MSP\SBS_Word2007*. On a computer running Windows XP, the default installation location is *My Documents\MSP\SBS_Word2007*. If your computer is running Windows XP, whenever an exercise tells you to navigate to your *Documents* folder, you should instead go to your *My Documents* folder.

To uninstall the practice files from a computer running Windows XP:

1. On the Windows taskbar, click the **Start** button, and then click **Control Panel**.
2. In **Control Panel**, click (or in Classic view, double-click) **Add or Remove Programs**.

3. In the **Add or Remove Programs** window, click **Microsoft Office Word 2007 Step by Step**, and then click **Remove**.

4. In the **Add or Remove Programs** message box asking you to confirm the deletion, click **Yes**.

> **Important** If you need help installing or uninstalling the practice files, please see the "Getting Help" section later in this book. Microsoft Product Support Services does not provide support for this book or its companion CD.

Using the Start Menu

To start Word 2007 on a computer running Windows XP:

→ Click the **Start** button, point to **All Programs**, click **Microsoft Office**, and then click **Microsoft Office Word 2007**.

Folders on the Windows Vista Start menu expand vertically. Folders on the Windows XP Start menu expand horizontally. You will notice this variation between the images shown in this book and your Start menu.

Navigating Dialog Boxes

On a computer running Windows XP, some of the dialog boxes you will work with in the exercises not only look different from the graphics shown in this book but also work differently. These dialog boxes are primarily those that act as an interface between Word and the operating system, including any dialog box in which you navigate to a specific location. For example, here are the Open dialog boxes from Word 2007 running on Windows Vista and Windows XP and some examples of ways to navigate in them.

To navigate to the *Chapter01* folder in Windows Vista:

→ In the **Favorite Links** pane, click **Documents**. Then in the folder content pane, double-click **MSP**, **SBS_Word2007**, and double-click **Chapter01**.

To move back to the *SBS_Word2007* folder in Windows Vista:

→ In the upper-left corner of the dialog box, click the **Back** button.

Back

To navigate to the *Chapter01* folder in Windows XP:

→ On the **Places** bar, click **My Documents**. Then in the folder content pane, double-click **MSP**, **SBS_Word2007**, and double-click **Chapter01**.

To move back to the *SBS_Word2007* folder in Windows XP:

→ On the toolbar, click the **Up One Level** button.

Up One Level

The Microsoft Business Certification Program

Desktop computing proficiency is becoming increasingly important in today's business world. As a result, when screening, hiring, and training employees, more employers are relying on the objectivity and consistency of technology certification to ensure the competence of their workforce. As an employee or job seeker, you can use technology certification to prove that you already have the skills you need to succeed, saving current and future employers the trouble and expense of training you.

The Microsoft Business Certification program is designed to assist employees in validating their Windows Vista skills and 2007 Microsoft Office program skills. There are two paths to certification:

- A Microsoft Certified Application Specialist (MCAS) is an individual who has demonstrated worldwide skill standards for Windows Vista or the 2007 Microsoft Office suite through a certification exam in Windows Vista or in one or more of the 2007 Microsoft Office programs, including Microsoft Office Word 2007, Microsoft Office Excel 2007, Microsoft Office PowerPoint 2007, Microsoft Office Outlook 2007, and Microsoft Office Access 2007.

- A Microsoft Certified Application Professional (MCAP) is an individual who has taken his or her knowledge of the 2007 Microsoft Office suite and of Microsoft SharePoint products and technologies to the next level and has demonstrated through a certification exam that he or she can use the collaborative power of the Office suite to accomplish job functions such as Budget Analysis and Forecasting, or Content Management and Collaboration.

After attaining certification, you can include the MCAS or MCAP logo with the appropriate certification designator on your business cards and other personal promotional materials. This logo attests to the fact that you are proficient in the applications or cross-application skills necessary to achieve the certification.

Selecting a Certification Path

When selecting the Microsoft Business Certification path that you would like to pursue, you should assess the following:

- The program and program version(s) with which you are familiar
- The length of time you have used the program
- Whether you have had formal or informal training in the use of that program

Candidates for MCAS-level certification are expected to successfully complete a wide range of standard business tasks, such as formatting a document or spreadsheet. Successful candidates generally have six or more months of experience with Windows Vista or the specific Office the program, including either formal, instructor-led training or self-study using MCAS-approved books, guides, or interactive computer-based materials.

Candidates for MCAP-level certification are expected to successfully complete more complex, business-oriented tasks utilizing advanced functionality with the combined 2007 Microsoft Office suite of products. Successful candidates generally have between six months and one or more years of experience with the programs, including formal, instructor-led training or self-study using MCAP-approved materials.

Becoming a Microsoft Certified Application Specialist

Every MCAS and MCAP certification exam is developed from a set of exam skill standards that are derived from studies of how Windows Vista and the 2007 Office programs are used in the workplace. Because these skill standards dictate the scope of each exam, they provide you with critical information on how to prepare for certification.

To become certified as a Microsoft Certified Application Specialist for Microsoft Office Word 2007, you must demonstrate proficiency in these six areas:

- **Creating and customizing documents.** You must demonstrate the ability to quickly create and format documents; lay out documents by formatting pages; make documents and content easier to find; and personalize Word 2007 by customizing options.

- **Formatting content.** You must demonstrate the ability to format text and paragraphs, including creating and modifying styles and setting tabs; manipulate text by cutting, copying, and pasting it, and by finding and replacing it; and control pagination with page breaks and sections.

- **Working with visual content.** You must demonstrate the ability to insert and format pictures, clip art, SmartArt graphics, and shapes; insert graphic text by using WordArt, pull quotes, and drop caps; and insert, format, and link text boxes.

- **Organizing content.** You must demonstrate the ability create and use Quick Parts (building blocks); create, modify, and sort lists; create and format tables, including merging and splitting cells and performing calculations; insert and format captions, bibliographies, and tables of figures and authorities; and use mail merge to create form letters, envelopes, and labels.

- **Reviewing documents.** You must demonstrate the ability to move around in a document and switch to a different view; compare and merge documents; and manage tracked changes and work with comments.

- **Sharing and securing content.** You must demonstrate the ability to prepare a document for sharing by saving it in the appropriate format, removing inappropriate or private information, and marking it as final; restrict permissions to a document, set a password, and protect it; and attach a digital signature.

Taking a Microsoft Business Certification Exam

The MCAS and MCAP certification exams for Windows Vista and the 2007 Office programs are performance-based and require you to complete business-related tasks using an interactive simulation (a digital model) of the Windows Vista operating system or one or more programs in the Office suite.

Test-Taking Tips

- Follow all instructions provided in each question completely and accurately.

- Enter requested information as it appears in the instructions, but without duplicating the formatting unless you are specifically instructed to do otherwise. For example, the text and values you are asked to enter might appear in the instructions in bold and underlined (for example, **text**), but you should enter the information without applying these formats.

- Close all dialog boxes before proceeding to the next exam question unless you are specifically instructed otherwise.

- Don't close task panes before proceeding to the next exam question unless you are specifically instructed to do otherwise.

- If you are asked to print a document, spreadsheet, chart, report, or slide, perform the task, but be aware that nothing will actually be printed.

- Don't worry about extra keystrokes or mouse clicks. Your work is scored based on its result, not on the method you use to achieve that result (unless a specific method is indicated in the instructions), and not on the time you take to complete the question.

- If your computer becomes unstable during the exam (for example, if the exam does not respond or the mouse no longer functions) or if a power outage occurs, contact a testing center administrator immediately. The administrator will restart the computer and return the exam to the point where the interruption occurred with your score intact.

Certification

At the conclusion of the exam, you will receive a score report, which you can print with the assistance of the testing center administrator. If your score meets or exceeds the passing standard (the minimum required score), you will be mailed a printed certificate within approximately 14 days.

For More Information

To learn more about the Microsoft Certified Application Specialist exams and courseware, visit

http://www.microsoft.com/learning/mcp/mcas/

To learn more about the Microsoft Certified Application Professional exams and courseware, visit

http://www.microsoft.com/learning/mcp/mcap/

Features and Conventions of This Book

This book has been designed to lead you step by step through all the tasks you are most likely to want to perform in Microsoft Office Word 2007. If you start at the beginning and work your way through all the exercises, you will gain enough proficiency to be able to create and work with all the common types of Word documents. However, each topic is self contained. If you have worked with a previous version of Word, or if you completed all the exercises and later need help remembering how to perform a procedure, the following features of this book will help you locate specific information:

- **Detailed table of contents.** A listing of the topics and sidebars within each chapter.
- **Chapter thumb tabs.** Easily locate the beginning of the chapter you want.
- **Topic-specific running heads.** Within a chapter, quickly locate the topic you want by looking at the running head of odd-numbered pages.
- **Quick Reference.** General instructions for each procedure covered in specific detail elsewhere in the book. Refresh your memory about a task while working with your own documents.
- **Detailed index.** Look up specific tasks and features and general concepts in the index, which has been carefully crafted with the reader in mind.
- **Companion CD.** Contains the practice files needed for the step-by-step exercises, as well as a fully searchable electronic version of this book and other useful resources.
- **Full-color poster.** This handy reference guide introduces you to the basic features of the 2007 Microsoft Office system user interface, which you will learn more about in this book.

In addition, we provide a glossary of terms for those times when you need to look up the meaning of a word or the definition of a concept.

You can save time when you use this book by understanding how the *Step by Step* series shows special instructions, keys to press, buttons to click, and so on.

Convention	Meaning
	This icon at the end of a chapter introduction indicates information about the practice files provided on the companion CD for use in the chapter.
USE	This paragraph preceding a step-by-step exercise indicates the practice files that you will use when working through the exercise.
BE SURE TO	This paragraph preceding or following an exercise indicates any requirements you should attend to before beginning the exercise or actions you should take to restore your system after completing the exercise.
OPEN	This paragraph preceding a step-by-step exercise indicates files that you should open before beginning the exercise.
CLOSE	This paragraph following a step-by-step exercise provides instructions for closing open files or programs before moving on to another topic.
1 **2**	Blue numbered steps guide you through step-by-step exercises and Quick Reference versions of procedures.
1 2	Black numbered steps guide you through procedures in sidebars and expository text.
→	An arrow indicates a procedure that has only one step.
See Also	These paragraphs direct you to more information about a given topic in this book or elsewhere.
Troubleshooting	These paragraphs explain how to fix a common problem that might prevent you from continuing with an exercise.
Tip	These paragraphs provide a helpful hint or shortcut that makes working through a task easier, or information about other available options.
Important	These paragraphs point out information that you need to know to complete a procedure.
 Save	The first time you are told to click a button in an exercise, a picture of the button appears in the left margin. If the name of the button does not appear on the button itself, the name appears under the picture.
Enter	In step-by-step exercises, keys you must press appear as they would on a keyboard.
Ctrl + Home	A plus sign (+) between two key names means that you must hold down the first key while you press the second key. For example, "press Ctrl + Home" means "hold down the Ctrl key while you press the Home key."
Program interface elements	In steps, the names of program elements, such as buttons, commands, and dialog boxes, are shown in black bold characters.
User input	Anything you are supposed to type appears in blue bold characters.
Glossary terms	Terms that are explained in the glossary at the end of the book are shown in blue italic characters.

Using the Book's CD

The companion CD included with this book contains the practice files you'll use as you work through the book's exercises, as well as other electronic resources that will help you learn how to use Microsoft Office Word 2007.

What's on the CD?

The following table lists the practice files supplied on the book's CD.

Chapter	Files
Chapter 1: Exploring Word 2007	02_Opening.docx
	03_Viewing1.docx
	03_Viewing2.docx
	05_Printing.docs
Chapter 2: Editing and Proofreading Documents	01_Changes.docx
	02_SavedText.docx
	03_FindingWord.docx
	04_Outline.docx
	05_FindingText.docx
	06_Spelling.docx
	07_Finalizing.docx
Chapter 3: Changing the Look of Text	01_QuickFormatting.docx
	02_Characters.docx
	03_Paragraphs.docx
	04_Lists.docx
Chapter 4: Changing the Look of a Document	01_Background.docx
	02_Theme.docx
	03_Template.docx
	04_Header.docx
	05_ControllingPage.docx

Chapter	Files
Chapter 5: Presenting Information in Columns and Tables	01_Columns.docx
	02_TabularList.docx
	03_Table.docx
	05_Calculations.docx
	05_LoanData.xlsx
	06_Loan.xlsx
	06_Memo.docx
	06_TableAsLayout.docx
Chapter 6: Working with Graphics, Symbols, and Equations	01_Logo.png
	01_Picture.docx
	02_WordArt.docx
	03_Shapes.docx
	04_Relationships.docx
	05_Symbols.docx
Chapter 7: Working with Diagrams and Charts	01_Diagram.docx
	02_ModifyingDiagram.docx
	03_Chart.docx
	04_ModifyingChart.docx
	05_ExistingData.docx
	05_Sales.xlsx
Chapter 8: Working with Longer Documents	01_Parts.docx
	02_Contents.docx
	03_Index.docx
	04_Bookmarks.docx
	05_Hyperlinks.docx
	05_OtherLogos.docx
	06_Bibliography1.docx
	06_Bibliography2.docx
Chapter 9: Creating Form Letters, E-Mail Messages, and Labels	02_DataSource.xlsx
	02_PreparingData.docx
	03_DataSource.xlsx
	03_FormLetter.docx
	04_DataSource.xlsx
	04_MergingData.docx
	05_E-mail.docx
	06_DataSource.xlsx

Chapter	Files
Chapter 10: Collaborating with Others	*01_Sending1.docx*
	01_Sending2.docx
	01_Sending3.docx
	02_TrackChanges.docx
	03_Comments.docx
	04_Comparing1.docx
	04_Comparing2.docx
	04_Comparing3.docx
	05_Password.docx
	06_PreventingChanges.docx
	07_Workspace.docx
Chapter 11: Creating Documents for Use Outside of Word	*02_Web.docx*
	03_Blog.docx
	04_XML.docx
	04_XMLSchema.xsd
Chapter 12: Customizing Word	*02_Commands.docx*
	03_Toolbar1.docx
	03_Toolbar2.docx

In addition to the practice files, the CD contains some exciting resources that will really enhance your ability to get the most out of using this book and Word 2007, including the following:

- *Microsoft Office Word 2007 Step by Step* in eBook format

- *Microsoft Computer Dictionary*, 5th ed. eBook

- *First Look 2007 Microsoft Office System* (Katherine Murray, 2006)

- Sample chapter and poster from *Look Both Ways: Help Protect Your Family on the Internet* (Linda Criddle, 2007)

Important The companion CD for this book does not contain the Word 2007 software. You should purchase and install that program before using this book.

Minimum System Requirements

2007 Microsoft Office System

The 2007 Microsoft Office system includes the following programs:

- Microsoft Office Access 2007
- Microsoft Office Communicator 2007
- Microsoft Office Excel 2007
- Microsoft Office Groove 2007
- Microsoft Office InfoPath 2007
- Microsoft Office OneNote 2007
- Microsoft Office Outlook 2007
- Microsoft Office Outlook 2007 with Business Contact Manager
- Microsoft Office PowerPoint 2007
- Microsoft Office Publisher 2007
- Microsoft Office Word 2007

No single edition of the 2007 Office system installs all of the above programs. Specialty programs available separately include Microsoft Office Project 2007, Microsoft Office SharePoint Designer 2007, and Microsoft Office Visio 2007.

To install and run these programs, your computer needs to meet the following minimum requirements:

- 500 megahertz (MHz) processor
- 256 megabytes (MB) RAM
- CD or DVD drive
- 2 gigabytes (GB) available hard disk space; a portion of this disk space will be freed if you select the option to delete the installation files

> **Tip** Hard disk requirements will vary depending on configuration; custom installation choices may require more or less hard disk space.

- Monitor with 800×600 screen resolution; 1024×768 or higher recommended
- Keyboard and mouse or compatible pointing device

- Internet connection, 128 kilobits per second (Kbps) or greater, for download and activation of products, accessing Microsoft Office Online and online Help topics, and any other Internet-dependent processes

- Windows Vista or later, Microsoft Windows XP with Service Pack 2 (SP2), or Microsoft Windows Server 2003 or later

- Windows Internet Explorer 7 or Microsoft Internet Explorer 6 with service packs

The 2007 Microsoft Office suites, including Office Basic 2007, Office Home & Student 2007, Office Standard 2007, Office Small Business 2007, Office Professional 2007, Office Ultimate 2007, Office Professional Plus 2007, and Office Enterprise 2007, all have similar requirements.

Step-by-Step Exercises

In addition to the hardware, software, and connections required to run the 2007 Microsoft Office system, you will need the following to successfully complete the exercises in this book:

- Word 2007, Excel 2007, and Outlook 2007

- Access to a printer

- 10 MB of available hard disk space for the practice files

Installing the Practice Files

You need to install the practice files in the correct location on your hard disk before you can use them in the exercises. Follow these steps:

1. Remove the companion CD from the envelope at the back of the book, and insert it into the CD drive of your computer.

   The Step By Step Companion CD License Terms appear. Follow the on-screen directions. To use the practice files, you must accept the terms of the license agreement. After you accept the license agreement, a menu screen appears.

   > **Important** If the menu screen does not appear, click the Start button and then click Computer. Display the Folders list in the Navigation Pane, click the icon for your CD drive, and then in the right pane, double-click the StartCD executable file.

2. Click **Install Practice Files**.

3. Click **Next** on the first screen, and then click **Next** to accept the terms of the license agreement on the next screen.

4. If you want to install the practice files to a location other than the default folder (*Documents\MSP\SBS_Word2007*), click the **Change** button, select the new drive and path, and then click **OK**.

> **Important** If you install the practice files to a location other than the default, you will need to substitute that path within the exercises.

5. Click **Next** on the **Choose Destination Location** screen, and then click **Install** on the **Ready to Install the Program** screen to install the selected practice files.

6. After the practice files have been installed, click **Finish**.

7. Close the **Step by Step Companion CD** window, remove the companion CD from the CD drive, and return it to the envelope at the back of the book.

Using the Practice Files

When you install the practice files from the companion CD that accompanies this book, the files are stored on your hard disk in chapter-specific subfolders under *Documents \MSP\SBS_Word2007*. Each exercise is preceded by a paragraph that lists the files needed for that exercise and explains any preparations needed before you start working through the exercise. Here are examples:

> **USE** the *03_FormLetter* document and the *03_DataSource* workbook. These practice files are located in the *Chapter09* subfolder under *SBS_Word2007*.
>
> **BE SURE TO** start Word and display non-printing characters before beginning this exercise.
>
> **OPEN** the *03_FormLetter* document.

You can browse to the practice files in Windows Explorer by following these steps:

Start

1. On the Windows taskbar, click the **Start** button, and then click **Documents**.

2. In your **Documents** folder, double-click **MSP**, double-click **SBS_Word2007**, and then double-click a specific chapter folder.

You can browse to the practice files from a Word 2007 dialog box by following these steps:

1. On the **Favorite Links** pane in the dialog box, click **Documents**.

2. In your **Documents** folder, double-click **MSP**, double-click **SBS_Word2007**, and then double-click the specified chapter folder.

Removing and Uninstalling the Practice Files

You can free up hard disk space by uninstalling the practice files that were installed from the companion CD. The uninstall process deletes any files that you created in the *Documents\MSP\SBS_Word2007* chapter-specific folders while working through the exercises. Follow these steps:

Start

1. On the Windows taskbar, click the **Start** button, and then click **Control Panel**.

2. In **Control Panel**, under **Programs**, click the **Uninstall a program** task.

3. In the **Programs and Features** window, click **Microsoft Office Word 2007 Step by Step**, and then on the toolbar at the top of the window, click the **Uninstall** button.

4. If the **Programs and Features** message box asking you to confirm the deletion appears, click **Yes**.

See Also If you need additional help installing or uninstalling the practice files, see the "Getting Help" section later in this book.

> **Important** Microsoft Product Support Services does not provide support for this book or its companion CD.

Getting Help

Every effort has been made to ensure the accuracy of this book and the contents of its companion CD. If you do run into problems, please contact the sources listed below for assistance.

Getting Help with This Book and Its Companion CD

If your question or issue concerns the content of this book or its companion CD, please first search the online Microsoft Press Knowledge Base, which provides support information for known errors in or corrections to this book, at the following Web site:

www.microsoft.com/mspress/support/search.asp

If you do not find your answer at the online Knowledge Base, send your comments or questions to Microsoft Press Technical Support at:

mspinput@microsoft.com

Getting Help with Word 2007

If your question is about Microsoft Office Word 2007, and not about the content of this Microsoft Press book, your first recourse is the Word Help system. This system is a combination of tools and files stored on your computer when you installed the 2007 Microsoft Office system and, if your computer is connected to the Internet, information available from Microsoft Office Online. There are several ways to find general or specific Help information:

- To find out about an item on the screen, you can display a *ScreenTip*. For example, to display a ScreenTip for a button, point to the button without clicking it. The ScreenTip gives the button's name, the associated keyboard shortcut if there is one, and unless you specify otherwise, a description of what the button does when you click it.

- In the Word program window, you can click the Microsoft Office Word Help button (a question mark in a blue circle) at the right end of the Ribbon to display the Word Help window.

● After opening a dialog box, you can click the Help button (also a question mark) at the right end of the dialog box title bar to display the Word Help window with topics related to the functions of that dialog box already identified.

To practice getting help, you can work through the following exercise.

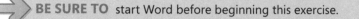

BE SURE TO start Word before beginning this exercise.

Microsoft Office
Word Help

1. At the right end of the Ribbon, click the **Microsoft Office Word Help** button.

   The Word Help window opens.

2. In the list of topics in the **Word Help** window, click **Activating Word**.

   Word Help displays a list of topics related to activating Microsoft Office system programs.

You can click any topic to display the corresponding information.

Show Table of
Contents

3. On the toolbar, click the **Show Table of Contents** button.

The Table Of Contents appears in the left pane, organized by category, like the table of contents in a book.

Clicking any category (represented by a book icon) displays that category's topics (represented by help icons) as well as any available online training (represented by training icons).

Online training   Topic

Category

If you're connected to the Internet, Word displays categories, topics, and training available from the Office Online Web site as well as those stored on your computer.

Back   Forward

4. In the **Table of Contents**, click a few categories and topics, then click the **Back** and **Forward** buttons to move among the topics you have already viewed.

Close

5. At the right end of the **Table of Contents** title bar, click the **Close** button.

6. At the top of the **Word Help** window, click the **Type word to search for** box, type Help window, and then press the Enter key.

The Word Help window displays topics related to the words you typed.

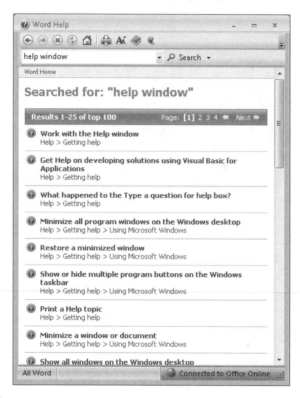

7. In the results list, click **Print a Help topic**.

The selected topic appears in the Word Help window, explaining that you can click the Print button on the toolbar to print any topic.

8. Below the title at the top of the topic, click **Show All**.

Word displays any hidden auxiliary information available in the topic and changes the Show All button to Hide All. You can display or hide an individual item by clicking it. When you click the Print button, Word will print all displayed information.

CLOSE the Word Help window.

More Information

If your question is about Microsoft Office Word 2007 or another Microsoft software product and you cannot find the answer in the product's Help system, please search the appropriate product solution center or the Microsoft Knowledge Base at:

support.microsoft.com

In the United States, Microsoft software product support issues not covered by the Microsoft Knowledge Base are addressed by Microsoft Product Support Services. Location-specific software support options are available from:

support.microsoft.com/gp/selfoverview/

Quick Reference

1 Exploring Word 2007

To start Word, page 6

→ At the left end of the Windows taskbar, click the **Start** button, point to **All Programs**, click **Microsoft Office**, and then click **Microsoft Office Word 2007**.

To open an existing file, page 13

1. Click the **Microsoft Office Button**, and then click **Open**.
2. In the **Open** dialog box, navigate to the folder that contains the file you want to open, and then double-click the file.

To move the insertion point to the beginning or end of the document, page 14

→ Press Ctrl + Home or Ctrl + End.

To convert a document created in an earlier version of Word, page 15

→ Click the **Microsoft Office Button**, and then click **Convert**.

To view multiple pages, page 17

1. On the **View** toolbar, click the **Zoom** button.
2. In the **Zoom** dialog box, click the **Many pages** arrow, select the number of pages, and then click **OK**

To adjust the magnification of a document, page 19

1. On the **View** toolbar, click the **Zoom** button.
2. In the **Zoom** dialog box, click a **Zoom to** percentage or type an amount in the **Percent** box, and then click **OK**.

To display the Document Map, page 19

→ On the **View** tab, in the **Show/Hide** group, select the **Document Map** check box.

To display thumbnails of pages, page 20

→ On the **View** tab, in the **Show/Hide** group, select the **Thumbnails** check box.

To display or hide non-printing characters, page 20

→ On the **Home** tab, in the **Paragraph** group, click the **Show/Hide ¶** button.

To display a document in a different view, page 20

→ On the **View** tab, in the **Document Views** group, click the button for the desired view; or

→ Click a view button on the **View** toolbar at the right end of the status bar.

To switch among open documents, page 22

→ On the **View** tab, in the **Window** group, click the **Switch Windows** button, and then click the name of the document you want to switch to.

To view multiple open documents, page 22

→ On the **View** tab, in the **Window** group, click the **Arrange All** button.

To open a new document, page 24

→ Click the **Microsoft Office Button**, click **New**, and then in the **New Document** window, double-click **Blank document**.

To save a document for the first time, page 25

1. On the **Quick Access Toolbar**, click the **Save** button; or click the **Microsoft Office Button**, and then click **Save As**.
2. If **Browse Folders** is shown in the lower-left corner of the **Save As** dialog box, click it, and then navigate to the location where you want to save the file.
3. In the **File name** box, type a name for the document, and then click **Save**.

To create a new folder while saving a document, page 26

1. Click the **Microsoft Office Button**, and then click **Save As**.
2. In the **Save As** dialog box, navigate to the folder where you want to create the new folder.
3. On the dialog box's toolbar, click the **New Folder** button.
4. Type the name of the new folder, press Enter, and then click **Open**.
5. In the **File name** box, type a name for the document, and then click **Save**.

To preview how a document will look when printed, page 28

→ Click the **Microsoft Office Button**, point to **Print**, and then click **Print Preview**.

To print a document with the default settings, page 31

→ Click the **Microsoft Office Button**, point to **Print**, and then click **Quick Print**.

To print a document with custom settings, page 30

1. Click the **Microsoft Office Button**, and then click **Print**.
2. In the **Print** dialog box, modify the settings as needed, and then click **OK**.

2 Editing and Proofreading Documents

To select text, page 35

→ Word: Double-click the word.

→ Sentence: Click in the sentence while holding down the [Ctrl] key.

→ Paragraph: Triple-click in the paragraph, or double-click in the selection area to the left of the paragraph.

→ Block: Click to the left of the first word, hold down the [Shift] key, and then click immediately to the right of the last word or punctuation mark.

→ Line: Click in the selection area to the left of the line.

→ Document: Triple-click in the selection area.

To delete text, page 38

→ Select the text, and then press [Del] or [Backspace].

To copy or cut and paste text, page 38

1. Select the text, and then on the **Home** tab, in the **Clipboard** group, click the **Copy** or **Cut** button.

2. Click where you want to paste the text, and then in the **Clipboard** group, click the **Paste** button.

To undo an action, page 39

→ On the **Quick Access Toolbar**, click the **Undo** button.

To move text by dragging, page 39

1. Select the text, and then point to the selection.

2. Hold down the mouse button, drag the text to its new location, and then release the mouse button.

To save text as a building block, page 41

1. Select the text. Then on the **Insert** tab, in the **Text** group, click the **Quick Parts** button, and then click **Save Selection to Quick Part Gallery**.

2. In the **Create New Building Block** dialog box, type a name for the building block, make any necessary changes to the settings, and then click **OK**.

To insert a building block in a document, page 42

→ Click where you want to insert the building block. Then either type the name of the building block, and press [F3]; or on the **Insert** tab, in the **Text** group, click the **Quick Parts** button, and select the building block from the **Quick Part** gallery.

To insert the date and time, page 43

1. Click where you want the date or time to appear, and then on the **Insert** tab, in the **Text** group, click the **Date & Time** button.

2. In the **Date and Time** dialog box, under **Available formats**, click the format you want, and then click **OK**.

To use the Thesaurus, page 44

1. Double-click the word you want to replace, and then on the **Review** tab, in the **Proofing** group, click the **Thesaurus** button.

2. In the **Research** task pane, point to the word you want to insert in place of the selected word, click the arrow that appears, and then click **Insert**.

To research information, page 45

1. On the **Review** tab, in the **Proofing** group, click **Research**.

2. In the **Research** task pane, in the **Search for** box, type the research topic.

3. Click the arrow of the box below the **Search for** box, click the resource you want to use, and then in the results list, click a source to view its information.

To translate a word or phrase into another language, page 46

1. Select the word or phrase, and then on the **Review** tab, in the **Proofing** group, click the **Translate** button.

2. In the **Translation** area of the **Research** task pane, select the desired languages in the **From** and **To** boxes to display the translation.

To display a document in Outline view, page 47

→ On the **View** toolbar, click the **Outline** button.

To display specific heading levels in Outline view, page 47

→ On the **Outlining** tab, in the **Outline Tools** group, click the **Show Level** arrow, and in the list, click a heading level.

To collapse or expand heading levels in Outline view, page 48

→ Click anywhere in the heading to be collapsed or expanded. Then on the **Outlining** tab, in the **Outline Tools** group, click the **Collapse** or **Expand** button.

To demote or promote headings in Outline view, page 48

→ Click the heading to be demoted or promoted. Then on the **Outlining** tab, in the **Outline Tools** group, click the **Demote** or **Promote** button.

To move content in Outline view, page 48

→ Collapse the heading whose text you want to move. Then on the **Outlining** tab, in the **Outline Tools** group, click the **Move Up** or **Move Down** button.

To find text, page 51

1. On the **Home** tab, in the **Editing** group, click the **Find** button.
2. On the **Find** tab of the **Find and Replace** dialog box, specify the text you want to find, and then click **Find Next**.

To replace text, page 52

1. On the **Home** tab, in the **Editing** group, click the **Replace** button.
2. On the **Replace** tab of the **Find and Replace** dialog box, specify the text you want to find and the text you want to replace it with, and then click **Find Next**.
3. Click **Replace** to replace the first instance of the text, **Replace All** to replace all instances, or **Find Next** to leave that instance unchanged and move to the next one.

To check spelling and grammar, page 57

1. On the **Review** tab, in the **Proofing** group, click the **Spelling & Grammar** button.
2. In the **Spelling and Grammar dialog** box, click the appropriate buttons to correct the errors Word finds or to add words to the custom dictionary or AutoCorrect list.
3. Click **OK** when Word reaches the end of the Spelling and Grammar check, and then click **Close**.

To remove personal information from a document, page 61

1. Click the **Microsoft Office Button**, point to **Prepare**, and then click **Inspect Document**.
2. In the **Document Inspector** dialog box, select the items you want checked, and then click **Inspect**.
3. In the **Document Inspector** summary, click the **Remove All** button to the right of any items you want removed, and then close the **Document Inspector** dialog box.

To mark a document as final, page 62

1. Click the **Microsoft Office Button**, point to **Prepare**, and then click **Mark as Final**.
2. Click **OK** in the message box, click **Save**, then click **OK** in the finalization message.

3 Changing the Look of Text

To preview and apply styles, page 66

→ Click the paragraph or select the text to which you want to apply a style. Then on the **Home** tab, in the **Styles** group, click the thumbnail of the style you want to apply in the Quick **Styles** gallery.

To change the style set, page 68

→ On the **Home** tab, in the **Styles** group, click the **Change Styles** button, click **Style Set**, and then click the set you want to use.

To apply character formatting, page 69

→ Select the text. Then on the **Home** tab, in the **Font** group (or on the **Mini toolbar** that appears), click the button of the formatting you want to apply.

To copy formatting, page 70

→ Select the text that has the formatting you want to copy. Then on the **Home** tab, in the **Clipboard** group (or on the **Mini toolbar** that appears), click the **Format Painter** button, and select the text to which you want to apply the copied formatting.

To change the font, page 70

→ Select the text. Then on the **Home** tab, in the **Font** group, click the **Font** arrow, and click the font you want.

To change the font size, page 70

→ Select the text. Then on the **Home** tab, in the **Font** group, click the **Font Size** arrow, and click the font size you want.

To apply text effects, page 70

1. Select the text, and then on the **Home** tab, click the **Font** Dialog Box Launcher.
2. In the **Font** dialog box, under **Effects**, select the check box for the effect you want, and then click **OK**.

To clear formatting from text, page 72

→ On the **Home** tab, in the **Font** group, click the **Clear Formatting** button.

To change the color of text, page 72

→ Select the text. Then on the **Home** tab, in the **Font** group, click the **Font Color** arrow, and in the color palette, click the color you want.

To highlight text with a color, page 73

→ Select the text. Then on the **Home** tab, in the **Font** group, click the **Highlight** arrow, and click the color you want.

To select all text with the same formatting, page 73

→ Click the formatted text. Then on the **Home** tab, in the **Editing** group, click the **Select** button, and click **Select Text With Similar Formatting**.

To insert a line break, page 78

→ Click at the right end of the text where you want the line break to appear. Then on the **Page Layout** tab, in the **Page Setup** group, click the **Breaks** button, and click **Text Wrapping**.

To align paragraphs, page 79

→ Click the paragraph, or select multiple paragraphs. Then on the **Home** tab, in the **Paragraph** group, click the **Align Left**, **Center**, **Align Right**, or **Justify** button.

To indent the first line of a paragraph, page 79

→ Click the paragraph. Then on the horizontal ruler, drag the **First Line Indent** marker to the location of the indent.

To indent an entire paragraph, page 80

→ Click the paragraph, or select multiple paragraphs. Then on the horizontal ruler, drag the **Left Indent** or **Right Indent** marker to the location of the indent.

To increase or decrease indenting, page 81

→ Click the paragraph, or select multiple paragraphs. Then in the **Paragraph** group, click the **Increase Indent** or **Decrease Indent** button.

To set a tab stop, page 81

→ Click the paragraph, or select multiple paragraphs. Then click the **Tab** button until it displays the type of tab you want, and click the horizontal ruler where you want to set the tab stop for the selected paragraph(s).

To change the position of a tab stop, page 83

→ Click the paragraph, or select multiple paragraphs. Then on the horizontal ruler, drag the tab stop to the new mark.

To add a border or shading to a paragraph, page 84

1. Click the paragraph. Then on the **Home** tab, in the **Paragraph** group, click the **Borders** arrow, and click **Borders and Shading**.

2. In the **Borders and Shading** dialog box, on the **Borders** tab, click the icon of the border style you want to apply, and then click **OK**.

3. In the **Borders and Shading** dialog box, on the **Shading** tab, click the **Fill** arrow, click the shading color you want, and then click **OK**.

To format paragraphs as a list, page 88

→ Select the paragraphs. Then on the **Home** tab, in the **Paragraph** group, click the **Bullets** or **Numbering** button.

To change the style of a list, page 88

1. Select the list paragraphs. Then on the **Home** tab, in the **Paragraph** group, click the **Bullets** or **Numbering** arrow.

2. In the **Bullets Library** or **Numbering Library**, click the bullet or number style you want to use.

To change the indent level of a list, page 90

→ Select the list paragraphs. Then on the **Home** tab, in the **Paragraph** group, click the **Decrease Indent** or **Increase Indent** button.

To sort items in a list, page 90

1. Select the list paragraphs. Then on the **Home** tab, in the **Paragraph** group, click the **Sort** button.

2. In the **Sort Text** dialog box, click the **Type** arrow, and then in the list, click the type of text by which to sort.

3. Select **Ascending** or **Descending**, and then click **OK**.

To create a multilevel list, page 91

1. Click where you want to create the list. Then on the **Home** tab, in the **Paragraph** group, click the **Multilevel List** button.

2. In the **Multilevel List** gallery, click the thumbnail of the multilevel list style you want to use.

3. Type the text of the list, pressing `Enter` to create another item at the same level, pressing `Enter` and then `Tab` to create a subordinate item, or pressing `Enter` and then `Shift` + `Tab` to create a higher-level item.

4 Changing the Look of a Document

To add a background color to a document, page 97

→ On the **Page Layout** tab, in the **Page Background** group, click the **Page Color** button, and then in the palette, click the background color you want.

To change a document's background fill effects, page 97

1. On the **Page Layout** tab, in the **Page Background** group, click the **Page Color** button, and then click **Fill Effects**.

2. In the **Fill Effects** dialog box, click the tab for the type of fill effect you want.

3. Click the options or thumbnails you want, and then click **OK**.

To add a text watermark, page 97

→ On the **Page Layout** tab, in the **Page Background** group, click the **Watermark** button, and then click the thumbnail for one of the predefined text watermarks.

or

1. On the **Page Layout** tab, in the **Page Background** group, click the **Watermark** button, and then click **Custom Watermark**.

2. In the **Printed Watermark** dialog box, select the **Text watermark** option, and then either click the **Text** arrow and click the text you want, or type the text in the **Text** box.

3. Format the text by changing the settings in the **Font**, **Size**, and **Color** boxes.

4. Select a layout option, select or clear the **Semitransparent** check box, and then click **OK**.

To use a picture as a watermark, page 100

1. On the **Page Layout** tab, in the **Page Background** group, click the **Watermark** button, and then click **Custom Watermark**.

2. In the **Printed Watermark** dialog box, select the **Picture watermark** option, and then click **Select Picture**.

3. In the **Insert Picture** dialog box, navigate to the folder where the picture is stored, double-click the name of the picture, and then click **OK**.

To apply a theme, page 101

→ On the **Page Layout** tab, in the **Themes** group, click the **Themes** button, and then in the **Themes** gallery, click the theme you want.

To save a custom theme, page 103

1. On the **Page Layout** tab, in the **Themes** group, click the **Themes** button, and then click **Save Current Theme**.

2. In the **Save Current Theme** dialog box, in the **File name** box, type a name for the theme, and then click **Save**.

To create a document based on a template, page 106

1. Click the **Microsoft Office Button**, click **New**, and then in the left pane of the **New Document** window, click **Installed Templates**.

2. In the center pane, double-click the thumbnail for the template you want.

3. Replace the placeholder text with your own text, and then save the document.

To save a document as a template, page 108

1. Click the **Microsoft Office Button**, and then click **Save As**.

2. In the **Save As** dialog box, in the **File name** box, type a name for the template.

3. Click the **Save as type** arrow, and then click **Word Template**.

4. Under **Favorite Links**, click **Templates**, and then click **Save**.

To create a new style, page 110

1. Click the text that you want to save as a new style.

2. In the **Styles** group, click the **More** button, and then click **Save Selection as a New Quick Style**.

3. In the **Create New Style from Formatting** dialog box, in the **Name** box, type the new style's name.

4. To make the style available in the template, rather than in only the current document, click **Modify**.

5. At the bottom of the dialog box, select the **New documents based on this template** option, and then click **OK**.

To apply a different template to a document, page 112

1. Click the **Microsoft Office Button**, and then click **Word Options**.

2. In the **Word Options** window, click **Add-Ins**.

3. Click the **Manage** arrow, click **Templates**, and then click **Go**.

4. In the **Templates and Add-ins** dialog box, under **Document template**, click **Attach**.

5. In the **Attach Template** dialog box, locate and double-click the template you want to attach.

6. In the **Templates and Add-ins** dialog box, select the **Automatically update document styles** check box, and then click **OK**.

To insert a header or footer in a document, page 113

1. On the **Insert** tab, in the **Header & Footer** group, click the **Header** or **Footer** button.

2. In the **Header** or **Footer** gallery, click the style you want to use.

3. In the placeholders, type the text you want.

4. On the **Design** contextual tab, in the **Close** group, click the **Close Header and Footer** button.

To insert only a page number, page 117

1. On the **Insert** tab, in the **Header & Footer** group, click the **Page Number** button.

2. Point to a position option in the list, and in the gallery, select a page number style.

To change the format of page numbers, page 117

1. On the **Insert** tab, in the **Header & Footer** group, click the **Page Number** button, and then click **Format Page Numbers**.

2. In the **Page Number Format** dialog box, click the **Number format** arrow, and then in the list, click the number format you want.

3. Select any other options you want, and then click **OK**.

To prevent widows and orphans, page 119

1. Select the paragraphs you want to format. Then on the **Home** tab, click the **Paragraph** Dialog Box Launcher.

2. In the **Paragraph** dialog box, click the **Line and Page Breaks** tab.

3. Select the **Widow/Orphan control** and **Keep lines together** check boxes. Then clear all the other check boxes by clicking them twice, and click **OK**.

To insert a page break, page 119

→ Click to the left of where you want to insert the page break. Then on the **Insert** tab, in the **Pages** group, click **Page Break**.

To insert a section break, page 120

→ Click to the left of where you want to insert the section break. Then on the **Page Layout** tab, in the **Page Setup** group, click the **Breaks** button, and under **Section Breaks**, click the type of section break you want.

To adjust page margins, page 120

→ On the **Page Layout** tab, in the **Page Setup** group, click the **Margins** button, and then click the margin style you want.

5 Presenting Information in Columns and Tables

To format text in multiple columns, page 125

→ Select the text. Then on the **Page Layout** tab, in the **Page Setup** group, click the **Columns** button, and click the number of columns you want.

To change the width of columns, page 126

1. Click anywhere in the first column. Then on the **Page Layout** tab, in the **Page Setup** group, click the **Columns** button, and then click **More Columns**.

2. Under **Width and spacing**, change the setting in the **Width** column or the **Spacing** column, and then click **OK**.

To hyphenate text automatically, page 127

→ On the **Page Layout** tab, in the **Page Setup** group, click the **Hyphenation** button, and then click **Automatic**.

To insert a column break, page 127

→ Click where you want the column break to appear. Then on the **Page Layout** tab, in the **Page Setup** group, click the **Breaks** button, and then click **Column**.

To create a tabular list, page 129

1. Type the text of the list, pressing Tab between each item on a line and pressing Enter at the end of each line.

2. Select the lines of the list, change the **Tab** button to the type of tab stop you want, and then click the horizontal ruler where you want to set tab stops that will line up the items in columns.

To insert a table, page 133

1. Click where you want to insert the table. Then on the **Insert** tab, in the **Tables** group, click the **Table** button.

2. In the grid, point to the upper-left cell, move the pointer across and down to select the number of columns and rows you want, and click the lower-right cell in the selection.

To merge table cells, page 134

→ Select the cells you want to merge. Then on the **Layout** contextual tab, in the **Merge** group, click the **Merge Cells** button.

To add rows to a table, page 135

→ Click in the row above or below which you want to add a single row, and then on the **Layout** tab, in the **Rows & Columns** group, click the **Insert Above** or **Insert Below** button; or select the number of rows you want to insert, and then in the **Rows & Columns** group, click the **Insert Above** or **Insert Below** button.

To convert text to a table, page 136

1. Select the text you want to convert. Then on the **Insert** tab, in the **Tables** group, click the **Table** button, and click **Convert Text to Table**.

2. In the **Convert Text to Table** dialog box, enter the dimensions of the table in the **Number of columns** and **Number of Rows** boxes, select the type of text separator, and then click **OK**.

To insert a Quick Table, page 139

1. Click where you want to insert the table. Then on the **Insert** tab, in the **Tables** group, click the **Table** button, and then point to **Quick Tables**.

2. In the **Quick Tables** gallery, click the table style you want.

To apply a table style, pages 140 and 143

→ Click the table whose style you want to change. Then on the **Design** contextual tab, in the **Table Styles** group, click the style you want in the **Table Styles** gallery.

To total a column of values in a table, page 144

1. Click the cell in the table where you want the total to appear.

2. On the **Layout** contextual tab, in the **Data** group, click the **Formula** button.

3. With the SUM formula in the **Formula** box, click **OK** to total the values.

To insert an Excel worksheet, page 146

→ Copy the worksheet data in Excel, and then in Word, click where you want to insert the copied data, and on the **Home** tab, in the **Clipboard** group, click the **Paste** button.

or

1. In Excel, copy the worksheet data. Then in Word, click where you want to insert the copied data, and on the **Home** tab, in the **Clipboard** group, click the **Paste** arrow, and click **Paste Special**.

2. In the **Paste Special** dialog box, in the **As** list, click **Microsoft Office Excel Worksheet Object**, select the **Paste link** option, and then click **OK**.

   or

→ Click where you want to insert the worksheet, and then on the **Insert** tab, in the **Tables** group, click the **Table** button, and click **Excel Spreadsheet**.

To draw a table, page 152

1. Click where you want to draw the table. Then on the **Insert** tab, in the **Tables** group, click the **Table** button, and then click **Draw Table**.

2. Drag the pointer (which has become a pencil) across and down to create a cell.

3. Point to the upper-right corner of the cell, and drag to create another cell, or draw column and row boundaries inside the first cell.

6 Working with Graphics, Symbols, and Equations

To insert a picture, page 159

1. Click where you want to insert the picture. Then on the **Insert** tab, in the **Illustrations** group, click the **Picture** button.

2. Navigate to the folder where the picture is stored, and then double-click the picture to insert it.

To adjust the size of an object, page 159

→ Click the object. Then point to one of the handles surrounding the object, and when the pointer becomes a two-headed arrow, drag until the picture is the size you want.

To insert clip art, page 161

1. Click where you want to insert the clip art. Then on the **Insert** tab, in the **Illustrations** group, click the **Clip Art** button.

2. In the **Clip Art** task pane, in the **Search for** box, type a word describing what you are looking for, and then click **Go**.

3. In the task pane, click a clip art image to insert it in the document, and then close the task pane.

To move an object, page 163

→ Click the object to select it. Then point to the object, and when the pointer changes to a four-headed arrow, drag the object to the new position.

To quickly copy an object, page 163

→ Click the object, hold down the Ctrl key, and then drag a copy of the object to its new location, releasing first the mouse button and then the Enter key.

To insert a WordArt object, page 165

1. Click where you want to insert the WordArt. Then on the **Insert** tab, in the **Text** group, click the **WordArt** button.
2. In the **WordArt** gallery, click the style you want.
3. In the **Edit WordArt Text** dialog box, type your text.
4. Set the size and other attributes of the text, and then click **OK**.

To apply a drop cap, page 170

→ Click in the paragraph. Then on the **Insert** tab, in the **Text** group, click the **Drop Cap** button, and click the style you want.

To draw a shape, page 172

1. On the **Insert** tab, in the **Illustrations** group, click the **Shapes** button, and then click the shape you want.
2. Point where you want the shape to appear, and then drag to draw the shape.

To group drawing objects, page 174

1. Hold down the Ctrl key, and click each object you want to group.
2. On the **Format** contextual tab, in the **Arrange** group, click the **Group** button, and then click **Group**.

To change the text wrapping of a picture, page 177

→ Select the picture. Then on the **Format** contextual tab, in the **Arrange** group, click the **Text Wrapping** button, and click the wrapping style and attributes you want.

To change the position of a picture, page 177

→ Select the picture. Then point to the picture, and when the pointer changes to a four-headed arrow, drag the picture to its new location.

or

1. Select the picture. Then on the **Format** contextual tab, in the **Arrange** group, click the **Picture** button, and click **More Layout Options**.
2. In the **Advanced Layout** dialog box, on the **Picture Position** tab, set the position options you want, and then click **OK**.

To insert a symbol, page 180

1. Click where you want to insert the symbol. Then on the **Insert** tab, in the **Symbols** group, click the **Symbol** button, and click **More Symbols**.

2. In the **Symbols** dialog box, on the **Symbols** tab, select the font you want.

3. Scroll through the list of symbols until you find the symbol you want, double-click it, and then click **Close**.

To insert an equation, page 182

1. Click where you want to insert the equation. Then on the **Insert** tab, in the **Symbols** group, click the **Equation** button.

2. Type your equation in the equation box that appears in the document.

7 Working with Diagrams and Charts

To insert a diagram, page 189

1. Click where you want to insert the diagram. Then on the **Insert** tab, in the **Illustrations** group, click the **SmartArt** button.

2. In the **Choose a SmartArt Graphic** dialog box, click the diagram layout you want, and then click **OK**.

To add text to a diagram, page 190

→ Click the placeholder text in the **Type your text here** pane or in the diagram shape, and then type your text.

To resize a diagram, page 192

→ Drag a sizing handle around the diagram frame, and then drag the handle to increase or decrease the size of the diagram.

To add a shape to a diagram, page 194

→ Click the diagram shape above or below which you want the new shape to appear. Then on the **Design** contextual tab, in the **Create Graphic** group, click the **Add Shape** arrow, and in the list, click **Add Shape After**, **Add Shape Before**, **Add Shape Above**, or **Add Shape Below**.

To change the diagram layout, page 194

→ Click a blank area in the diagram's frame. Then on the **Design** contextual tab, in the **Layouts** group, click the **More** button, and in the gallery, click the layout you want.

To move a diagram, page 196

→ Point to the diagram's frame (not one of the handles), and when the pointer changes to a four-headed arrow, drag the diagram to its new location.

To change the style of a diagram, page 196

→ Click a blank area inside the diagram's frame. Then on the **Design** tab, in the **SmartArt Styles** group, click the **More** button, and in the gallery, click the style you want.

To insert a chart, page 200

1. Click where you want the chart to appear. Then on the **Insert** tab, in the **Illustrations** group, click **Chart**.

2. In the **Insert Chart** dialog box, click the category of chart you want, click the style you want, and then click **OK**.

To enter data in a new chart, page 201

→ In the Excel worksheet, replace the sample data by clicking a cell, and then typing your own data.

To automatically fit a column to its longest entry, page 201

→ Point to the border between two column headings, and when the pointer changes to a double-headed arrow, double-click.

To edit the data in a chart, page 204

1. Click anywhere in the chart to activate it. Then on the **Design** tab, in the **Data** group, click the **Edit Data** button.

2. In the Excel worksheet, click the cell you want to edit, type the new data, and then press Enter.

To change the chart type, page 207

1. Click the chart. Then on the **Design** tab, in the **Type** group, click the **Change Chart Type** button.

2. In the **Change Chart Type** dialog box, click the chart type you want, and then click **OK**.

To change the style of a chart, page 208

→ Click the chart. Then on the **Design** tab, in the **Chart Styles** group, click the **More** button, and in the **Chart Styles** gallery, click the style you want.

To turn a chart's gridlines on and off, page 209

→ Click the chart. Then on the **Layout** contextual tab, in the **Axes** group, click the **Gridlines** button, point to **Primary Horizontal Gridlines** or **Primary Vertical Gridlines**, and click the option you want.

8   Working with Longer Documents

To delete a building block, page 225

1. In the **Text** group, click **Quick Parts**, and then click **Building Blocks Organizer**.

2. In the **Building blocks** list, select the building block you want to delete, and then click **Delete**.

To create a table of contents, page 227

1. Assuming that the document has paragraphs styled as headings, click where you want to insert the table of contents. Then on the **References** tab, in the **Table of Contents** group, click the **Table of Contents** button.

2. In the **Table of Contents** gallery, click the table of contents style you want.

To update a table of contents, page 229

1. Click in the table of contents. Then on the **References** tab, in the **Table of Contents** group, click the **Update Table** button.

2. In the **Update Table Of Contents** dialog box, click **Update page numbers only** or **Update entire table**, and then click **OK**.

To mark an index entry, page 235

1. Select the word you want to mark. Then on the **References** tab, in the **Index** group, click the **Mark Entry** button.

2. In the **Mark Index Entry** dialog box, click **Mark**.

To create an index, page 236

1. Click where you want to insert the index. Then on the **Home** tab, in the **Paragraph** group, click the **Show/Hide** button to turn off the display of non-printing characters.

2. On the **References** tab, in the **Index** group, click **Insert Index**.

3. In the **Index** dialog box, click the **Formats** arrow, click an index format, select any other options you want, and then click **OK**.

To insert a bookmark, page 239

1. Select the text or item that you want to bookmark. Then on the **Insert** tab, in the **Links** group, click **Bookmark**.

2. In the **Bookmark** dialog box, in the **Bookmark name** box, type the bookmark name (with no spaces) or select one from the list of bookmarks, and then click **Add**.

To insert a cross-reference, page 241

1. Click where you want to insert the cross-reference. Then type the introductory text for the cross reference; for example, For more information, see.

2. On the **Insert** tab, in the **Links** group, click the **Cross-reference** button.

3. In the **Cross-reference** dialog box, click the **Reference type** arrow, and then click the type of reference you want.

4. Click the **Insert reference to** arrow, and then click the type of item you are referencing, if necessary.

5. In the **For which** list, click the item you are referencing to, click **Insert**, and then click **Close**.

To insert a hyperlink to another location, page 243

1. Select the text or item you want to convert to a hyperlink. Then on the **Insert** tab, in the **Links** group, click **Hyperlink**.

2. In the **Insert Hyperlink** dialog box, select the type of link on the **Link to** bar, and then designate the hyperlink target.

3. Click **Target Frame**, and then in the **Set Target Frame** dialog box, specify where the hyperlink target will be displayed.

4. Click **OK** twice.

To jump to a hyperlink target from a Word document, page 244

→ Hold down the [Ctrl] key, and then click the link.

To edit a hyperlink, page 245

1. Right-click the hyperlink, and then click **Edit Hyperlink**.

2. In the **Edit Hyperlink** dialog box, make the necessary changes, and then click **OK**.

To create a footnote or endnote, page 247

1. Click where you want to insert the reference mark. Then on the **References** tab, in the **Footnotes** group, click **Insert Footnote** or **Insert Endnote**.

2. In the linked area at the bottom of the page or end of the document or section, type the note text.

To add a new bibliography source to the Source Manager, page 249

1. On the **References** tab, in the **Citations & Bibliography** group, click the **Manage Sources** button.

2. In the **Source Manager** dialog box, click **New**.

3. In the **Create Source** dialog box, click the **Type of Source** arrow, and in the list, click the source type. Then enter the bibliography information for the source, and click **OK**.

To insert a bibliography citation in a document, page 251

→ Click where you want to insert the citation. Then on the **References** tab, in the **Citations and Bibliography** group, click **Insert Citation**, and in the **Insert Citation** gallery, click the citation you want to insert.

To create a bibliography, page 252

→ Click where you want to insert the bibliography. Then on the **References** tab, in the **Citations & Bibliography** group, click the **Bibliography** button, and in the gallery, click the type of bibliography you want.

9 Creating Form Letters, E-Mail Messages, and Labels

To use an existing data source, page 258

1. Open the main document. Then on the **Mailings** tab, in the **Start Mail Merge** group, click the **Start Mail Merge** button, and click **Step by Step Mail Merge wizard**.

2. In the **Mail Merge** task pane, select an option in the **Select document type** area, and then click **Next: Starting document**.

3. Select the **Use the current document** option, and then click **Next: Select recipients**.

4. Select the **Use an existing list** option, and then click **Browse**.

5. In the **Select Data Source** dialog box, navigate to the location of the data source, and then double-click the file.

To add a record to a data source, page 259

1. On the **Mailings** tab, in the **Start Mail Merge** group, click the **Edit Recipient List** button.

2. In the **Mail Merge Recipients** dialog box, in the **Data Source** box, click the data source, and then click **Edit**.

3. In the **Edit Data Source** dialog box, click **New Entry**, enter the new record information into the fields, click **OK**, and then click **Yes** to update the list.

To sort data in a data source, page 260

1. On the **Mailings** tab, in the **Start Mail Merge** group, click the **Edit Recipient List** button.

2. In the **Mail Merge Recipients** dialog box, under **Refine Recipient List**, click **Sort**.

3. In the **Filter and Sort** dialog box, click the **Sort by** arrow, and select the field you want to sort by. Then click **Ascending** or **Descending**, and click **OK**.

To filter records in a data source, page 261

1. On the **Mailings** tab, in the **Start Mail Merge** group, click the **Edit Recipient List** button.

2. In the **Mail Merge Recipients** dialog box, under **Refine Recipient List**, click **Filter**.

3. In the **Filter and Sort** dialog box, click the **Field** arrow, and select the criteria you want to use for the filter. Then click **OK**.

To insert a merge field into a form letter, page 263

1. Click where you want to insert the merge field. Then on the **Mailings** tab, in the **Write and Insert Fields** group, click the button for the field you want to insert.

2. In the dialog box that opens, click **OK** to accept the default settings, or make any changes you want and then click **OK**.

To print an envelope based on an address in a document, page 270

1. Select the lines of the address in the document. Then on the **Mailings** tab, in the **Create** group, click the **Envelopes** button.

2. In the **Envelopes and Labels** dialog box, type a return address, if necessary, and make any other necessary selections.

3. Insert an envelope in the printer according to your printer manufacturer's directions, and then click **Print**.

To send personalized e-mail messages, page 271

1. Open a new blank document. Then on the **Mailings** tab, in the **Start Mail Merge** group, click the **Start Mail Merge** button, and click **E-mail Messages**.

2. Type the text of the message in the Word document.

3. In the **Start Mail Merge** group, click the **Select Recipients** button, and then designate the data source you want to use.

4. Add any necessary merge fields to the message by using the buttons in the **Write & Insert Fields** group.

5. In the **Finish** group, click the **Finish & Merge** button, and then click **Send E-mail Messages**.

6. In the **Merge to E-mail** dialog box, select **Email_Address** in the **To** box, type a subject in the **Subject line** box, select the mail format, select which records to use, and then click **OK**.

To create mailing labels, page 275

1. Open a new blank document. Then on the **Mailings** tab, in the **Start Mail Merge** group, click **Labels**.

2. In the **Label Options** dialog box, select the label vendor and product number you want, and then click **OK**.

3. In the **Start Mail Merge** group, click the **Select Recipients** button, and then designate the data source you want to use.

4. With the insertion point in the first cell on the left, in the **Write & Insert Fields** group, click the **Address block** button.

5. In the **Insert Address Block** dialog box, click **OK** to accept the default settings.

6. In the **Write & Insert Fields** group, click the **Update Labels** button.

7. In the **Preview Results** group, click the **Preview Results** button.

8. In the **Finish & Merge** group, click the **Finish & Merge** button, and select whether you want to merge to a document or the printer.

10   Collaborating with Others

To send a copy of a document as an e-mail attachment, page 281

1. On the **Microsoft Office Button** menu, point to **Send**, and then click **E-mail**.
2. In the **To** box, type the e-mail address of the recipient(s), and then click the **Send** button.

To turn change tracking on or off, page 285

→ On the **Review** tab, in the **Tracking** group, click the **Track Changes** button.

To display revisions in balloons, page 286

→ In the **Tracking** group, click the **Balloons** button, and then in the list, click **Show Revisions in Balloons**.

To show or hide revisions marks, page 286

→ In the **Tracking** group, click the **Display for Review** arrow, and then in the list, click **Final Showing Markup** or **Final**.

To accept or reject a change in a document, page 287

→ Select the changed text. Then in the **Changes** group, click the **Accept** or **Reject** button.

To move among comments in a document, page 287

→ On the **Review** tab, in the **Comments** group, click the **Next** or **Previous** button.

To insert a comment, page 289

→ Select the word(s) you want to comment on. Then on the **Review** tab, in the **Comments** group, click the **New Comment** button, and type the comment in the comment balloon.

To delete a comment, page 289

→ Click the comment balloon. Then on the **Review** tab, in the **Comments** group, click the **Delete** button.

To open and close the reviewing pane, page 289

→ On the **Review** tab, in the **Tracking** group, click the **Reviewing Pane** button.

To edit a comment, page 290

→ Click the comment you want to edit, and then type your changes.

To respond to a comment, page 290

→ Click the comment balloon. Then on the **Review** tab, in the **Comments** group, click the **New Comment** button, and type your response.

To hide comments, page 290

→ On the **Review** tab, in the **Tracking** group, click the **Show Markup** arrow, and then click **Comments**.

To combine versions of a document, page 292

1. On the **Review** tab, in the **Compare** group, click the **Compare** button, and then click **Combine**.

2. In the **Combine Documents** dialog box, click the **Original document** arrow, and then in the list, click the name of the original document.

3. Click the **Revised document** arrow, and then in the list, click the name of a different version of the document.

4. In the lower-left corner of the dialog box, click **More**, and then under **Comparison settings**, select the check boxes for the items you want Word to check.

5. Under **Show changes in**, select the option you want, and then click **OK**.

To hide a reviewer's changes, page 293

→ On the **Review** tab, in the **Tracking** group, click the **Show Markup** button, point to **Reviewers**, and then click the name of a reviewer whose changes you want to hide.

→ To display hidden changes, in the **Tracking** group, click the **Show Markup** button, point to **Reviewers**, and then click **All Reviewers**.

To accept all changes in a document, page 293

→ On the **Review** tab, in the **Changes** group, click the **Accept** arrow, and then click **Accept All Changes in Document**.

To protect a document with a password, page 294

1. Click the **Microsoft Office Button**, and then click **Save As**.

2. In the **Save As** dialog box, navigate to the folder where you want to save the file, and then in the **File name** box, type a name for the document.

3. At the bottom of the dialog box, click **Tools**, and then click **General Options**.

4. In the **General Options** dialog box, in the **Password to open** or **Password to modify** box, type a password.

5. Click **OK** to close the **General Options** dialog box.

6. In the **Confirm Password** dialog box, in the **Reenter password to modify** box, type the password again, and then click **OK**.

7. Back in the **Save As** dialog box, click **Save**.

To remove a password, page 296

1. Click the **Microsoft Office Button**, click **Save As**, click **Tools**, and then click **General Options**.

2. In the **General Options** dialog box, select the contents of the **Password to open** or **Password to modify** box, press `Del`, click **OK**, and then click **Save**.

To restrict formatting and editing, page 297

1. On the **Review** tab, in the **Protect** group, click the **Protect Document** button, and then click **Restrict Formatting and Editing**.

2. In the **Restrict Formatting and Editing** task pane, under **Formatting restrictions**, select the **Limit formatting to a selection of styles** check box, and then click **Settings**.

3. Click the **Recommended Minimum** button. Then under **Checked styles are currently allowed**, select the check boxes for other styles you want to include.

4. Under **Formatting**, select the check boxes for any other restrictions you want to set on the document, and then click **OK**.

5. If a message box asks if you want to remove any styles in the document that aren't allowed, click **Yes**.

6. Under **Editing restrictions** in the task pane, select the **Allow only this type of editing in the document** check box.

7. Click the arrow to the right of the box below the check box, and then in the list, click the type of changes you want to allow.

8. Under **Start enforcement** in the task pane, click **Yes, Start Enforcing Protection**.

9. Enter a password if you want, and then click **OK**.

To create a document workspace, page 300

1. Open the document for which you want to create a document workspace. Then click the **Microsoft Office Button**, point to **Publish**, and click **Create Document Workspace**.

2. In the **Document Management** task pane, in the **Location for new workspace** box, type the URL of the SharePoint site where you want to create the document workspace, and then click **Create**.

3. If you are asked to supply your user name and password to connect to the site, fill in the **User name** and **Password** boxes, and then click **OK**.

11 Creating Documents for Use Outside of Word

To save a document as a Web page, page 313

1. Open the document you want to save as a Web page. Then click the **Microsoft Office Button**, and click **Save As**.

2. In the **Save As** dialog box, navigate to the folder where you want to save the Web page, and then in the **File name** box, type a name.

3. Click the **Save as type** arrow, and then in the list, click **Web Page**.

4. If you want the Web page title to be something other than what is shown in the dialog box, click **Change Title**, and then in the **Page title** box in the **Set Page Title** dialog box, type a new title, and click **OK**.

5. In the **Save As** dialog box, click **Save**.

To register a blog space, page 316

1. Click the **Microsoft Office Button**, and then click **New**.

2. In the **New Document** dialog box, double-click **New blog post**.

3. In the **Register a Blog Account** dialog box, click **Register Now**.

4. In the **New Blog Account** dialog box, click the **Blog** arrow, select the name of your blog service provider, and then click **Next**.

5. In the **New Account** dialog box, type in the requested information, and click **OK**.

To publish a blog post, page 318

1. Open the blog post that you want to publish. Then on the **Blog Post** tab, in the **Blog** group, click the **Publish Entry** button.

2. In the **Connect to Your Space** dialog box, enter your user information, and then click **OK**.

To save a document in XML format, page 320

1. Open the document you want to save as XML. Then click the **Microsoft Office Button**, and click **Save As**.

2. In the **Save As** dialog box, navigate to the folder where you want to save the XML file, and then in the **File name** box, type a name.

3. Click the **Save as type** arrow, and then in the list, click **Word XML Document**.

4. In the **Save As** dialog box, click **Save**.

To show the Developer tab on the Ribbon, page 321

1. Click the **Microsoft Office Button**, and then click **Word Options**.

2. On the **Popular** page of the **Word Options** window, under **Top options for working with Word**, select the **Show Developer tab in the Ribbon** check box, and then click **OK**.

12 Customizing Word

To change default program options, page 330

→ Click the **Microsoft Office Button**, and then click **Word Options**.

To add a button for a command to the Quick Access Toolbar, page 337

1. At the right end of the **Quick Access Toolbar**, click the **Customize Quick Access Toolbar** button.
2. If the command you want to add appears in the list, click it; otherwise, click **More Commands**.
3. Set **Choose command from** to the tab or menu containing the command you want to add. Then click the command in the list below, and click **Add** to move it to the box on the right.
4. Click **OK** to add a button for the selected command to the Quick Access Toolbar for all documents.

To create a keyboard shortcut, page 345

1. At the right end of the **Quick Access Toolbar**, click the **Customize Quick Access Toolbar** button, and then click **More Commands**.
2. In the **Word Options** window, to the right of **Keyboard shortcuts**, click **Customize**.
3. In the **Customize Keyboard** dialog box, in the **Categories** list, click the name of the tab or menu that contains the command you want, and then in the **Commands** list, click the command.
4. If there is not already a shortcut for the command, click the **Press new shortcut key** box, and then press the keys you want to use for the shortcut.
5. If the shortcut is not already assigned to another command, click **Assign**.

Chapter at a Glance

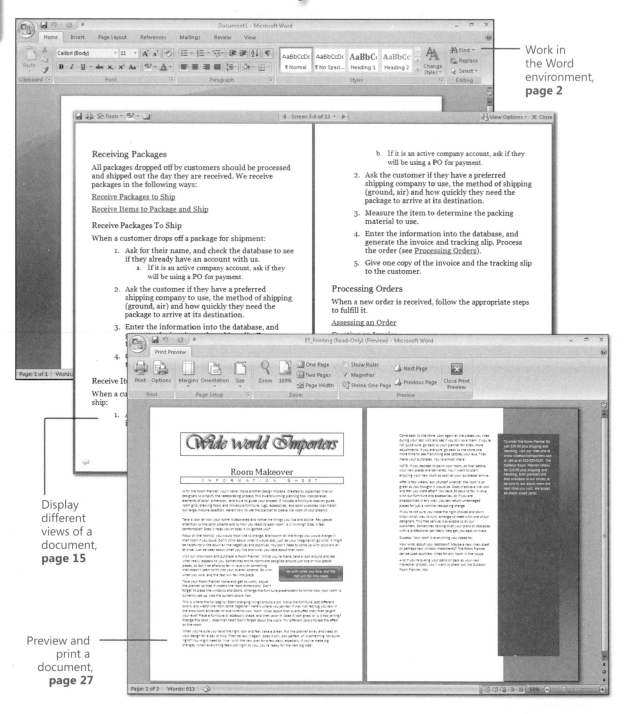

Work in the Word environment, **page 2**

Display different views of a document, **page 15**

Preview and print a document, **page 27**

1 Exploring Word 2007

In this chapter, you will learn to:

✔ Work in the Word environment.

✔ Open, move around in, and close a document.

✔ Display different views of a document.

✔ Create and save a document.

✔ Preview and print a document.

When you use a computer program to create, edit, and produce text documents, you are *word processing*. Microsoft Office Word 2007 is one of the most sophisticated word-processing programs available today. With Word 2007, it is easier than ever to efficiently create a wide range of business and personal documents, from the simplest letter to the most complex report. Word includes many *desktop publishing* features that you can use to enhance the appearance of documents so that they are appealing and easy to read. The program has been completely redesigned to make these and other powerful features more accessible. As a result, even novice users will be able to work productively in Word after only a brief introduction.

In this chapter, you will first familiarize yourself with the Word working environment. Then you will open an existing Word document, learn ways of moving around in it, and close it. You will explore various ways of viewing documents so that you know which view to use for different tasks and how to tailor the program window to meet your needs. You will create and save a new document and then save an existing document in a different location. Finally, you will preview and print a document.

See Also Do you need only a quick refresher on the topics in this chapter? See the Quick Reference entries on pages xxxix–lxiii.

 Important Before you can use the practice files in this chapter, you need to install them from the book's companion CD to their default location. See "Using the Book's CD" on page xxv for more information.

> **Troubleshooting** Graphics and operating system–related instructions in this book reflect the Windows Vista user interface. If your computer is running Microsoft Windows XP and you experience trouble following the instructions as written, please refer to the "Information for Readers Running Windows XP" section at the beginning of this book.

Working in the Word Environment

As with all programs in the 2007 Microsoft Office release, the most common way to start Word is from the Start menu displayed when you click the Start button at the left end of the Microsoft Windows taskbar. If Word is the first program in the 2007 Office system that you have used, you are in for a surprise! The look of the program window has changed radically from previous versions.

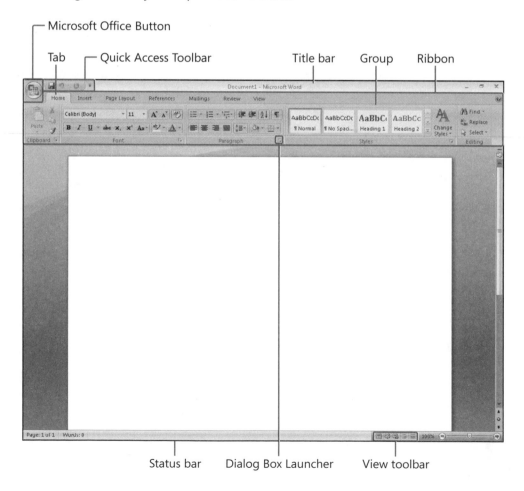

> **Tip** What you see on your screen might not match the graphics in this book exactly. The screens in this book were captured on a monitor set to a resolution of 1024 by 768 pixels with the Windows taskbar is hidden to increase the display space.

The new Word environment is designed to more closely reflect the way people generally work with the program. When you first start Word, this environment consists of the following elements:

Microsoft Office
Button

- Commands related to managing Word and Word documents as a whole (rather than document content) are gathered together on a menu that is displayed when you click the *Microsoft Office Button*.

- Commands can be represented as buttons on the *Quick Access Toolbar* to the right of the Microsoft Office Button. By default, this toolbar displays the Save, Undo, and Repeat buttons, but you can customize the toolbar to include any command that you use frequently.

  See Also For information about customizing the Quick Access Toolbar, see "Making Favorite Word Commands Easily Accessible" in Chapter 12, "Customizing Word."

- The *title bar* displays the name of the active document. At the right end of the title bar are the three familiar buttons that have the same function in all Windows programs. You can temporarily hide the Word window by clicking the Minimize button, adjust the size of the window with the Restore Down/Maximize button, and close the active document or quit Word with the Close button.

- Below the title bar is the *Ribbon*, which makes all the capabilities of Word available in a single area so that you can work efficiently with the program.

- Commands related to working with document content are represented as buttons on the *tabs* that make up the Ribbon. The Home tab is active by default. Clicking one of the other tabs, such as Insert, displays that tab's buttons.

  > **Tip** If Microsoft Outlook with Business Contact Manager is installed on your computer, you will have a Business Tools tab in addition to those shown in our graphics.

- On each tab, buttons are organized into *groups*. Depending on the size of the program window, in some groups the button you are likely to use most often is bigger than the rest.

> **Tip** Depending on your screen resolution and the size of the program window, a tab might not have enough room to display all of its groups. In that case, the name of the group resembles a button, and clicking the button displays the group's commands.

Dialog Box
Launcher

● Related but less common commands are not represented as buttons in the group. Instead they are available in a dialog box, which you can display by clicking the *Dialog Box Launcher* at the right end of the group's title bar.

● Some button names are displayed and some aren't. Pausing the mouse pointer over any button for a few seconds (called *hovering*) displays a *ScreenTip* with not only the button's name but also its function.

● Some buttons have arrows, but not all arrows are alike. If you point to a button and both the button and its arrow are in the same box and are the same color, clicking the button will display options for refining the action of the button. If you point to a button and the button is in one box and its arrow is in a different box with a different shade, clicking the button will carry out that action with the button's current settings. If you want to change those settings, you need to click the arrow to see the available options.

⎯⎯ Clicking this type of button always displays a list of options.

⎯⎯⎯⎯ Clicking this type of button carries out the command with the current settings.

⎯⎯ Clicking this button's arrow displays a list of options.

● The *Microsoft Office Word Help button* appears at the right end of the Ribbon.

● You create a document in the *document window*. When more than one document is open, each document has its own window.

● Across the bottom of the program window, the *status bar* gives you information about the current document. You can turn off the display of an item of information by right-clicking the status bar and then clicking that item.

Customize Status Bar	
Formatted Page Number	1
Section	1
✓ Page Number	1 of 1
Vertical Page Position	1"
Line Number	1
Column	1
✓ Word Count	0
✓ Spelling and Grammar Check	
✓ Language	
✓ Signatures	Off
✓ Information Management Policy	Off
✓ Permissions	Off
Track Changes	Off
Caps Lock	Off
Overtype	Insert
Selection Mode	
Macro Recording	Not Recording
✓ View Shortcuts	
✓ Zoom	100%
✓ Zoom Slider	

Click this item to display it on the status bar

- At the right end of the status bar is the *View toolbar*, which provides tools for adjusting the view of document content.

    See Also For information about adjusting the view of a document, see "Displaying Different Views of a Document" later in this chapter.

The goal of the redesigned environment is to make working on a document more intuitive. Commands for tasks you perform often are no longer hidden on menus and in dialog boxes, and features that you might not have discovered before are now more visible.

For example, when a formatting option has several choices available, they are often displayed in a *gallery* of *thumbnails*. These galleries give you an at-a-glance picture of each choice. If you point to a thumbnail in a gallery, an awesome new feature called *live preview* shows you what that choice will look like if you apply it to your document.

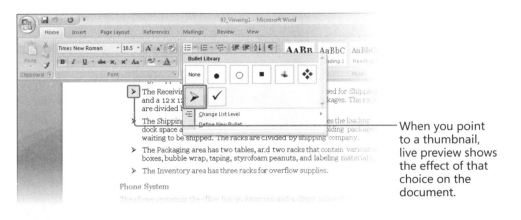

When you point to a thumbnail, live preview shows the effect of that choice on the document.

In this exercise, you will start Word and explore the Microsoft Office Button and the tabs and groups on the Ribbon. Along the way, you will see how to take advantage of galleries and live preview. There are no practice files for this exercise.

> **BE SURE TO** start your computer, but don't start Word yet.

Start

1. On the taskbar, click the **Start** button, click **All Programs**, click **Microsoft Office**, and then click **Microsoft Office Word 2007**.

   The Word program window opens, displaying a blank document.

Microsoft Office Button

2. Click the **Microsoft Office Button**.

   Commands related to managing documents (such as creating, saving, and printing) are available from the menu that opens. This menu, which we refer to throughout this book as the *Office menu*, takes the place of the File menu that appeared in previous versions of Word.

The commands on the left are for tasks related to the document as a whole. After you have worked with a document, its name appears in the Recent Documents list so that you can quickly open it again. At the bottom of the menu are buttons for changing program options and for quitting Word.

See Also For information about changing program options, see "Changing Default Program Options" in Chapter 12, "Customizing Word."

3. Press the [Esc] key to close the menu.

On the Ribbon, the Home tab is active. Buttons related to working with document content are organized on this tab in five groups: Clipboard, Font, Paragraph, Styles, and Editing. Only the buttons representing commands that can be performed on the currently selected document element are active.

4. Hover the mouse pointer over the active buttons on this tab to display the ScreenTips that name them and describe their functions.

> **Important** Depending on your screen resolution and the size of the program window, you might see more or fewer buttons in each of the groups, or the buttons you see might be represented by larger or smaller icons than those shown in this book. Experiment with the size of the program window to understand the effect on the appearance of the tabs.

5. Click the **Insert** tab, and then explore its buttons.

Buttons related to all the items you can insert are organized on this tab in seven groups: Pages, Tables, Illustrations, Links, Header & Footer, Text, and Symbols.

6. Click the **Page Layout** tab, and then explore its buttons.

Buttons related to the appearance of your document are organized on this tab in five groups: Themes, Page Setup, Page Background, Paragraph, and Arrange.

Margins

Dialog Box Launcher

7. In the **Page Setup** group, display the ScreenTip for the **Margins** button.

The ScreenTip tells you how you can adjust the margins.

8. At the right end of the **Page Setup** group's title bar, click the **Page Setup** Dialog Box Launcher.

The Page Setup dialog box opens.

Page Setup

Margins | Paper | Layout

Margins

Top: 1"   Bottom: 1"
Left: 1.25"   Right: 1.25"
Gutter: 0"   Gutter position: Left

Orientation

Portrait   Landscape

Pages

Multiple pages: Normal

Preview

Apply to: Whole document

Default...   OK   Cancel

The dialog box provides a single location where you can set the margins and orientation, and specify the setup of a multi-page document. You can preview the results of your changes before applying them.

See Also For information about setting up multi-page documents, see "Controlling What Appears on Each Page" in Chapter 4, "Changing the Look of a Document."

9. Click **Cancel** to close the dialog box.

10. In the **Themes** group, click the **Themes** button.

Themes

You see a gallery of thumbnails of the available themes.

11. Press Esc to close the gallery without making a selection.

12. In the **Page Background** group, click the **Page Color** button, and then in the top row of the **Theme Colors** palette, point to each box in turn.

The blank document page shows a live preview of what it will look like If you click the color you are pointing to. You can see the effect of the selection without actually applying it.

13. Press Esc to close the palette without making a selection.

14. Click the **References** tab, and then explore its buttons.

Buttons related to items you can add to long documents, such as reports, are organized on this tab in six groups: Table Of Contents, Footnotes, Citations & Bibliography, Captions, Index, and Table Of Authorities.

15. Click the **Mailings** tab, and then explore its buttons.

Buttons related to creating mass mailings are organized on this tab in five groups: Create, Start Mail Merge, Write & Insert Fields, Preview Results, and Finish.

16. Click the **Review** tab, and then explore its buttons.

Buttons related to proofing, commenting, and changing documents are organized on this tab in six groups: Proofing, Comments, Tracking, Changes, Compare, and Protect.

17. Click the **View** tab, and then explore its buttons.

Buttons related to changing the view or the display of documents are organized on this tab in five groups: Document Views, Show/Hide, Zoom, Window, and Macros.

Opening, Moving Around in, and Closing a Document

To open an existing document, you click the Microsoft Office Button and then click Open to display the Open dialog box. The first time you use this command, the dialog box displays the contents of your *Documents* folder. If you display the dialog box again in the same Word session, it displays the contents of whatever folder you last used. To see the contents of a different folder, you use standard Windows techniques. After you locate the file you want to work with, you can double-click it to open it.

Tip Clicking a file name and then clicking the Open arrow in the lower-right corner of the Open dialog box displays a list of alternative ways in which you can open the file. To look through the document without making any inadvertent changes, you can open the file as *read-only*, or you can open an independent copy of the file. You can open an file in a Web browser, or open an XML file with a transform (see Chapter 11). In the event of a computer crash or other similar incident, you can tell Word to open the file and attempt to repair any damage. And you can display earlier versions of the file.

To move around in an open document without changing the location of the insertion point, you can use the vertical and horizontal scroll bars in the following ways:

- Click the scroll arrows to move the document window up or down by a line, or left or right by a few characters.

- Click above or below the vertical scroll box to move up or down one windowful, or to the left or right of the horizontal scroll box to move left or right one windowful.

- Drag the scroll box on the scroll bar to display the part of the document corresponding to the location of the scroll box. For example, dragging the scroll box to the middle of the scroll bar displays the middle of the document.

You can also move around in a document in ways that do move the insertion point. To place the insertion point at a particular location, you simply click there. To move the insertion point back or forward a page, you can click the Previous Page and Next Page buttons below the vertical scroll bar.

You can also press a key or a *key combination* on the keyboard to move the insertion point. For example, you can press the Home key to move the insertion point to the left end of a line or press Ctrl+Home to move it to the beginning of the document.

> **Tip** The location of the insertion point is displayed on the status bar. By default, the status bar tells you which page the insertion point is on, but you can also display its location by section, line, and column, and in inches from the top of the page. Simply right-click the status bar, and then click the option you want to display.

This table lists ways to use your keyboard to move the insertion point.

To move the insertion point...	Press...
Left one character	Left Arrow
Right one character	Right Arrow
Down one line	Down Arrow
Up one line	Up Arrow
Left one word	Ctrl+Left Arrow
Right one word	Ctrl+Right Arrow
To the beginning of the current line	Home
To the end of the current line	End
To the beginning of the document	Ctrl+End
To the beginning of the previous page	Ctrl+Page Up
To the beginning of the next page	Ctrl+Page Down
Up one screen	Page Down
Down one screen	Page Up

In a long document, you might want to move quickly among elements of a certain type; for example, from graphic to graphic. You can click the Select Browse Object button at the bottom of the vertical scroll bar and then make a choice in the palette of browsing options that appears, such as Browse by Page or Browse by Graphic.

If more than one document is open, you can close it by clicking the Close button at the right end of the title bar. If only one document is open, clicking the Close button closes the document and also quits Word. If you want to close the document but leave Word open, you must click the Microsoft Office Button and then click Close.

In this exercise, you will open an existing document and explore various ways of moving around in it. Then you will close the document.

> **USE** the *02_Opening* document. This practice file is located in the *Chapter01* subfolder under *SBS_Word2007*.

Microsoft Office
Button

1. Click the **Microsoft Office Button**, and then click **Open**.

   The Open dialog box opens, showing the contents of the folder you used for your last open or save action.

2. If the contents of the *Documents* folder are not displayed, in the **Navigation Pane**, click **Documents**.

3. Double-click the **MSP** folder, double-click the **SBS_Word2007** folder, and then double-click the **Chapter01** folder.

4. Click the *02_Opening* document, and then click the **Open** button.

   The *02_Opening* document opens in the Word program window.

Insertion point   Scroll bar   Scroll arrow

The Taguien Cycle

A Fantasy Series for Young Adults

The Taguien Cycle is the most exciting and promising new project to have come before the committee in several years. It meets our two primary goals: Develop a book line that will appeal to young adult readers, especially boys; and develop a book line that has the potential for media spin-offs that will contribute to future profits and on-going financial success.

Interest in the fantasy genre has increased steadily over the past ten years, a trend that shows no sign of reversal. Anecdotal industry sales statistics show an increase of 2 to 3 percent per year for adult fantasy books and 5 to 6 percent for young adult fantasy books. Each year Lucerne has published several fairytale/magic books for younger readers, but we do not currently offer anything sophisticated enough to appeal to young adult readers. Although we have found it very difficult to sell other genres to this audience of reluctant readers, there is every indication that offering a fantasy series at this time would met with success.

The most successful fantasy series are aimed squarely at the young adult market but also appeal to high-level grade-school readers and adults. Several publishers have already achieved solid success in this arena with books by a variety of authors, such as:

1) Harry Potter series, by J. K. Rowling.
2) Bartimaeus Trilogy, by Jonathan Stroud.
3) Artemis Fowl series, by Eoin Colfer.
4) Old Kingdom trilogy, by Garth Nix.
5) Inheritance series, by Christopher Paolini

Of special note are the Harry Potter series and the Inheritance series. The Harry Potter series now includes six books that are known and loved world-wide, making it arguably the most successful of all the fantasy offerings since J.R.R. Tolkien's classic trilogy, Lord of the Rings. The Inheritance series was penned by a 19-year-old, who

Page: 1 of 2 | Words: 669

Vertical scroll bar   Select Browse Object button

5. In the second line of the document title, click at the end of the paragraph to position the insertion point.

6. Press the ⎡Home⎤ key to move the insertion point to the beginning of the line.

7. Press the ⎡→⎤ key two times to move the insertion point to the beginning of the word *Fantasy* in the heading.

8. Press the ⎡End⎤ key to move the insertion point to the end of the line.

9. Press ⎡Ctrl⎤+⎡End⎤ to move the insertion point to the end of the document.

10. Press ⎡Ctrl⎤+⎡Home⎤ to move the insertion point to the beginning of the document.

Next Page

11. At the bottom of the vertical scroll bar, click the **Next Page** button.

12. Click above the vertical scroll box to change the view of the document by one windowful.

13. Drag the vertical scroll box to the top of the vertical scroll bar.

The beginning of the document comes into view. Note that the location of the insertion point has not changed—just the view of the document.

Select Browse
Object

14. Click to the left of the title to place the insertion point at the top of the document, and then at the bottom of the vertical scroll bar, click the **Select Browse Object** button.

A palette of browse choices opens.

15. Move the pointer over the buttons representing the objects you can browse among.

As you point to each button, the name of the object appears at the top of the palette.

Browse by Page

16. Click the **Browse by Page** button.

The insertion point moves from the beginning of Page 1 to the beginning of Page 2.

17. Click the **Microsoft Office Button**, and then click **Close**.

> **Troubleshooting** If you click the Close button at the right end of the title bar instead of clicking the Microsoft Office Button and then clicking Close, you will close the open Word document and quit the Word program. To continue working, start Word again.

Compatibility with Earlier Versions

Word 2007 uses a different file format than previous versions of the program. You can open a document created with previous versions, but the new features of Word 2007 will not be available. The name of the document appears in the title bar with [Compatibility Mode] to its right. You can work in Compatibility Mode, or you can convert the document to the Word 2007 file format by clicking the Microsoft Office Button, and clicking Convert. You can then click the Save button on the Quick Access Toolbar to overwrite the existing document, or click Save As on the Office menu to save the document in the new format as a different file.

You cannot open a Word 2007 document in a previous version of Word unless you install the Compatibility Pack for the 2007 Office system, which is available for free download from Microsoft Office Online. After installing the Compatibility Pack, you can open and work with Word 2007 documents, but you cannot open Word 2007 templates.

Displaying Different Views of a Document

In Word, you can view a document in a variety of ways:

- *Print Layout view*. This view displays a document on the screen the way it will look when printed. You can see elements such as margins, page breaks, headers and footers, and watermarks.

- *Full Screen Reading view*. This view displays as much of the content of the document as will fit on the screen at a size that is comfortable for reading. In this view, the Ribbon is replaced by a single toolbar at the top of the screen with buttons that you can use to save and print the document, access references and other tools, highlight text, and make comments. You can also move from page to page and adjust the view.

- *Web Layout view*. This view displays a document on the screen the way it will look when viewed in a Web browser. You can see backgrounds, AutoShapes, and other effects. You can also see how text wraps to fit the window and how graphics are positioned.

  See Also For information about Web documents, see "Creating and Modifying a Web Document" in Chapter 11, "Creating Documents for Use Outside of Word."

- *Outline view*. This view displays the structure of a document as nested levels of headings and body text, and provides tools for viewing and changing its hierarchy.

See Also For information about outlining, see "Reorganizing a Document Outline" in Chapter 2, "Editing and Proofreading Documents."

● *Draft view.* This view displays the content of a document with a simplified layout so that you can type and edit quickly. You cannot see layout elements such as headers and footers.

You switch among views by using buttons in the Document Views group on the View tab or by using the buttons on the View toolbar in the lower-right corner of the window.

You can use other buttons on the View tab to do the following:

● Display rulers and gridlines to help you position and align elements.

● Display a separate pane containing the *Document Map*—a list of the headings that make up the structure of the document—while viewing and editing its text.

● Display a separate pane containing *thumbnails* of the document's pages.

● Arrange and work with windows.

● Change the magnification of the document.

You can also adjust the magnification of the document by using tools on the View toolbar at the right end of the status bar. You can click the Zoom button and select (or type) a percentage; drag the slider to the left or right; or click the Zoom Out or Zoom In button at either end of the slider.

When you are creating more complex documents, it is easier to place elements exactly if you turn on the display of non-printing characters. These characters fall into two categories: those that control the layout of your document and those that provide the structure for behind-the-scenes processes such as indexing. You can turn the display of non-printing characters on and off by clicking the Show/Hide ¶ button in the Paragraph group on the Home tab.

> **Tip** You can hide any text by selecting it, clicking the Font Dialog Box Launcher at the right end of the Font group's title bar on the Home tab, selecting the Hidden check box, and clicking OK. When the Show/Hide ¶ button is turned on, hidden text is visible and is identified in the document by a dotted underline.

In this exercise, you will first explore various ways that you can customize Print Layout view to make the work of developing documents more efficient. You will turn white space on and off, zoom in and out, display the rulers and Document Map, and view non-printing characters and text. Then you will switch to other views, noticing the differences so that you have an idea of which one is most appropriate for which task. Finally, you will switch between open documents and view documents in more than one window at the same time.

> **USE** the *03_Viewing1* and *03_Viewing2* documents. These practice files are located in the *Chapter01* subfolder under *SBS_Word2007*.
>
> **OPEN** the *03_Viewing1* document.

1. In Print Layout view, scroll through the document.

    As you can see, on all pages but the first, the printed document will have the title in the header at the top of the page, the page number in the right margin, and the date in the footer at the bottom of each page.

    See Also For information about headers and footers, see "Adding Headers and Footers" in Chapter 4, "Changing the Look of a Document."

2. Point to the gap between any two pages, and when the pointer changes to two opposing arrows, double-click the mouse button. Then scroll through the document again.

    The white space at the top and bottom of each page and the gray space between pages is now hidden.

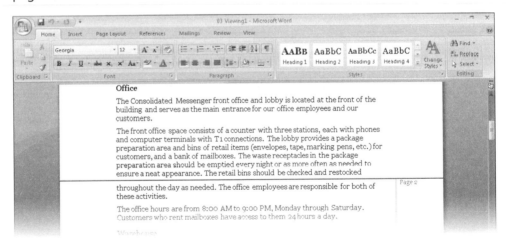

3. Restore the white space by pointing to the black line that separates one page from the next, double-clicking the mouse button.

4. Press [Ctrl]+[Home] to move to the top of the document, and then on the **View** toolbar, click the **Zoom** button.

    The Zoom dialog box opens.

100%

Zoom

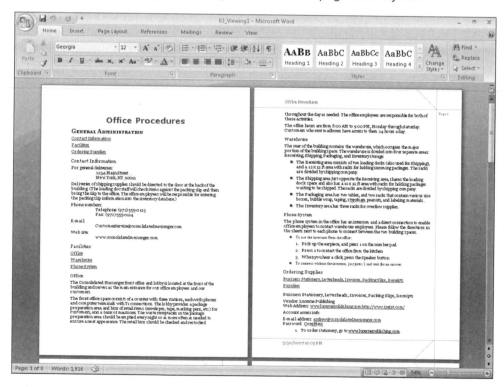

5. Under **Many pages**, click the monitor button, click the second page thumbnail in the top row, and then click **OK**.

The magnification changes so that you can see two pages side by side.

Next Page

6. Below the vertical scroll bar, click the **Next Page** button to display the third and fourth pages of the document.

7. On the **View** toolbar, click the **Zoom** button. Then in the **Zoom** dialog box, click **75%**, and click **OK**.

Notice that the Zoom slider position is adjusted to reflect the new setting.

Zoom Out

8. At the left end of the **Zoom** slider, click the **Zoom Out** button a couple of times.

As you click the button, the slider moves to the left and the Zoom percentage decreases.

Zoom In

9. At the right end of the **Zoom** slider, click the **Zoom In** button until the magnification is 100%.

10. On the **View** tab, in the **Show/Hide** group, select the **Ruler** check box.

Horizontal and vertical rulers appear above and to the left of the page. On the rulers, the active area of the page is white and the margins are blue.

11. In the **Show/Hide** group, click the **Document Map** check box.

A pane opens on the left side of the screen, displaying an outline of the headings in the document. The first heading on the active page is highlighted.

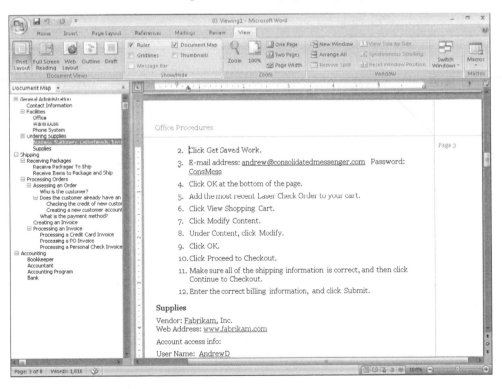

12. In the **Document Map**, click the **Shipping** heading.

Word displays the page containing the selected heading.

13. In the **Show/Hide** group, click the **Thumbnails** check box, and then scroll the **Thumbnails** pane, and click Page **5**.

Close

14. In the **Thumbnails** pane, click the **Close** button.

The pane on the left closes.

¶

Show/Hide ¶

15. On the **Home** tab, in the **Paragraph** group, click the **Show/Hide ¶** button.

You can now see non-printing characters such as spaces, tabs, and paragraph marks.

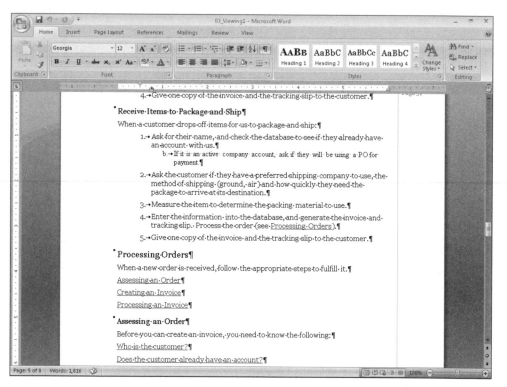

Full Screen
Reading

16. On the **View** tab, in the **Document Views** group, click the **Full Screen Reading** button.

The screen changes to display the document in a format that makes it easy to read.

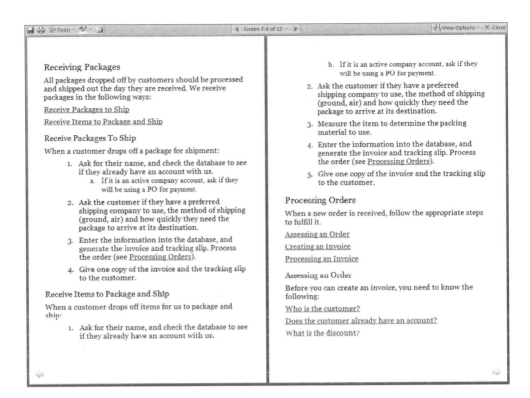

Screen 7-8 of 13

Receiving Packages

All packages dropped off by customers should be processed and shipped out the day they are received. We receive packages in the following ways:

Receive Packages to Ship

Receive Items to Package and Ship

Receive Packages To Ship

When a customer drops off a package for shipment:

1. Ask for their name, and check the database to see if they already have an account with us.
   a. If it is an active company account, ask if they will be using a PO for payment.
2. Ask the customer if they have a preferred shipping company to use, the method of shipping (ground, air) and how quickly they need the package to arrive at its destination.
3. Enter the information into the database, and generate the invoice and tracking slip. Process the order (see Processing Orders).
4. Give one copy of the invoice and the tracking slip to the customer.

Receive Items to Package and Ship

When a customer drops off items for us to package and ship:

1. Ask for their name, and check the database to see if they already have an account with us.

   b. If it is an active company account, ask if they will be using a PO for payment.
2. Ask the customer if they have a preferred shipping company to use, the method of shipping (ground, air) and how quickly they need the package to arrive at its destination.
3. Measure the item to determine the packing material to use.
4. Enter the information into the database, and generate the invoice and tracking slip. Process the order (see Processing Orders).
5. Give one copy of the invoice and the tracking slip to the customer.

Processing Orders

When a new order is received, follow the appropriate steps to fulfill it.

Assessing an Order

Creating an Invoice

Processing an Invoice

Assessing an Order

Before you can create an invoice, you need to know the following:

Who is the customer?

Does the customer already have an account?

What is the discount?

Next Screen

17. At the top of the screen, click the **Next Screen** button.

You move to the next two screens of information.

X Close

18. Explore the other buttons at the top of the Full Screen Reading view, and then click the **Close** button to return to Print Layout view.

Web Layout

19. Press Ctrl + Home. Then on the **View** toolbar, click the **Web Layout** button, and scroll through the document.

In a Web browser, the text column will fill the window and there will be no page breaks.

Outline

20. Press Ctrl + Home, and then on the **View** toolbar, click the **Outline** button.

The screen changes to show the document's hierarchical structure, and the Outlining tab appears at the left end of the Ribbon.

21. On the **Outlining** tab, in the **Outline Tools** group, click the **Show Level** arrow, and in the list, click **Level 2**.

The document collapses to display only the Level 1 and Level 2 headings.

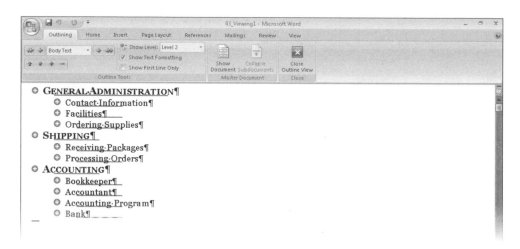

Draft

22. On the **View** toolbar, click the **Draft** button, and then scroll through the document.

You can see the basic content of the document without any extraneous elements, such as margins and headers and footers. The active area on the ruler indicates the width of the text column, dotted lines indicate page breaks, and scrolling is quick and easy.

23. Click the **Microsoft Office Button**, click **Open**, and then in the **Open** dialog box, double-click *03_Viewing2*.

The *03_Viewing2* document opens in Print Layout view in its own document window. Notice that the telephone number in the body of the memo has a dotted underline because it is formatted as hidden.

24. On the **Home** tab, in the **Paragraph** group, click the **Show/Hide ¶** button to turn it off.

Non-printing characters and hidden text are no longer visible.

25. On the **View** tab, in the **Window** group, click **Switch Windows**, and then click *03_Viewing1*.

The other open document is displayed in Draft view, with non-printing characters visible.

26. On the **View** tab, in the **Window** group, click the **Arrange All** button.

The two document windows are sized and stacked one above the other. Each window has a Ribbon, so you can work with each document independently.

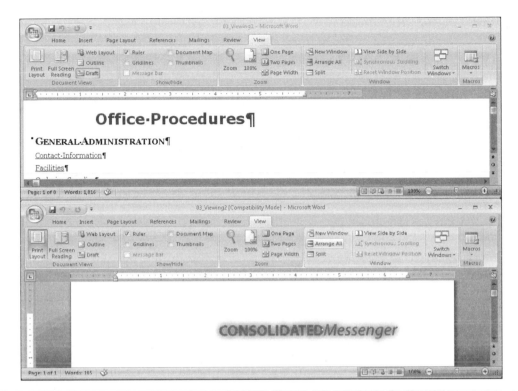

27. At the right end of the *03_Viewing1* window's title bar, click the **Close** button.

Clicking the Close button does not quit Word because more than one document is open.

Close

28. At the right end of the *03_Viewing2* window's title bar, click the **Maximize** button.

The document window expands to fill the screen.

Maximize

29. On the **View** tab, in the **Show/Hide** group, clear the **Ruler** check box to turn off the rulers.

CLOSE the *03_Viewing2* document.

Creating and Saving a Document

To create a Word document, you simply open a new blank document and type your content. The blinking insertion point shows where the next character you type will appear. When the insertion point reaches the right margin, the word you are typing moves to the next line. Because of this *word wrap* feature, which is common in word-processing and desktop-publishing programs, you press Enter only to start a new paragraph, not a new line.

Each document you create is temporary unless you save it as a file with a unique name or location. To save a document for the first time, you click the Save button on the Quick Access Toolbar or click the Microsoft Office Button and then click Save. Either action displays the Save As dialog box, where you can assign the name and storage location.

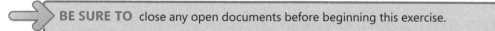

If you want to save the document in a folder other than the one shown in the Address bar, you can click the chevrons to the left of the current folder name and then navigate to the folder you want. You can also click Browse Folders to display the Navigation Pane and a toolbar. If you want to create a new folder in which to store the file, you can click the New Folder button on this toolbar.

After you save a document the first time, you can save changes simply by clicking the Save button. The new version of the document then overwrites the previous version. If you want to keep both the new version and the previous version, click Save As on the Office menu, and then save the new version with a different name in the same location or with the same name in a different location. (You cannot store two files with the same name in the same folder.)

In this exercise, you will enter text in a new document, and you will save the document in a folder that you create. There are no practice files for this exercise.

BE SURE TO close any open documents before beginning this exercise.

Microsoft Office
Button

1. Click the **Microsoft Office Button**, click **New**, and then in the **New Document** window, double-click **Blank Document**.

A new document window opens in Print Layout view.

2. With the insertion point at the beginning of the new document, type Decorators, Get Ready for Change!, and then press Enter.

The text appears in the new document.

3. Type With spring just around the corner, let's start making those home decor changes you've been thinking about all winter. Let's introduce fresh new color. Let's add some accessories. Let's come up with a great plan for a room to love.

Notice that you did not need to press Enter when the insertion point reached the right margin because the text wrapped to the next line.

> **Tip** If a red wavy line appears under a word or phrase, Word is flagging a possible error. For now, ignore any errors.

4. Press Enter, and then type Here at Wide World Importers, we realize that you need to have the right tools to guarantee a successful room makeover. And with that in mind, we are proud to present the latest addition to our line of decorating tools, the Room Planner.

Save

5. On the **Quick Access Toolbar**, click the **Save** button.

The Save As dialog box opens, displaying the contents of the *Documents* folder. In the File Name box, Word suggests *Decorators*, the first word in the document, as a possible name for this file.

6. In the lower-left corner of the dialog box, click **Browse Folders**.

The dialog box expands to show the Navigation Pane and a toolbar.

7. Double-click **MSP**, double-click **SBS_Word2007**, and double-click **Chapter01**.

8. On the dialog box's toolbar, click the **New Folder** button, type My New Documents as the name of the new folder, and then press [Enter].

   My New Documents is now the current folder in the Save As dialog box.

9. In the **File name** box, double-click the existing entry, and then type My Announcement.

   > **Troubleshooting** Programs that run on the Windows operating systems use file name extensions to identify different types of files. For example, the extension *.docx* identifies Word 2007 documents. Windows Vista programs do not display these extensions by default, and you shouldn't type them in the Save As dialog box. When you save a file, Word automatically adds whatever extension is associated with the type of file selected in the Save As Type box.

10. Click **Save**.

    The Save As dialog box closes, Word saves the *My Announcement* file in the *My New Documents* folder, and the name of the document, *My Announcement*, appears on the program window's title bar.

11. Click the **Microsoft Office Button**, and then click **Save As**.

The Save As dialog box opens, displaying the contents of the *My New Documents* folder.

12. In the Address bar in the **Save As** dialog box, click the chevrons to the left of *My New Documents*, and then in the list, click **Chapter01**.

The dialog box now displays the contents of the *My New Documents* folder's *parent folder*, *Chapter01*.

13. Click **Save**.

Word saves the *My Announcement* file in the *Chapter01* folder. You now have two versions of the document saved with the same name but in different folders.

CLOSE the *My Announcement* file.

> **Tip** By default, Word periodically saves the document you are working on in case the program stops responding or you lose electrical power. To adjust the time interval between saves, click the Microsoft Office Button, click Word Options, click Save in the left pane of the Word Options window, and specify the period of time in the box to the right of the Save AutoRecover Information Every check box. Then click OK.

Previewing and Printing a Document

When you are ready to print a document, you can click the Microsoft Office Button, point to Print, and then click Quick Print. Word then uses your computer's default printer and the settings specified in the Print dialog box. To use a different printer or change the print settings, you click the Microsoft Office Button, and then click Print to open the Print dialog box. You can then specify which printer to use, what to print, and how many copies, and you can make other changes to the settings.

Before you print a document, you almost always want to check how it will look on paper by previewing it. Previewing is essential for multi-page documents but is helpful even for one-page documents. To preview a document, you click the Microsoft Office Button, point to Print, and then click Print Preview. This view shows exactly how each page of the document will look when printed. Word displays a Print Preview tab on the Ribbon to provide tools for checking each page and making adjustments if you don't like what you see.

By using the buttons in the Page Setup group on the Print Preview tab, you can make the following changes:

- Change the margins of the document to fit more or less information on a page or to control where the information appears. You define the size of the top, bottom, left, and right margins by clicking the Margins button and making a selection from the Margins gallery, or by clicking Custom Margins and specifying settings on the Margins tab of the Page Setup dialog box.

- Switch the *orientation* (the direction in which a page is laid out on the paper). The default orientation is *portrait*, in which the page is taller than it is wide. You can set the orientation to *landscape*, in which the page is wider than it is tall, by clicking the Orientation button and selecting that option.

> **Tip** The pages of a document all have the same margins and are oriented the same way unless you divide your document into sections. Then each section can have independent margin and orientation settings.

See Also For more information about sections, see "Controlling What Appears on Each Page" in Chapter 4, "Changing the Look of a Document."

- Select the paper size you want to use by clicking the Size button and making a selection in the Paper Size gallery.

You can click buttons in other groups to change the printer options, change the view of the document, and change the mouse pointer so that you can edit the text.

In this exercise, you will preview a document, adjust the margins, change the orientation, and select a new printer before sending the document to be printed.

> **USE** the *05_Printing* document. This practice file is located in the *Chapter01* subfolder under *SBS_Word2007*.
> **BE SURE TO** install a printer and turn it on before starting this exercise.
> **OPEN** the *05_Printing* document.

Microsoft Office
Button

1. Click the **Microsoft Office Button**, point to the **Print** arrow, and then click **Print Preview**.

   The window's title bar now indicates that you are viewing a preview of the document, and the Print Preview tab appears on the Ribbon.

2. On the **Print Preview** tab, in the **Zoom** group, click the **Two Pages** button.

   Word displays the two pages of the document side by side.

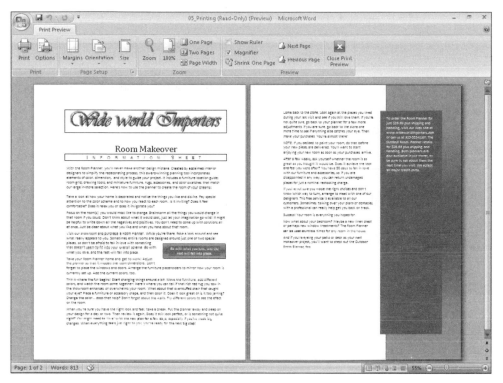

3. In the **Page Setup** group, click the **Margins** button.

The Margins gallery appears.

4. In the gallery, click **Wide**.

   The text rewraps within the new margins, and the left end of the status bar indicates that the document now has 3 pages.

5. In the **Preview** group, click the **Next Page** button to see the last page of the document.

Dialog Box
Launcher

6. Click the **Page Setup** Dialog Box Launcher.

   The Page Setup dialog box opens, displaying the Margins tab.

7. Under **Margins**, replace the value in the **Left** box by typing 1". Then replace the value in the **Right** box with 1", and click **OK**.

   The width of the margins decreases, and the text rewraps to fill 2 pages.

Orientation

8. In the **Page Setup** group, click the **Orientation** button, and then click **Landscape**.

   The pages of the document are now wider than they are tall.

9. Point to the top of the first page of the document so that the pointer becomes a magnifying glass, and then click.

   The first page is magnified. Notice that the Zoom box at the right end of the status bar now displays 100%.

10. Click near the top of the document.

    The Zoom percentage changes, and you now see both pages at the same time.

Close Print
Preview

11. In the **Preview** group, click the **Close Print Preview** button.

    You don't have to be in Print Preview to change the orientation of a document. You can do it in Print Layout view.

Orientation ▾

12. On the **Page Layout** tab, in the **Page Setup** group, click the **Orientation** button, and then click **Portrait**.

13. Click the **Microsoft Office Button**, and then click **Print**.

> **Tip** You can click the Microsoft Office Button, point to Print, and then click Quick Print to print the document without first viewing the settings.

The Print dialog box opens.

14. If you have more than one printer available and you want to switch printers, click the **Name** arrow, and in the list, click the printer you want.

15. Under **Page Range**, click the **Current Page** option.

16. Under **Copies**, change the **Number of copies** setting to 2, and then click **OK**.

    Word prints two copies of the first page on the designated printer.

> **CLOSE** the 03_Printing document without saving your changes, and if you are not continuing directly on to the next chapter, quit Word.

Key Points

- You can open more than one Word document, and you can view more than one document at a time, but only one document can be active at a time.

- You create Word documents by typing text at the insertion point. It's easy to move the insertion point by clicking in the text or pressing keys and key combinations.

- When you save a Word document, you specify its name, location, and file format in the Save As dialog box.

- You can view a document in a variety of ways, depending on your needs as you create the document and on the purpose for which you are creating it.

Chapter at a Glance

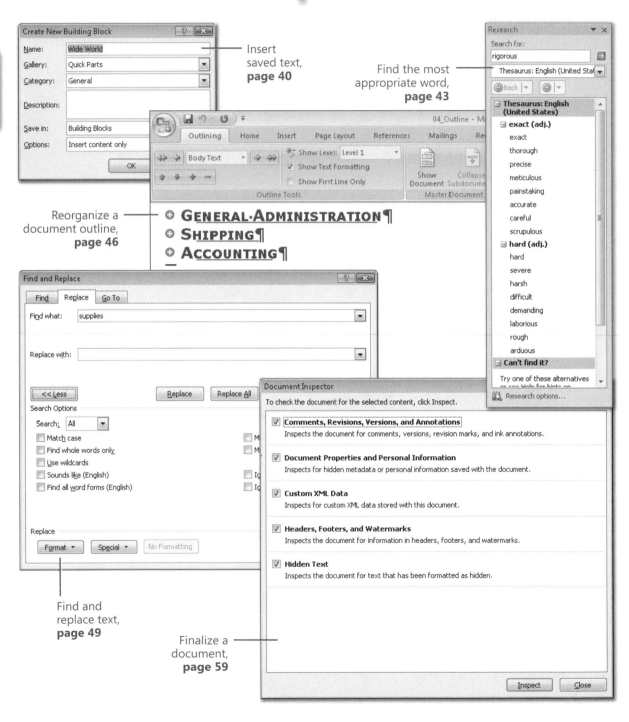

Insert saved text, **page 40**

Find the most appropriate word, **page 43**

Reorganize a document outline, **page 46**

Find and replace text, **page 49**

Finalize a document, **page 59**

2 Editing and Proofreading Documents

In this chapter, you will learn to:

✔ Make changes to a document.

✔ Insert saved text.

✔ Find the most appropriate word.

✔ Reorganize a document outline.

✔ Find and replace text.

✔ Correct spelling and grammatical errors.

✔ Finalize a document.

Unless the documents you create are intended for no one's eyes but your own, you need to ensure that they are correct, logical, and persuasive. Whether you are a novice writer or an experienced writer, Microsoft Office Word 2007 has several tools that make creating professional documents easy and efficient:

- Editing tools provide quick-selection techniques and drag-and-drop editing to make it easy to move and copy text anywhere you want it.

- The building blocks feature can be used to save and recall specialized terms or standard paragraphs.

- Reference and research tools include a thesaurus that makes it easy to track down synonyms and research services that provide access to a variety of Web-based reference materials.

- Outlining tools allow easy rearranging of headings and text to ensure that your argument is logical.

- Search tools can be used to locate and replace words and phrases, either one at a time or throughout a document.

- The AutoCorrect and Spelling And Grammar features make it easy to correct typos and grammatical errors before you share a document with others.

- Finalizing tools ensure that a document is ready for distribution.

In this chapter, you will edit the text in a document by inserting and deleting text, copying and pasting a phrase, and moving a paragraph. You will save a couple of building blocks, and you'll rearrange a document in Outline view. You will find a phrase and replace one phrase with another throughout the entire document. You'll change an AutoCorrect setting and add a misspelled word to its list. You'll check the spelling and grammar in a document and add a term to the custom dictionary. Finally, you'll inspect a document for inappropriate information and mark it as final.

See Also Do you need only a quick refresher on the topics in this chapter? See the Quick Reference entries on pages xxxix–lxiii.

Important Before you can use the practice files in this chapter, you need to install them from the book's companion CD to their default location. See "Using the Book's CD" on page xxv for more information.

Troubleshooting Graphics and operating system–related instructions in this book reflect the Windows Vista user interface. If your computer is running Microsoft Windows XP and you experience trouble following the instructions as written, please refer to the "Information for Readers Running Windows XP" section at the beginning of this book.

Making Changes to a Document

You will rarely write a perfect document that doesn't require any editing. You will almost always want to insert a word or two, change a phrase, or move text from one place to another. You can edit a document as you create it, or you can write it first and then revise it. Or you might want to edit a document that you created for one purpose so that it will serve a different purpose. For example, a letter from last year's marketing campaign might be edited to create a new letter for this year's campaign.

Inserting text is easy; you click to position the insertion point and simply begin typing. Any existing text to the right of the insertion point moves to make room for the new text.

What Happened to Overtype?

By default, Word is in Insert mode. In previous versions of Word, it was possible to accidentally switch to Overtype mode by inadvertently pressing the Insert key. In Overtype mode, existing text does not move to the right when you type new text; instead, each character you type replaces an existing character.

In Word 2007, you must deliberately switch to Overtype mode if you want to use it. Here's how:

1. Right-click the status bar, and then click **Overtype** to display the Insert mode status at the left end of the status bar.

2. Click **Insert** on the status bar.

   The word *Overtype* then replaces *Insert*. You can click the word to switch back to Insert mode when you have finished overtyping.

By default, pressing the Insert key has no effect on the mode. If you want the Insert key to turn Overtype mode on and off, follow these steps:

1. Click the **Microsoft Office Button**, and then click **Word Options**.

2. In the **Word Options** dialog box, click **Advanced** in the left pane, and then under **Editing options**, select the **Use the Insert key to control overtype mode** check box.

3. Click **OK**.

Deleting text is equally easy. If you want to delete only one or a few characters, you can simply position the insertion point and then press the Backspace or Delete key until the characters are all gone. Pressing Backspace deletes the character to the left of the insertion point; pressing Delete deletes the character to the right of the insertion point.

To delete more than a few characters efficiently, you need to know how to *select* the text. Selected text appears highlighted on the screen. You can select specific items as follows:

- To select a word, double-click it. Word selects the word and the space following it. It does not select punctuation following a word.

- To select a sentence, click anywhere in the sentence while holding down the Ctrl key. Word selects all the characters in the sentence, from the first character through the space following the ending punctuation mark.

- To select a paragraph, triple-click it.

You can select adjacent words, lines, or paragraphs by positioning the insertion point at the beginning of the text you want to select, holding down the Shift key, and then pressing the Arrow keys or clicking at the end of the text that you want to select. If you want to select words, lines, or paragraphs that are not adjacent, you make the first selection and then hold down the Ctrl key while selecting the next block.

As an alternative, you can use the *selection area* to quickly select various items. This is an invisible area in the document's left margin, where the pointer becomes a hollow right-pointing arrow. You can use the selection area as follows:

- To select a line, click the selection area to the left of the line.
- To select a paragraph, double-click the selection area to the left of the paragraph.
- To select an entire document, triple-click the selection area.

> The Taguien Cycle
> A Fantasy Series for Young Adults
>
> The Taguien Cycle is the most exciting and promising new book project to have come before the committee in several years. It meets our two principal goals: Develop a book line that will appeal to young adult readers between the ages of twelve to fifteen, especially boys; and develop a book line that has the potential for media spin-offs that will contribute to future profits and on-going financial success.
>
> Each year Lucerne has published several fairytale/magic books for younger readers, but we do not currently offer anything sophisticated enough to appeal to young adult readers. Although we have found it very difficult to sell other genres to this audience of reluctant readers, there is every indication that offering a fantasy series at this time would meet with success.
>
> Interest in the fantasy genre has increased steadily over the past ten years, a trend that shows no sign of reversal. Anecdotal industry sales statistics show an increase of 2 to 3 percent per year for adult fantasy books and 5 to 6 percent for young adult fantasy books.

Selection area

After selecting the text you want to work with, simply press the Backspace or Delete key.

> **Tip** To deselect text, click anywhere in the document window except the selection area.

After selecting text, you can move or copy it in the following ways:

- Use the *Clipboard* when you need to move or copy text between two locations that you cannot see at the same time—for example, between pages or between documents. The Clipboard is a temporary storage area in your computer's memory. Select the text, and then click the Cut or Copy button in the Clipboard group on the Home tab. Then reposition the insertion point and click the Paste button to insert the selection in its new location. When you cut text, it is removed from its original location, and when you copy it, it also remains in its original location.

See Also For more information, see the sidebar entitled "About the Clipboard" later in this topic.

● Use *drag-and-drop editing* (frequently referred to simply as *dragging*) when you need to move or copy text only a short distance—for example, within a paragraph or line. Dragging does not involve the Clipboard. Start by selecting the text. Then hold down the mouse button, drag the text to its new location, and release the mouse button. To copy the selection, hold down the Ctrl key while you drag.

If you make a change to a document and then realize that you made a mistake, you can easily reverse the change. You can undo your last editing action by clicking the Undo button on the Quick Access Toolbar. To undo an earlier action, click the Undo arrow and then click that actions in the list.

> **Tip** Selecting an action from the Undo list undoes that action and all the editing actions you performed after that one. You cannot undo a single action except the last one you performed.

If you undo an action and then change your mind, you can click the Redo button on the Quick Access Toolbar. You can redo only the last action that you undid.

In this exercise, you will edit the text in a document. You'll insert and delete text, undo the deletion, copy and paste a phrase, and move a paragraph.

> **USE** the *01_Changes* document. This practice file is located in the *Chapter02* subfolder under *SBS_Word2007*.
> **BE SURE TO** start Word before beginning this exercise.
> **OPEN** the *01_Changes* document.

Show/Hide ¶

1. If non-printing characters are not visible in the document, on the **Home** tab, in the **Paragraph** group, click the **Show/Hide** ¶ button.

2. In the third sentence of the first paragraph, click immediately to the left of the word *between*, hold down the ⎣shift⎦ key, and then click immediately to the right of the word *fifteen* (and to the left of the comma that follows it).

   Word selects the text between the two clicks.

¶

The·Taguien··Cycle¶
A·Fantasy·Series·for·Young··Adults¶

¶
The·Taguien··Cycle··is·the·most··exciting··and·promising··new·book·project·to·have··come·before·
the·committee··in·several··years.··It·meets··our·two·principal··goals:··Develop··a·book·line··that·will·
appeal·to·young··adult··readers·between··the·ages··of·twelve··to·fifteen,··especially··boys;··and·
develop··a·book·line··that·has·the·potential··for·media··spin-offs··that·will··contribute··to·future·
profits··and·on-going··financial··success.¶
¶
Each·year·Lucerne··has·published··several·fairytale/magic··books·for·younger··readers,··but·we·do·
not·currently··offer··anything··sophisticated··enough··to·appeal·to·young··adult··readers.··Although·
we·have··found··it·very··difficult··to·sell··other·genres··to·this·audience··of·reluctant··readers,··there·is·
every·indication··that·offering··a·fantasy··series··at·this··time··would·meet·with··success.¶
¶
Interest·in·the·fantasy··genre··has·increased··steadily··over·the·past·ten·years,··a·trend·that·shows·no·
sign··of·reversal.··Anecdotal··industry··sales·statistics··show··an·increase··of·2·to·3·percent·per·year·
for·adult··fantasy··books·and·5·to·6·percent·for·young··adult·fantasy··books.¶

3. Press the ⌨Del key to delete the selection.

Word also deletes the space before the selection.

4. Select the word **book** in the first sentence of the first paragraph by double-clicking it, and then press the ⌨Backspace key.

5. Double-click the word **principal** in the same paragraph, and then replace it by typing **primary**.

Notice that you don't have to type a space after *primary*. Word inserts the space for you.

> **Tip** Word inserts and deletes spaces because the Use Smart Cut And Paste check box is selected on the Advanced page of the Word Options dialog box. If you want to be able to control the spacing yourself, click the Microsoft Office Button, click Word Options, click Advanced, clear this check box, and click OK.

6. Position the mouse pointer in the selection area to the left of the phrase *A Fantasy Series for Young Adults*, and then click once to select the entire line of text.

7. On the **Home** tab, in the **Clipboard** group, click the **Copy** button.

Copy

The selection is copied to the Clipboard.

8. Click the **Next Page** button below the vertical scroll bar to move to the beginning of the next page, press the ⌨↓ key, and then in the **Clipboard** group, click the **Paste** button (not its arrow).

Paste

The Paste Options button appears below and to the right of the insertion. You can click this button if you want to change Word's default way of pasting, but in this case, you can just ignore it.

Cut

9. Return to Page 1, and then in the numbered list, triple-click anywhere in the *Bartimaeus Trilogy* paragraph to select the entire paragraph.

10. In the **Clipboard** group, click the **Cut** button.

11. Press the ⬆ key to move to the beginning of the *Harry Potter series* paragraph, and then in the **Clipboard** group, click the **Paste** button.

The two paragraphs have effectively switched places and the list has been renumbered.

See Also For more information about numbered lists, see "Creating and Modifying Lists" in Chapter 3, "Changing the Look of Text."

Undo

12. On the **Quick Access Toolbar**, click the **Undo** arrow, and in the list, click the third action (**Paste**).

Word undoes the previous cut-and-paste operation and the pasting of the copied text.

13. Press Ctrl + Home to move to the top of the document. Then move the pointer into the selection area adjacent to the paragraph that begins *Interest in the fantasy genre*, and double-click to select the paragraph.

14. Point to the selection, hold down the mouse button, and then drag the paragraph up to the beginning of the paragraph above it.

When you release the mouse, the text appears in its new location.

15. With the text still selected, press the End key.

Word releases the selection and moves the insertion point to the end of the paragraph.

16. Press Space , and then press Del

Word deletes the paragraph mark, and the two paragraphs are now one paragraph.

¶

The·Taguien· Cycle¶
A·Fantasy·Series·for· Young· Adults¶

¶
The·Taguien· Cycle· is·the·most·exciting· and·promising· new·project·to·have· come·before·the· committee· in·several·years.· It·meets·our·two·primary· goals:· Develop· a·book·line· that·will· appeal·to·young· adult·readers,·especially· boys;· and·develop· a·book·line· that·has·the·potential· for·media· spin-offs· that·will· contribute· to·future· profits· and·on-going· financial· success.¶

¶
Interest·in· the·fantasy· genre· has·increased· steadily· over·the·past·ten· years,· a·trend·that·shows· no· sign· of·reversal.· Anecdotal· industry· sales· statistics· show· an·increase· of·2·to·3·percent· per·year· for·adult· fantasy· books·and·5·to·6·percent· for·young· adult·fantasy· books.· Each·year· Lucerne· has· published· several· fairytale/magic· books·for·younger· readers,· but· we·do·not· currently· offer· anything· sophisticated· enough· to·appeal·to·young· adult·readers.· Although· we·have·found· it· very·difficult· to·sell· other·genres· to·this· audience· of·reluctant· readers,·there· is· every· indication· that·offering· a·fantasy· series· at·this· time· would· meet·with· success.¶

¶
¶

17. In the selection area, click adjacent to the paragraph mark below the combined paragraph, and then press ⌷Del⌷.

CLOSE the *01_Changes* document without saving your changes.

About the Clipboard

You can view the items that have been cut and copied to the Clipboard by clicking the Clipboard Dialog Box Launcher to open the Clipboard task pane, which displays up to 24 cut or copied items.

To paste an individual item at the insertion point, you simply click the item. To paste all the items, click the Paste All button. You can point to an item, click the arrow that appears, and then click Delete to remove it from the Clipboard, or you can remove all the items by clicking the Clear All button.

You can control the behavior of the Clipboard task pane by clicking Options at the bottom of the pane. You can choose to have the Clipboard task pane appear when you cut or copy a single item or multiple items. You can also choose to display the Clipboard icon in the status area of the taskbar when the Clipboard task pane is displayed.

To close the Clipboard task pane, click the Close button at the right end of its title bar.

Inserting Saved Text

To save time and ensure consistency in your documents, you can save any text you use frequently as a *building block*. You do this by selecting the text, clicking Quick Parts in the Text group on the Insert tab, clicking Save Selection To Quick Part Gallery, and assigning the text a name. It then appears under its assigned name in the Quick Parts gallery.

See Also For information about the many different kinds of pre-defined building blocks that you can use to enhance your documents, see "Inserting Ready-Made Document Parts" in Chapter 8, "Working with Longer Documents."

After you have saved the text, you can insert it at any time by clicking Quick Parts to display its gallery and then clicking the building block you want.

> **Tip** You can also type the name of the building block and then press the F3 key to insert it at the insertion point.

In this exercise, you will save the names of a company and a product as building blocks so that you can insert them elsewhere in a document.

> **USE** the *02_SavedText* document. This practice file is located in the *Chapter02* subfolder under *SBS_Word2007*.
>
> **OPEN** the *02_SavedText* document.

1. Toward the end of the first paragraph of the document, select **Wide World Importers**.

[Quick Parts ▾]

2. On the **Insert** tab, in the **Text** group, click the **Quick Parts** button, and then click **Save Selection to Quick Part Gallery**.

The Create New Building Block dialog box opens.

Create New Building Block		
Name:	Wide World	
Gallery:	Quick Parts	▾
Category:	General	▾
Description:		
Save in:	Building Blocks	▾
Options:	Insert content only	▾
	OK	Cancel

3. In the **Name** box, type www, and then click **OK**.

Word saves the selection in the Quick Parts gallery.

4. In the third paragraph of the document, select **chimonobambusa marmorea**, and then in the **Text** group, click the **Quick Parts** button.

Notice that the company name now appears as a building block in the Quick Parts gallery.

General
www
Wide World Importers

📄 Document Property   ▸
🔲 Field...
📘 Building Blocks Organizer...
🖥 Get More on Office Online...
📄 Save Selection to Quick Part Gallery...

5. Click **Save Selection to Quick Part Gallery**, and save the selected text with the name **cm**.

6. Press Ctrl + End to move the insertion point to the end of the document, and then press Space.

7. Type **In particular** and a space. Then in the **Text** group, click the **Quick Parts** button, and in the gallery, click the **www** entry.

   The company name appears at the insertion point.

8. Type a space followed by **recommends cm**.

9. Press the F3 key, and then type a period.

   Word replaces *cm* with its building block, *chimonobambusa marmorea*.

about anyone who wishes to grow one in their backyard. Some dwarf species include chimonobambusa marmorea, indocalamus tessellatus, and pleioblastus chino vaginatus. Also suitable for the personal garden are those categorized as mid size. Examples of these types of plants are bambusa glaucophylla and otatea acuminata aztectorum. Plant starts and seeds are easier to find than ever, being available at nurseries and through mail order. ¶
¶
Bamboo is quickly becoming an important economic factor in many developing nations. A 60-foot tree cut for marketing can take up to 60 years to replace, whereas a 60-foot bamboo can take as little as 60 days to reach marketability. And the majority of bamboo destined for the world market is harvested by women and children, most of who live at or below subsistence levels in poor nations. So as production increases, so does support for the economies of those countries that produce it. ¶
¶
Choosing bamboo as part of home or garden design makes sense on many levels. Not only does it have an appealing look, but it supports the environment as well as the countries that produce it. In particular Wide World Importers recommends chimonobambusa marmorea. ¶

www   cm

Troubleshooting Pressing the F3 key substitutes the corresponding building block only if the name you type contains no spaces. There must be a space to its left, and the insertion point must be to its right.

CLOSE the *02_SavedText* document without saving your changes.

Important When you quit Word, you will be asked whether you want to save the Building Blocks template, which by default is where your custom building blocks are saved. If you want to discard the building blocks you have created in this Word session, click No. If you want to save them, click Yes.

Inserting the Date and Time

One of the easiest ways to insert today's date or the current time in a document is to use the Insert Date And Time button in the Text group on the Insert tab. After you specify the format you want to use, Word retrieves the date or time from your computer's internal calendar or clock. You can insert the information as regular text or as a *field*. A field is a placeholder that tells Word to supply the specified information in the specified way. The advantage of using a field is that it can be updated with the click of a button.

Here are the steps for inserting the date or time:

1. With the insertion point located where you want the date or time to appear, on the **Insert** tab, in the **Text** group, click the **Date & Time** button.

   The Date And Time dialog box opens.

2. Under **Available formats**, click the date and/or time format you want.

3. If you want to insert a date or time field, select the **Update automatically** check box.

4. Click **OK**.

If you selected Update Automatically, Word inserts a Date or Time field depending on the format you selected. When you point to the field, it is highlighted as a unit. You can click the field to select it, and you can click the Update button that appears above it to update the field with the most current information. If you right-click the field, you can click Toggle Field Codes to see the codes that control the field; click the command again to redisplay the date or time information.

You can insert other types of date and time fields, such as a PrintDate field or an EditTime field. Insert a Date or Time field in the usual way, right-click the field, and then click Edit Field. In the Field dialog box, change the setting in the Categories box to Date And Time, and in the Field Names list, click the field you want. When you click OK, the information corresponding to the field type you specified is shown in the document.

Finding the Most Appropriate Word

Language is often contextual—you use different words and phrases in a marketing brochure, in a letter requesting immediate payment of an invoice, and in an informal memo about a social gathering after work. To help you ensure that you are using the words that best convey your meaning in any given context, Word provides a *Thesaurus* where you can look up synonyms (alternative words) for a selected word. The Thesaurus is one of a set of Research services provided by Word.

To look up alternatives for a word in the Thesaurus, you select the word and then click the Thesaurus button in the Proofing group on the Review tab. The Research task pane opens, displaying a list of synonyms. You then click the synonym that you want to replace the selected word.

In this exercise, you'll use the Thesaurus to replace one word with another.

> **USE** the *03_FindingWord* document. This practice file is located in the *Chapter02* subfolder under *SBS_Word2007*.
>
> **OPEN** the *03_FindingWord* document.

1. Double-click the word **rigorous** in the last line of the first paragraph of the letter.

2. On the **Review** tab, in the **Proofing** group, click the **Thesaurus** button.

   The Research task pane opens, listing synonyms for the word *rigorous*.

3. In the task pane, under **exact**, click **meticulous**.

   The word *meticulous* replaces *rigorous* in the Search For box at the top of the task pane, and synonyms for *meticulous* are now listed in the task pane.

4. Point to the word **thorough**, click the arrow that appears, and then click **Insert**.

   The word *thorough* replaces *rigorous* in the document.

5. Close the **Research** task pane.

CLOSE the *03_FindingWord* document without saving your changes.

Researching Information

In addition to the Thesaurus, the Research task pane provides access to a variety of informational resources from within Word. You can enter a topic in the Search For box and specify in the box below which resource Word should use to look for information about that topic. By clicking Research Options at the bottom of the Research task pane, you can specify which of a predefined list of reference materials, such as Microsoft Encarta and various Internet resources, will be available from a list, and you can add your own reference-material sources.

To research information:

1. On the **Review** tab, in the **Proofing** group, click the **Research** button to display the Research task pane.

2. In the **Search for** box, type the topic you are interested in researching.

   For example, you might type *bamboo*.

3. Click the arrow to the right of the box below the Search For box, and then in the list, click the resource you want to use to search for information.

   For example, you might click MSN Search. When you have made your selection, the Start Searching button to the right of the Search For box flashes, and seconds later, the search results are displayed in the task pane.

4. Click any information sources that interest you.

   You can click a hyperlink to a Web address to go to the Web to track down further information. You can also select part of a topic, right-click the selection, click Copy, and then paste the selection into your document. Or you can click right-click the selection and click Look Up to research information about the selection.

Translating Text

Word now comes with built-in dictionaries for many common languages, so you can easily translate words and phrases from one language to another.

To translate a word into another language:

1. Select the word, and then on the **Review** tab, in the **Proofing** group, click the **Translate** button.

   The Research task pane opens with boxes in which you can specify the source language and the translation language.

2. Under **Translation** in the **Research** task pane, change the settings in the **From** and **To** boxes as necessary.

   The translated text appears under Bilingual Dictionary.

To translate a different word or phrase, you can type it in the Search For box and then click the Start Searching button to the right.

To view the translation of any word you point to, click the Translation ScreenTip button in the Proofing group on the Review tab, and then select the language you want to see. You can then point to any word in a document to display the equivalent word in the language you selected. Click the button again, and then click Turn Off Translation ScreenTip to turn off the translation display.

Reorganizing a Document Outline

If you are creating a document that contains headings, you can format it with built-in heading styles that include outline levels. Then it is easy to view and organize the document in Outline view. In this view, you can hide all the body text and display only the headings at and above a particular level. You can then rearrange the sections of a document by moving their headings.

See Also For more information about formatting with styles, see "Working with Templates" in Chapter 4, "Changing the Look of a Document."

To view a document in Outline view, click the Outline button in the Document Views group on the View tab, or click the Outline button on the View toolbar. The document is then displayed with a hierarchical structure, and the Outlining tab appears on the Ribbon.

The Outline Tools group on this tab includes buttons you can click to display only the headings at a specific level and above, to *promote* or *demote* headings or body text by changing their level, and to move headings and their text up or down in the document. The indentations and symbols used in Outline view to indicate the level of a heading or paragraph in the document's structure do not appear in the document in other views or when you print it.

> **Tip** You can click the buttons in the Master Document group to create a master document with subdocuments that you can then display and hide. The topic of master documents and subdocuments is beyond the scope of this book. For information, see Word Help.

In this exercise, you'll switch to Outline view, promote and demote headings, move headings, and expand and collapse the outline.

> **USE** the *04_Outline* document. This practice file is located in the *Chapter02* subfolder under *SBS_Word2007*.
>
> **OPEN** the *04_Outline* document.

Outline

1. In the lower-right corner of the window, on the **View** toolbar, click the **Outline** button.

   The screen changes to display the document in Outline view, and the Outlining tab appears at the left end of the Ribbon.

2. On the **Outlining** tab, in the **Outline Tools** group, click the **Show Level** arrow, and in the list, click **Level 1**.

   The document collapses to display only level-1 headings.

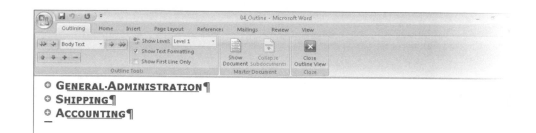

○ **GENERAL·ADMINISTRATION**¶
○ **SHIPPING**¶
○ **ACCOUNTING**¶

3. Click anywhere in the **Accounting** heading.

4. In the **Outline Tools** group, click the **Expand** button.

Expand

Word expands the *Accounting* section to display its level-2 headings.

5. In the **Outline Tools** group, click the **Demote** button.

Demote

The *Accounting* heading changes to a level-2 heading.

6. On the **Quick Access Toolbar**, click the **Undo** button.

Undo

The *Accounting* heading changes back to a level-1 heading.

7. In the **Outline Tools** group, click the **Collapse** button.

Collapse

8. Click the **Demote** button.

Again, the *Accounting* heading changes to a level-2 heading.

9. Click the **Expand** button.

Because the subheadings were hidden under *Accounting* when you demoted the heading, all the subheadings have been demoted to level 3 to maintain the hierarchy of the section.

10. Click the **Collapse** button, and then in the **Outline Tools** group, click the **Promote** button.

Promote

The *Accounting* heading is now a level-1 heading again.

11. Press [Ctrl]+[Home] to move to the top of the document, and then in the **Outline Tools** group, in the **Show Level** list, click **Level 2**.

The outline shows all the level-1 and level-2 headings.

12. Click the plus sign to the left of the *Accounting* heading, and then in the **Outline Tools** group, click the **Move Up** button three times.

Move Up

The *Accounting* heading and all its subheadings move above the *Shipping* heading.

13. In the **Outline Tools** group, in the **Show Level** list, click **All Levels**.

You can now scroll through the document to see the effects of the reorganization.

14. In the **Close** group, click the **Close Outline View** button.

Word displays the reorganized document in Print Layout view.

CLOSE the *04_Outline* document without saving your changes.

Finding and Replacing Text

One way to ensure that the text in your documents is consistent and accurate is to use the Find feature of Word to search for every instance of a particular word or phrase. For example, if you were responsible for advertising a trademarked product, you would probably want to search your marketing materials to check that every instance of the product's name was correctly identified as a trademark.

Clicking the Find button in the Editing group on the Home tab displays the Find tab of the Find And Replace dialog box. After you enter the text you want to find in the Find What box, you can do the following:

- Click Find Next to select the first occurrence of that text.
- In the Reading Highlight list, click Highlight All to highlight all occurrences.

If you find an error in the document while conducting a search, you can make editing changes on the fly without closing the Find And Replace dialog box. Simply click the document, make the change, and then click the Find And Replace dialog box to make it active again.

If you know that you want to substitute one word or phrase for another, you can use the Replace feature to find each occurrence of the text you want to change and replace it with different text. Clicking the Replace button in the Editing group displays the Replace tab of the Find And Replace dialog box, which is similar to the Find tab. On the Replace tab, you can do the following:

- Click Replace to replace the selected occurrence with the text in the Replace With box and move to the next occurrence.
- Click Replace All to replace all occurrences with the text in the Replace With box.
- Click Find Next to leave the selected occurrence as it is and locate the next one.

You can use other options in the Find And Replace dialog box to carry out more complicated searches and replaces. Clicking More expands the box to make these additional options available.

You can make a selection from the Search list to guide the direction of the search. You can select the Match Case check box to match capitalization and select the Find Whole Words Only check box to find only whole-word occurrences of the Find What text. If you want to check that your usage of two similar words, such as *effect* and *affect*, is correct, you can select the Use Wildcards check box and then enter a *wildcard character* in the Find What box to locate variable information. The two most common wildcard characters are:

● The ? wildcard stands for any single character in this location in the Find What text.

● The * wildcard stands for any number of characters in this location in the Find What text.

> **Tip** To see a list of the other available wildcards, use Help to search for wildcards.

Selecting the Sounds Like check box finds occurrences of the search text that sound the same but are spelled differently, such as *there* and *their*. Selecting the Find All Word Forms check box finds occurrences of a particular word in any form, such as *plan*, *planned*, and *planning*. You can match a prefix or a suffix, and you can ignore punctuation and white space. Finally, you can locate formatting, such as bold, or special characters, such as tabs, by selecting them from the Format or Special list.

In this exercise, you will find a phrase and make a correction to the document. Then you'll replace one phrase with another throughout the entire document.

> **USE** the *05_FindingText* document. This practice file is located in the *Chapter02* subfolder under *SBS_Word2007*.
>
> **OPEN** the *05_FindingText* document.

1. With the insertion point at the beginning of the document, on the **Home** tab, in the **Editing** group, click the **Find** button.

The Find And Replace dialog box opens, displaying the Find tab.

2. In the **Find what** box, type The Taguien Cycle, click **Reading Highlight**, and then in the list, click **Highlight All**.

3. Scroll to Page 2.

Word has found and selected all the occurrences of *The Taguien Cycle* in the document. (We dragged the title bar of the dialog box to move it to the side.)

4. Click the document behind the **Find and Replace** dialog box, double-click the word **the** in *the Taguien Cycle* in the first paragraph (not the title) on Page 2, and then type The to correct the capitalization.

5. Press Ctrl + Home to move the insertion point to the beginning of the document.

6. Click the title bar of the **Find and Replace** dialog box, and then click the **Replace** tab.

The Find What box retains the entry from the previous search.

7. Click the **Replace with** box, type The Taguien Cycle, and then click the **More** button.

8. At the bottom of the expanded dialog box, click the **Format** button, and then click **Font**.

The Replace Font dialog box opens.

9. Under **Font Style**, click **Italic**, and then click **OK**.

10. Click **Find Next**, and then click **Replace**.

   The selected plain text title is replaced with italicized text, and the next occurrence of *The Taguien Cycle* is selected.

11. Click **Replace All**.

   Word displays a message box indicating that six replacements were made.

12. Click **OK** to close the message box, and then in the **Find and Replace** dialog box, click the **Find** tab.

13. In the **Find what** box, click **Reading Highlight**, and then in the list, click **Highlight All**.

   Word highlights six occurrences of the Find What text.

14. Click **Reading Highlight**, and then in the list, click **Clear Highlighting**.

CLOSE the Find And Replace dialog box and then close the *05_FindingText* document without saving your changes.

Correcting Spelling and Grammatical Errors

In the days of handwritten and typewritten documents, people might have tolerated a typographical or grammatical error or two because correcting such errors without creating a mess was difficult. Word processors like Word have built-in spelling and grammar checkers, so now documents that contain these types of errors are likely to reflect badly on their creators.

> **Tip** Although Word can help you eliminate misspellings and grammatical errors, its tools are not infallible. You should always read through your documents to catch the problems that the Word tools can't detect.

Word provides two tools to help you with the chore of eliminating spelling and grammar errors: the AutoCorrect and Spelling And Grammar features.

Have you noticed that Word automatically corrects some misspellings as you type them? This is the work of the AutoCorrect feature. AutoCorrect corrects commonly misspelled words, such as *adn* to *and*, so that you don't have to correct them yourself. AutoCorrect comes with a long list of frequently misspelled words and their correct spellings. If you frequently misspell a word that AutoCorrect doesn't change, you can add it to the list in the AutoCorrect dialog box.

If you deliberately mistype a word and don't want to accept the AutoCorrect change, you can reverse it by clicking the Undo button on the Quick Access Toolbar before you type anything else.

Although AutoCorrect ensures that your documents are free of common misspellings, it doesn't detect random typographical and grammatical errors. For those types of errors, you can turn to the Spelling And Grammar feature for help. You might have noticed that as you type, Word underlines potential spelling errors with red wavy underlines and grammatical errors with green wavy underlines. You can right-click an underlined word or phrase to display suggested corrections.

If you want to check the spelling or grammar of the entire document, it is easier to click the Spelling & Grammar button in the Proofing group on the Review tab than to deal with underlined words and phrases individually. Word then works its way through the document from the insertion point and displays the Spelling And Grammar dialog box if it encounters a potential error. If the error is a misspelling, the Spelling And Grammar dialog box suggests corrections; if the error is a breach of grammar, the Spelling And Grammar dialog box tells you which rule you have broken as well as suggesting corrections. The buttons available in the Spelling And Grammar dialog box are dynamic and change to those most appropriate for fixing the error. For example, for a grammatical error, you are given the opportunity to ignore the rule you have broken throughout the document.

In this exercise, you'll change an AutoCorrect setting and add a misspelled word to its list. You'll check the spelling in the document and add terms to the custom dictionary, and you'll find, review, and correct a grammatical error.

> **USE** the *06_Spelling* document. This practice file is located in the *Chapter02* subfolder under *SBS_Word2007*.
>
> **OPEN** the *06_Spelling* document.

1. Click at the end of the first paragraph in the letter, press [Space], and then type in your reserch, followed by a period.

   As soon as you type the period, AutoCorrect changes *reserch* to *research*.

2. Click the **Microsoft Office Button**, and then click **Word Options**.

3. In the left pane of the **Word Options** window, click **Proofing**, and then on the Proofing page, click **AutoCorrect Options**.

   The AutoCorrect dialog box opens, displaying the AutoCorrect tab.

Microsoft Office
Button

Notice the corrections that AutoCorrect will make. You can clear the check box of any item you don't want corrected. For example, if you don't want AutoCorrect to capitalize a lowercase letter or word that follows a period, clear the Capitalize First Letter Of Sentences check box.

4. Click in the **Replace** box, and then type avalable.

   Word scrolls the list below to show the entry that is closest to what you typed.

5. Press the Tab key to move the insertion point to the **With** box, and then type available.

6. Click **Add** to add the entry to the correction list, and then click **OK**.

7. Click **OK** to close the Word Options window.

8. Press Ctrl+End to move to the end of the document, and then in the paragraph that begins *Thank you for your* interest, position the insertion point to the right of the period at the end of the third sentence.

9. Press Space , and then type Shelly will not be avalable May 10-15 followed by a period.

   The word *avalable* changes to *available*.

10. Press Ctrl + Home to move to the top of the document, and then right-click *sorces*, the first word with a red wavy underline.

Word lists possible correct spellings for this word, as well as actions you might want to carry out.

sources
sores
scores
forces
sources'
Ignore
Ignore All
Add to Dictionary
AutoCorrect ▶
Language ▶
Spelling...
Look Up...
Cut
Copy
Paste

11. In the list, click **sources**.

Word removes the red wavy underline and inserts the correction.

12. Press Ctrl + Home again, and then on the **Review** tab, in the **Proofing** group, click the **Spelling & Grammar** button.

The Spelling And Grammar dialog box opens, with the first word that Word does not recognize, *commited*, displayed in red in the Not In Dictionary box.

Spelling and Grammar: English (United States)

Not in Dictionary:

It is a very complex balancing act, but we are commited to doing our part to succeed.

- Ignore Once
- Ignore All
- Add to Dictionary

Suggestions:

- committed
- commuted
- commixed

- Change
- Change All
- AutoCorrect

☑ Check grammar

Options...   Undo   Cancel

13. With **committed** selected in the **Suggestions** box, click **AutoCorrect**.

Word adds the misspelling and the selected correction to the AutoCorrect list, so that the next time you type *commited* by mistake, the spelling will be corrected for you as you type. Word then flags *Dyck* as the next possible misspelling.

> **Troubleshooting** If the errors we mention don't appear to be in the practice file, click Options at the bottom of the Spelling And Grammar dialog box. Then in the Word Options window, under When Correcting Spelling And Grammar In Word, click Recheck Document, click Yes to reset the checkers, and then click OK.

14. Click **Ignore All**.

    Word will now skip over this and any other occurrences of this proper noun. It moves on to highlight the duplicate word *for*.

15. Click **Delete**.

    Word deletes the second *for* and then flags a possible grammatical error.

This grammatical error is identified as incorrect use of a comma. You need to read the sentence and then decide whether and how to correct it. In this case, the error is not related to the comma after *venture* but to the fact that there is no verb in the first half of the sentence.

> **Tip** Word's grammar checker helps identify phrases and clauses that do not follow traditional grammatical rules, but it is not always accurate. It is easy to get in the habit of ignoring green wavy underlines. However, it is wise to scrutinize them all to be sure that your documents don't contain any embarrassing mistakes.

16. Behind the **Spelling and Grammar** dialog box, click the document, double-click the word **An** at the beginning of the sentence with the error, and then type The import business is an.

17. Click the title bar of the **Spelling and Grammar** dialog box, and then click **Resume**.

Word flags *Florian* as a word that it doesn't recognize. *Florian* is a proper noun and is spelled correctly. By adding words like this one to the custom dictionary, you can prevent Word from continuing to flag them.

18. Click **Add to Dictionary**.

Word displays a message, indicating that it has finished checking the spelling and grammar of the document.

19. Click **OK** to close the message box.

CLOSE the *06_Spelling* document without saving your changes.

Viewing Document Statistics

As you type, Word keeps track of the number of pages and words in your document, displaying this information at the left end of the status bar. To see the number of words in only part of the document, such as a few paragraphs, simply select that part. The status bar then displays the number of words in the selection, expressed as a fraction of the total, such as 250/800.

To see more statistics, you can open the Word Count dialog box by clicking the Word Count button in the Proofing group on the Review tab. In addition to the count of pages and words, the Word Count dialog box displays the number of characters, paragraphs, and lines. It also gives you the option of including or excluding words in text boxes, footnotes, and endnotes.

Finalizing a Document

When a document is complete and ready for distribution, you typically perform several final tasks. These might include inspecting the document for any remaining private or inappropriate information, restricting access, or adding a digital signature.

Many documents go through several revisions, and some are scrutinized by multiple reviewers. During this development process, documents can accumulate information that you might not want in the final version, such as the names of people who worked on the document, comments that reviewers have added to the file, or hidden text about status and assumptions. This extraneous information is not a concern if the final version is to be delivered as a printout. However, these days more and more files are delivered electronically, making this information available to anyone who wants to read it.

Word 2007 includes a tool called the Document Inspector, which finds and removes all extraneous and potentially confidential information. You can instruct the Document Inspector to look for comments, revisions, and annotations; for any personal information saved with the document; and for hidden text. The Document Inspector displays a summary of its findings and gives you the option of removing anything it finds.

Word also includes another finalizing tool called the Compatibility Checker, which checks for the use of features not supported in previous versions of Word.

After you have handled extraneous information and compatibility issues, you can mark a document as final and make its file read-only, so that other people know that they should not make changes to this released document.

In this exercise, you will inspect a document for inappropriate information and mark it as final.

> **USE** the *07_Finalizing* document. This practice file is located in the *Chapter02* subfolder under *SBS_Word2007*.
>
> **OPEN** the *07_Finalizing* document.

Microsoft Office
Button

1. Click the **Microsoft Office Button**, point to **Prepare**, and then click **Properties**.

The Document Information Panel opens above the document, showing that identifying information has been saved with the file. Some of the information, including the name of the author, was attached to the file by Word. Other information was added by a user.

2. In the upper-left corner of the **Document Information Panel**, click the **Document Properties** arrow, and then in the list, click **Advanced Properties**.

The Properties dialog box opens.

```
07_Finalizing Properties                              [?] [-][x]

 General | Summary | Statistics | Contents | Custom

    [W]        07_Finalizing


    Type:      Microsoft Office Word Document
    Location:  C:\Users\Carlos Carvallo\Documents\MSP\SBS_Word2007
    Size:      451KB (462,835 bytes)


    MS-DOS name:  07_FIN~1.DOC
    Created:      Friday, September 29, 2006 11:31:12 PM
    Modified:     Friday, September 29, 2006 5:26:28 PM
    Accessed:     Friday, September 29, 2006 11:31:12 PM


    Attributes:   [ ] Read only    [ ] Hidden
                  [✓] Archive      [ ] System


                              [    OK    ]  [  Cancel  ]
```

3. In turn, click the **Summary** and **Statistics** tabs, noticing that additional identifying information is displayed there.

4. Click **Cancel** to close the **Properties** dialog box, and then in the upper-right corner of the **Document Information Panel**, click the **Close** button.

[x]
Close

5. Save the document in the *Chapter02* subfolder with the name My Information Sheet.

6. Click the **Microsoft Office Button**, point to **Prepare**, and then click **Inspect Document**.

The Document Inspector dialog box opens, listing the items that will be checked.

7. Without changing the default selections in the **Document Inspector** dialog box, click **Inspect**.

   The Document Inspector reports the presence of the document properties and personal information that you viewed earlier in this exercise, as well as some custom XML data.

8. To the right of **Document Properties and Personal Information**, click **Remove All**.

   Word removes the document properties and personal information.

9. To the right of **Custom XML Data**, click **Remove All**.

   See Also For information about XML, see "Creating an XML Document" in Chapter 11, "Creating Documents for Use Outside of Word."

10. In the **Document Inspector** dialog box, click **Close**.

11. Click the **Microsoft Office Button**, point to **Prepare**, and then click **Mark As Final**.

   A message tells you that the document will be marked as final and then saved.

12. Click **OK** to complete the process.

   A message tells you that the document has been marked as final and that typing, editing commands, and proofing marks are turned off.

13. Click **OK** to close the message, and then click the **Insert** tab.

   Most of the buttons are inactive, indicating that you cannot make changes.

CLOSE the *My Information Sheet* document, and if you are not continuing directly on to the next chapter, quit Word.

Adding a Digital Signature

When you create a document that will be circulated to other people via e-mail or the Web, you might want to attach a *digital signature*, which is an electronic stamp of authentication. The digital signature confirms the origin of the document and indicates that no one has tampered with the document since it was signed.

To add a digital signature to a Word document, you must first obtain a digital ID. Certified digital IDs can be obtained from companies such as IntelliSafe Technologies and Comodo Inc. You can obtain the ID and attach it to a document by clicking the Microsoft Office Button, pointing to Finish, clicking Add a Digital Signature, and then following the instructions.

Key Points

- You can cut or copy text and paste it elsewhere in the same document or in a different document. Cut and copied text is stored on the Clipboard.

- Made a mistake? No problem! You can undo a single action or the last several actions you performed by clicking the Undo button (or its arrow) on the Quick Access Toolbar. You can even redo an action if you change you mind again.

- You don't have to type the same text over and over again. Instead, save the text as a Quick Part and insert it with a few mouse clicks.

- Need a more precise word to get your point across? You can use the Thesaurus to look up synonyms for a selected word, and use the Research service to access specialized reference materials and online resources.

- If you take the time to apply heading styles to a document, you can use the outline to rearrange the document.

- You can find each occurrence of a word or phrase and replace it with another.

- You can rely on AutoCorrect to correct common misspellings. Correct other spelling and grammatical errors individually as you type or by checking the entire document in one pass.

- Before you distribute an electronic document, you can remove any information you don't want people to be able to see.

Chapter at a Glance

Manually change
the look of characters,
page 68

Manually
change
the look of
paragraphs,
page 75

Quickly format text
and paragraphs,
page 66

Create and
modify lists,
page 86

3 Changing the Look of Text

In this chapter, you will learn to:

- ✔ Quickly format text and paragraphs.
- ✔ Manually change the look of characters.
- ✔ Manually change the look of paragraphs.
- ✔ Create and modify lists.

The appearance of your documents helps to convey their message. Microsoft Office Word 2007 can help you develop professional-looking documents whose appearance is appropriate to their contents. You can easily format your text so that key points stand out and your arguments are easy to grasp.

In this chapter, you will experiment with Quick Styles and then change the look of individual words. Then you'll indent paragraphs, change paragraph alignment and spacing, set tab stops, modify line spacing, and add borders and shading. Finally you'll create and format both bulleted and numbered lists.

See Also Do you need only a quick refresher on the topics in this chapter? See the Quick Reference entries on pages xxxix–lxiii.

> **Important** Before you can use the practice files in this chapter, you need to install them from the book's companion CD to their default location. See "Using the Book's CD" on page xxv for more information.

> **Troubleshooting** Graphics and operating system–related instructions in this book reflect the Windows Vista user interface. If your computer is running Microsoft Windows XP and you experience trouble following the instructions as written, please refer to the "Information for Readers Running Windows XP" section at the beginning of this book.

Quickly Formatting Text and Paragraphs

Word 2007 includes a number of new features, as well as enhancements to existing features, that make the process of formatting content effortless. For example, buttons for changing the font size, color, and other character attributes have been gathered in the Font group on the Home tab so that they are all easily accessible. And many common formatting buttons are available on the Mini toolbar that appears when you point to selected text.

See Also   For information about changing character attributes, see "Manually Changing the Look of Characters" later in this chapter.

However, you don't have to apply attributes one at a time. You can easily change several attributes at once with a couple of mouse clicks by using *Quick Styles*. This powerful tool is available in the Styles group on the Home tab. Quick Styles are galleries consisting of the following:

- *Paragraph styles.* You can use these styles to apply a consistent look to different types of paragraphs, such as headings, body text, captions, quotations, and list paragraphs.

- *Character styles.* You can use these styles to change the appearance of selected words.

All of the Quick Styles in a particular gallery coordinate with each other, lending a clean, consistent, professional look to your documents. You can switch from one set of styles to another by selecting from Quick Styles galleries with names like Traditional, Distinctive, Modern, and Elegant. To help you choose the style you want, you can point to the name of the set to see a live preview of how your document will look with a particular set of Quick Styles applied to it. After you have applied one set of Quick Styles, you can easily change the look of the entire document by selecting a different set of Quick Styles from the Change Styles list.

In this exercise, you will experiment with Quick Styles.

USE the *01_QuickFormatting* document. This practice file is located in the *Chapter03* subfolder under *SBS_Word2007*.

BE SURE TO start Word before beginning this exercise.

OPEN the *01_QuickFormatting* document.

1. With the insertion point at the top of the document, on the **Home** tab, in the **Styles** group, move the pointer over each thumbnail in the displayed row of the **Quick Styles** gallery.

The formatting of the heading changes to show you a live preview of how the heading will look if you click the style you are pointing to. You don't have to actually apply the formatting to see its effect.

Down

2. Without making a selection, click the **Down** arrow to the right of the gallery.

> **Tip** This arrow has a dynamic ScreenTip that currently reads *Row 1 of 5.*

The next row of the Quick Styles gallery scrolls into view.

3. Move the pointer over each thumbnail in this row of the **Quick Styles** gallery.

4. In the **Styles** group, click the **More** button.

More

Word displays the entire Quick Styles gallery. The style applied to the paragraph containing the insertion point is surrounded by a border.

AaBbCcDc	AaBbCcDc	**AaBbC**	AaBbCc
¶ Normal	¶ No Spaci...	Heading 1	Heading 2
AaBbCcL	AaB	*AaBbCc.*	AaBbCcDc
Heading 3	Title	Subtitle	Subtle Em...
AaBbCcL	*AaBbCcDc*	**AaBbCcDc**	*AaBbCcDc*
Emphasis	Intense E...	Strong	Quote
AaBbCcDc	AABBCCDC	AABBCCDC	**AABBCCDC**
Intense Q...	Subtle Ref...	Intense R...	Book Title
AaBbCcDc	AaBbCcDdEt		
¶ List Para...	¶ Caption		

Save Selection as a New Quick Style...
Clear Formatting
Apply Styles...

5. In the gallery, click the **Title** thumbnail to apply that style to the paragraph containing the insertion point.

6. Click anywhere in the **Information Sheet** heading, and then in the **Styles** group, click the **Subtitle** thumbnail.

> **Troubleshooting** If you select text and then apply a paragraph style, only the selected text takes on the formatting of the style. You can simply click again in the paragraph and reapply the style.

Up

7. Click anywhere in the **Moving to a New Home** heading, and then in the **Styles** group, click the **Up** arrow, and click the **Heading 1** thumbnail.

8. Apply the **Heading 1** style to the **Staying Healthy** and **Keeping Bugs at Bay** headings.

9. Apply the **Heading 3** style to the **Mites** and **Mealy Bugs** headings.

10. In the **Styles** group, click the **Change Styles** button, click **Style Set**, and then point to each set name in turn, watching the effect on the document.

11. When you have finished exploring, click **Modern**.

   The formatting of the document changes and the headings and text take on the look assigned to this set of styles.

> **CLOSE** the *01_QuickFormatting* document without saving your changes.

Manually Changing the Look of Characters

When you type text in a document, it is displayed in a particular font. Each *font* consists of 256 alphabetic characters, numbers, and symbols that share a common design. By default the font used for text in a new Word document is Calibri, but you can change the font at any time. The available fonts vary from one computer to another, depending on the programs installed. Common fonts include Arial, Verdana, and Times New Roman.

You can vary the look of a font by changing the following *attributes*:

- Almost every font comes in a range of *font sizes*, which are measured in *points* from the top of letters that have parts that stick up (ascenders), such as *h*, to the bottom of letters that have parts that drop down (descenders), such as *p*. A point is approximately 1/72 of an inch.

- Almost every font comes in a range of *font styles*. The most common are regular (or plain), italic, bold, and bold italic.

- Fonts can be enhanced by applying *font effects*, such as underlining, small capital letters (small caps), or shadows.

- A palette of harmonious *font colors* is available, and you can also specify custom colors.

- You can alter the *character spacing* by pushing characters apart or squeezing them together.

After you have selected an appropriate font for a document, you can use these attributes to achieve different effects. Although some attributes might cancel each other out, they are usually cumulative. For example, you might use a bold font in various sizes and various shades of green to make different heading levels stand out in a newsletter. Collectively, the font and its attributes are called *character formatting*.

In this exercise, you will format the text in a document by changing its font, font style, size, color, and character spacing.

> **USE** the *02_Characters* document. This practice file is located in the *Chapter03* subfolder under *SBS_Word2007*.
>
> **OPEN** the *02_Characters* document.

1. In the *Beautiful Bamboo* heading, click anywhere in the word **Beautiful**.

2. On the **Home** tab, in the **Font** group, click the **Underline** button.

Underline

> **Tip** If you click the Underline arrow, you can choose a style from the Underline gallery. You can also change the underline color.

The word containing the insertion point is now underlined. Notice that you did not have to select the entire word.

3. In the same heading, click anywhere in the word **Bamboo**, and then on the **Quick Access Toolbar**, click the **Repeat** button.

Repeat

The last formatting command is repeated. Again, although you did not select the entire word, it is now underlined.

4. In the selection area, click adjacent to *Beautiful Bamboo* to select the entire heading.

Word displays a Mini toolbar of buttons that you can use to quickly change the look of the selection.

5. On the **Mini toolbar**, click the **Bold** button.

Bold

The heading is now bold. The active buttons on the Mini toolbar and in the Font group on the Home tab indicate the attributes that you applied to the selection.

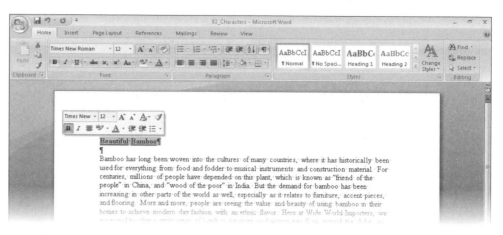

See Also For information about the use of character formatting, see the sidebar entitled "More About Case and Character Formatting" later in this chapter.

Format Painter

6. On the **Mini toolbar**, click the **Format Painter** button, and then click in the selection area adjacent to the *Types of Bamboo* heading.

Word "paints" the formatting of *Beautiful Bamboo* onto *Types of Bamboo*.

> **Tip** The Format Painter button is also available in the Clipboard group on the Home tab.

7. Select **Beautiful Bamboo**, and then on the **Home** tab, in the **Font** group, click the **Font** arrow, scroll the list of available fonts, and then click **Stencil**.

> **Troubleshooting** If Stencil is not available, select any heavy font that catches your attention.

The heading at the top of the document now appears in the new font.

Font Size

8. In the **Font** group, click the **Font Size** arrow, and then in the list, click **26**.

The size of the heading text increases to 26 points.

> **Tip** You can increase or decrease the font size in set increments by clicking the Grow Font and Shrink Font buttons in the Font group, or by clicking the same buttons on the Mini toolbar that appears when you select text.

Dialog Box Launcher

9. Click the **Font** Dialog Box Launcher.

The Font dialog box opens.

10. Click the **Underline style** arrow, and then in the list, click **(none)**.

11. Under **Effects**, select the **Outline** check box.

12. Click the **Character Spacing** tab.

13. Click the **Spacing** arrow, and then in the list, click **Expanded**.

14. To the right, click the **By** up arrow until the spacing is expanded by **2 pt** (points), and then click **OK**.

The selected text appears with an outline effect and with the spacing between the characters expanded by 2 points.

Clear Formatting

15. On the **Home** tab, in the **Font** group, click the **Clear Formatting** button.

The formatting of the selected text is removed.

Undo

16. On the **Quick Access Toolbar**, click the **Undo** button.

The formatting of the selected text is restored.

17. In the last sentence of the second paragraph, select the words **light green**.

Font Color

18. On the **Home** tab, in the **Font** group, click the **Font Color** arrow, and then under **Standard Colors** in the palette, click the light green box.

The selected words are now light green. (To see the color, clear the selection by clicking a blank area of the document.)

> **Tip** If you want to apply the Font Color button's current color, you can simply click the button (not the arrow).

19. In the same sentence, select **dark, rich shades of green**, click the **Font Color** arrow, and then below the palette, click **More Colors**.

The Colors dialog box opens.

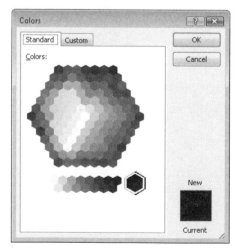

20. In the **Colors** wheel on the **Standard** tab, click one of the dark green shades on the left, and then click **OK**.

   The selection is now dark green.

Highlight

21. Select the phrase **supports the environment** in the second sentence of the last paragraph. Then in the **Font** group, click the **Highlight** arrow, and under **Recent Colors** in the palette, click the green box.

   This is the same green that you selected in Step 20. After you select a custom color in one palette, it is available in all the palettes. The highlighted phrase now stands out from the rest of the text.

   > **Tip** If you click the Highlight button without first making a selection, the mouse pointer becomes a highlighter that you can drag across text. Click the Highlight button again or press Esc to turn off the highlighter.

22. In the paragraph that begins *Because they are so easy to grow*, select the bamboo species name **chimonobambusa marmorea**. Then hold down the Ctrl key while selecting **indocalamus tessellatus**, **pleioblastus chino vaginatus**, **bambusa glaucophylla**, and **otatea acuminata aztectorum**.

23. Click the **Font** Dialog Box Launcher.

24. In the **Font** dialog box, click the **Font** tab, and under **Effects**, select the **Small caps** check box. Then click **OK**.

   The lowercase letters in the species names now appear in small capital letters, making those names easy to find in the text.

Select ▾ 25. Click anywhere in the first species name. Then on the **Home** tab, in the **Editing** group, click the **Select** button, and click **Select Text with Similar Formatting**.

   All the species names that have been formatted in small caps are selected.

26. In the **Font** group, click the **Bold** button, and then click away from the selection.

   The species names are now both small caps and bold.

¶

Types of Bamboo¶

There are many different sizes and varieties of bamboo. It is both tropical and subtropical, growing in climates as diverse as jungles and mountainsides. Actually giant, woody grasses, it is very adaptable, with some species deciduous and others evergreen. Although there isn't yet a complete knowledge about this plant, there are believed to be between 1100 and 1500 different species of bamboo. The color range is from light green leaves and culms (stems) to dark, rich shades of green or some combination thereof.¶

¶

Because they are so easy to grow in such a variety of climates, there is a plant available for just about anyone who wishes to grow one in their backyard. Some dwarf species include **CHIMONOBAMBUSA MARMOREA**, **INDOCALAMUS TESSELLATUS**, and **PLEIOBLASTUS CHINO-VAGINATUS**. Also suitable for the personal garden are those categorized as mid size. Examples of these types of plants are **BAMBUSA GLAUCOPHYLLA** and **OTATEA ACUMINATA AZTECTORUM**. Plant starts and seeds are easier to find than ever, being available at nurseries and through mail order. ¶

¶

Bamboo is quickly becoming an important economic factor in many developing nations. A 60-foot tree cut for marketing can take up to 60 years to replace, whereas a 60-foot bamboo can take as little as 60 days to reach marketability. And the majority of bamboo destined for the world market is harvested by women and children, most of who live at or below subsistence levels in poor nations. So as production increases, so does support for the economies of those countries that produce it.¶

¶

Choosing bamboo as part of home or garden design makes sense on many levels. Not only does it have an appealing look, but it supports the environment as well as the countries that produce it. In particular Wide World Importers recommends chimonobambusa marmoreal.¶

CLOSE the *02_Characters* document without saving your changes.

More About Case and Character Formatting

The way you use case and character formatting in a document can influence its visual impact on your readers. Used judiciously, case and character formatting can make a plain document look attractive and professional, but excessive use can make it look amateurish and detract from the message. For example, using too many fonts in the same document is the mark of inexperience, so don't use more than two or three.

Bear in mind that lowercase letters tend to recede, so using all uppercase letters (capitals) can be useful for titles and headings or for certain kinds of emphasis. However, large blocks of uppercase letters are tiring to the eye.

Where do the terms uppercase and lowercase come from? Until the advent of computers, individual characters were assembled to form the words that would appear on a printed page. The characters were stored alphabetically in cases, with the capital letters in the upper case and the small letters in the lower case.

> **Tip** If you want to see a summary of the formatting applied to a selection, you can display the Style Inspector pane by clicking the Styles Dialog Box Launcher and then clicking the Style Inspector button (the middle button at the bottom of the Styles task pane). You can then click anywhere in the document to see a formatting summary of the word containing the insertion point. To see details about the formatting, you can click the Reveal Formatting button at the bottom of the Style Inspector pane to open the Reveal Formatting task pane.

Manually Changing the Look of Paragraphs

As you know, you create a *paragraph* by typing text and then pressing the Enter key. The paragraph can be a single word, a single sentence, or multiple sentences. You can change the look of a paragraph by changing its alignment, its line spacing, and the space before and after it. You can also put borders around it and shade its background. Collectively, the settings you use to vary the look of a paragraph are called *paragraph formatting*.

In Word, you don't define the width of paragraphs and the length of pages by defining the area occupied by the text; instead you define the size of the white space—the left, right, top, and bottom *margins*—around the text. You use the Margins button in the Page Setup group on the Page Layout tab to define these margins, either for the whole document or for sections of the document.

See Also For information about setting margins, see "Previewing and Printing a Document" in Chapter 1, "Exploring Word 2007." For information about sections, see "Controlling What Appears on Each Page" in Chapter 4, "Changing the Look of a Document."

Although the left and right margins are set for a whole document or section, you can vary the position of the text between the margins. The easiest way to do this is by moving controls on the horizontal ruler. You can indent paragraphs from the left and right margins, as well as specify where the first line of a paragraph begins and where the second and subsequent lines begin.

Setting a right indent indicates where all the lines in a paragraph should end, but sometimes you might want to specify where only a single line should end. For example, you might want to break a title after a particular word to make it look balanced on the page. You can end an individual line by inserting a *text wrapping break* or *line break*. After positioning the insertion point where you want the break to occur, you click the Breaks button in the Page Setup group on the Page Layout tab, and then click Text Wrapping. Word indicates the line break with a bent arrow. Inserting a line break does not start a new paragraph, so when you apply paragraph formatting to a line of text that ends with a line break, the formatting is applied to the entire paragraph, not just that line.

> **Tip** You can also press Shift+Enter to insert a line break.

You can align lines of text in different locations across the page by using *tab stops*. The easiest way to set tab stops is to use the horizontal ruler. By default, Word sets left-aligned tab stops every 0.5 inch, as indicated by gray marks below this ruler. To set a custom tab stop, you start by clicking the Tab button located at the left end of the ruler until the type of tab stop you want appears. You have the following options:

- **Left Tab.** Aligns the left end of the text with the stop.
- **Center Tab.** Aligns the center of the text with the stop.
- **Right Tab.** Aligns the right end of the text with the stop.
- **Decimal Tab.** Aligns the decimal point in the text with the stop.
- **Bar Tab.** Draws a vertical bar aligned with the stop down the paragraph containing the insertion point.

After selecting the type of tab stop, you simply click the ruler where you want the tab stop to be. Word then removes any default tab stops to the left of the one you set. To change the position of an existing custom tab stop, you drag it to the left or right on the ruler. To delete a custom tab stop, you drag it away from the ruler.

To move the text to the right of the insertion point to the next tab stop, you press the Tab key. The text is then aligned on the tab stop according to its type. For example, if you set a center tab stop, pressing Tab moves the text so that its center is aligned with the tab stop.

Tip When you want to fine-tune the position of tab stops, click the Paragraph Dialog Box Launcher on either the Home or Page Layout tab. In the Paragraph dialog box, click the Tabs button to display the Tabs dialog box. You might also open this dialog box if you want to use *tab leaders*—visible marks such as dots or dashes connecting the text before the tab with the text after it. For example, tab leaders are useful in a table of contents to carry the eye from the text to the page number.

In addition to tab stops, the horizontal ruler also displays *indent markers* that are used to control where each line of text starts and ends. You use these markers to indent text from the left or right margins as follows:

- **First Line Indent.** Begins a paragraph's first line of text at this marker.
- **Hanging Indent.** Begins a paragraph's second and subsequent lines of text at this marker.
- **Left Indent.** Indents the text to this marker.
- **Right Indent** Wraps the text when it reaches this marker.

You can also determine the positioning of a paragraph between the left and right margins by changing its alignment. You can click buttons in the Paragraph group on the Home tab to align paragraphs as follows:

- **Align Left.** Aligns each line of the paragraph at the left margin, with a ragged right edge.
- **Align Right.** Aligns each line of the paragraph at the right margin, with a ragged left edge.
- **Center.** Aligns the center of each line in the paragraph between the left and right margins, with ragged left and right edges.
- **Justify.** Aligns each line between the margins, creating even left and right edges.

Tip If you know that you want to type a centered paragraph, you don't have to type it and then format it as centered. You can use the *Click and Type* feature to create appropriately aligned text. Move the pointer to the center of a blank area of the page, and when the pointer's shape changes to an I-beam with centered text attached, double-click to create an insertion point that is ready to enter centered text. Similarly, you can double-click at the left edge of the page to enter left-aligned text and at the right edge to enter right-aligned text.

To make it obvious where one paragraph ends and another begins, you can add space be-tween them by adjusting the Spacing After and Spacing Before settings in the Paragraph group on the Page Layout tab. You can adjust the spacing between the lines in a para-graph by clicking the Line Spacing button in the Paragraph group on the Home tab.

When you want to make several adjustments to the alignment, indentation, and spacing of selected paragraphs, it is sometimes quicker to use the Paragraph dialog box than to click buttons and drag markers. Click the Paragraph Dialog Box Launcher on either the Home or Page Layout tab to open the Paragraph dialog box.

To make a paragraph really stand out, you can put a border around it or shade its background. For real drama, you can do both.

> **Tip** A paragraph's formatting is stored in its paragraph mark. If you delete the paragraph mark, thereby making it part of the following paragraph, its text takes on the formatting of that paragraph. If you position the insertion point anywhere in the paragraph and press Enter to create a new one, the new paragraph takes on the existing paragraph's formatting.

In this exercise, you'll change text alignment and indentation, insert and modify tab stops, modify paragraph and line spacing, and add borders and shading around para-graphs to change their appearance.

> **USE** the *03_Paragraphs* document. This practice file is located in the *Chapter03* subfolder under *SBS_Word2007*.
>
> **BE SURE TO** turn on the display of non-printing characters for this exercise. Also display the rulers.
>
> **OPEN** the *03_Paragraphs* document.

Zoom Out

1. In the lower-right corner of the document window, click the **Zoom Out** button twice to set the zoom percentage to 80%.

You can now see all the text of the document.

2. In the fourth line of the document, click to the left of *Update*, and then on the **Page Layout** tab, in the **Page Setup** group, click the **Breaks** button, and then click **Text Wrapping**.

Word inserts a line break character and moves the part of the paragraph that follows that character to the next line.

See Also For information about page and section breaks, see "Controlling What Appears on Each Page" in Chapter 4, "Changing the Look of a Document." For information about column breaks, see "Presenting Information in Columns" in Chapter 5, "Presenting Information in Columns and Tables."

Center

3. Select the first four lines of the document, and then on the **Home** tab, in the **Paragraph** group, click the **Center** button.

   The lines are now centered between the margins. Notice that even though you did not select the fifth line, it is also centered because it is part of the *Author Meet and Greet* paragraph.

Text wrapping line break

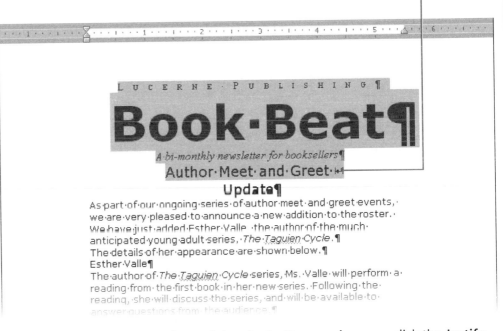

Justify

4. Select the next two paragraphs, and then in the **Paragraph** group, click the **Justify** button.

   The edges of the first paragraph are now flush against both the left and right margins. The second paragraph doesn't change because it is less than a line long.

First Line Indent

5. With both paragraphs still selected, on the horizontal ruler, drag the **First Line Indent** marker to the 0.25-inch mark.

   The first line of each paragraph is now indented 0.25 inch from the left margin.

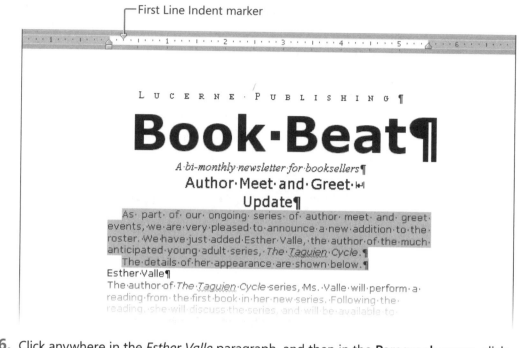

First Line Indent marker

6. Click anywhere in the *Esther Valle* paragraph, and then in the **Paragraph** group, click the **Center** button.

> **Tip** When applying paragraph formatting, you don't have to select the entire paragraph.

Left Indent

7. Select all the paragraphs below *Esther Valle*, and then on the horizontal ruler, drag the **Left Indent** marker to the 0.5-inch mark.

The First Line Indent and Hanging Indent markers move with the Left Indent marker, and all the selected paragraphs are now indented 0.5 inch from the left margin.

Right Indent

8. Drag the **Right Indent** marker to the 5-inch mark.

The paragraphs are now indented from the right margin as well.

Left Indent marker

Right Indent marker

> **Tip** Left and right margin indents are frequently used to draw attention to special paragraphs, such as quotations.

Increase Indent

9. Select the **Date:**, **Time:**, **Location:**, and **Ticket cost:** paragraphs, and then in the **Paragraph** group, click the **Increase Indent** button.

   These four paragraphs are now indented to the 1-inch mark.

Left Tab

10. Without changing the selection, make sure the **Left Tab** button at the junction of the horizontal and vertical rulers is active, and then click the ruler at the 2.5-inch mark to set a left tab stop.

11. Click at the right end of the *Date:* paragraph to position the insertion point before the paragraph mark, and then press the [Tab] key.

    Word will left-align any text you type after the tab character at the new tab stop.

12. Press the [↓] key, and then press [Tab].

13. Repeat Step 12 for the *Location* and *Ticket cost* paragraphs.

    All four paragraphs now have tabs that are aligned with the tab stop at the 2.5-inch mark.

Left-aligned tab stop   Default tab stop

As· part· of· our· ongoing· series· of· author· meet· and· greet· events,·we·are·very·pleased·to·announce·a·new·addition·to·the· roster.·We·have·just·added·Esther·Valle,·the·author·of·the·much· anticipated·young·adult·series,·*The·Taquien·Cycle*.¶
The·details·of·her·appearance·are·shown·below.¶
Esther·Valle¶
The·author·of·*The·Taquien·Cycle*·series,·Ms.·Valle·will· perform·a·reading·from·the·first·book·in·her·new· series.·Following·the·reading,·she·will·discuss·the· series,·and·will·be·available·to·answer·questions· from·the·audience.¶
Date:·   →   ¶
Time:·   →   ¶
Location:·   →   ¶
Ticket·cost:· → ¶
For·more·information,·contact:·¶
¶
Tickets·will·be·available·at·the·door,·but·to·reserve· your·seat·in·advance·please·send·your·check·to:·¶

14. Without moving the insertion point, type **Adult**, and then press [Tab].

Decimal Tab

15. Click the **Tab** button three times to activate a decimal tab, and then click the 4-inch mark on the horizontal ruler.

16. Type $10.00, press [Enter], press [Tab] type **Child**, press [Tab] again, and then type $5.00.

    The new paragraph takes on the same paragraph formatting as the *Ticket cost* paragraph, and the dollar amounts are aligned on their decimal points.

Decimal-aligned tab stop

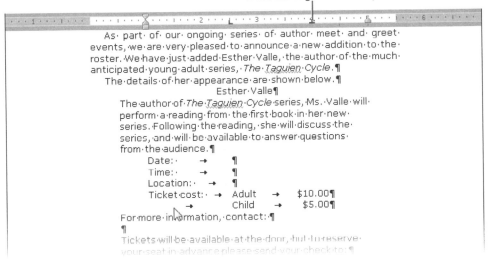

17. Drag through any part of the two paragraphs with dollar amounts, and then on the horizontal ruler, drag the decimal tab stop from the 4-inch mark to the 3.5-inch mark.

18. On the **Home** tab, in the **Editing** group, click the **Select** button, and then click **Select All**.

19. On the **Page Layout** tab, in the **Paragraph** group, change the **Spacing After** setting to **12 pt**.

    Word inserts 12 points of space after every paragraph in the document.

Line Spacing

20. Click anywhere in the paragraph that begins *As part of*, and then on the **Home** tab, in the **Paragraph** group, click the **Line Spacing** button, and then click **Remove Space After Paragraph**.

21. Select the **Date:**, **Time:**, **Location:**, and **Ticket cost:** paragraphs, and then repeat Step 20.

22. Select the **Jill Shrader**, **Lucerne Publishing**, and **4567 Oak Street** paragraphs, and then repeat Step 20 again.

23. Click anywhere in the paragraph that begins *The author of,* click the **Line Spacing** button again, and then click **1.5**.

You have adjusted both the paragraph and line spacing of the document.

Borders

24. Click the *Book Beat* paragraph. Then on the **Home** tab, in the **Paragraph** group, click the **Borders** arrow, and at the bottom of the list, click **Borders and Shading**.

The Borders And Shading dialog box opens.

25. Under **Setting**, click the **Shadow** icon to select that border style.

> **Tip** You can change the settings in the Style, Color, and Width boxes to create the kind of border you want. If you want only one, two, or three sides of the selected paragraphs to have a border, click the buttons surrounding the image in the Preview area.

26. Click the **Shading** tab.

You can use the options on this tab to format the background of the selected paragraph.

27. Click the **Fill** arrow, and under **Theme Colors**, click the second lightest purple box (**Purple, Accent 4, Lighter 60%**). Then click **OK** to close the **Borders and Shading** dialog box.

A border with a shadow surrounds the text, and the background color is light purple.

BE SURE TO change the Zoom percentage back to 100% before moving on to the next exercise, and if you want, turn off the rulers.

CLOSE the *03_Paragraphs* document without saving your changes.

Finding and Replacing Formatting

In addition to searching for words and phrases, you can use the Find And Replace dialog box to search for a specific format and replace it with a different format.

To search for a specific format and replace it with a different format:

1. On the **Home** tab, in the **Editing** group, click the **Replace** button.

   The Find And Replace dialog box opens, displaying the Replace tab.

2. Click **More** to expand the dialog box, click **Format**, and then click **Font** or **Paragraph**.

   The Find Font or Find Paragraph dialog box opens. (You can also click Style to search for paragraph styles or character styles.)

3. In the dialog box, click the format you want to find, and then click **OK**.

4. Click the **Replace with** text box, click **Format**, click **Font** or **Paragraph**, click the format you want to substitute for the Find What format, and then click **OK**.

5. Click **Find Next** to search for the first occurrence of the format, and then click **Replace** to replace that one instance or **Replace All** to replace every instance.

Creating and Modifying Lists

When you want to present a list of items in a document, you will usually want to put each item on its own line rather than burying the items in a paragraph. When the order of items is not important—for example, for a list of items needed to carry out a task—use a bulleted list. When the order is important—for example, for the steps in a procedure—use a numbered list.

With Word, you start a bulleted or numbered list as follows:

- To create a bulleted list, type * (an asterisk) at the beginning of a paragraph, and then press the Spacebar or the Tab key.

- To create a numbered list, type 1. (the numeral 1 followed by a period) at the beginning of a paragraph, and then press the Spacebar or the Tab key.

In either case, you then type the first item in the list and press Enter. Word starts the new paragraph with a bullet or 2 followed by a period and formats the first and second paragraphs as a numbered list. Typing items and pressing Enter adds subsequent bulleted or numbered items. To end the list, press Enter twice, or press Enter and then Backspace.

> **Troubleshooting** If you want to start a paragraph with an asterisk or number but don't want the paragraph to be formatted as a bulleted or numbered list, click the AutoCorrect Options button that appears after Word changes the formatting, and then click the Undo option.

After you create a list, you can modify, format, and customize the list as follows:

- You can move items around in a list, insert new items, or delete unwanted items. If the list is numbered, Word automatically updates the numbers.
- You can sort items in a bulleted list into ascending or descending order by clicking the Sort button in the Paragraph group on the Home tab.
- For a bulleted list, you can change the bullet symbol by clicking the Bullets arrow in the Paragraph group and making a selection from the Bullet Library. You can also define a custom bullet by clicking the Bullets arrow and then clicking Define New Bullet.
- For a numbered list, you can change the number style by clicking the Numbering arrow in the Paragraph group and making a selection from the Numbering Library. You can also define a custom style by clicking the Numbering arrow and then clicking Define New Number Format.
- You can create a multilevel bulleted list, numbered list, or outline by clicking the Multilevel List button in the Paragraph group, selecting a style from the List Library, and then typing the list. You press Enter to create a new item at the same level, the Tab key to move down a level, and the Backspace key to move up a level.

  See Also For information about another way to create an outline, see "Reorganizing a Document Outline" in Chapter 2, "Editing and Proofreading Documents."

- You can modify the indentation of the list by dragging the indent markers on the horizontal ruler. Lists are set up with the first line "outdented" to the left from the other lines, and you can change both the overall indentation of the list and the relationship of the first line to the other lines.

In this exercise, you will create a bulleted list and a numbered list and then modify lists in various ways. You will then create a multilevel list with letters instead of numbers.

> **USE** the *04_Lists* document. This practice file is located in the *Chapter03* subfolder under *SBS_Word2007*.
>
> **OPEN** the *04_Lists* document.

Bullets

1. Select the three paragraphs under *Rationale*, and then on the **Home** tab, in the **Paragraph** group, click the **Bullets** button.

The selected paragraphs are reformatted as a bulleted list.

The·Taguien·Cycle¶

A·Series·for·Young·Adults¶
Judy·Lew,·Project·Editor¶
Rationale¶
- → Lucerne·currently·has·no·offering·for·young·adults¶
- → Fantasy·series·have·been·hits·in·this·hard-to-please·market¶
- → Customers·are·turning·to·other·publishers·to·meet·demand¶
Characters·of·a·Hit·Fantasy¶
A·hero¶
An·ally¶
A·teacher¶

2. With the three paragraphs still selected, in the **Paragraph** group, click the **Bullets** arrow.

The Bullet Library appears.

Recently Used Bullets

●

Bullet Library

| None | ● | ○ | ■ | ⊥ | ❖ |

| ➢ | ✓ |

Document Bullets

●

⊡ Change List Level   ▶
Define New Bullet...

3. In the gallery, click the bullet composed of four diamonds.

   The bullet character in the selected list changes.

4. Select the four paragraphs under *Characters of a Hit Fantasy*, and then in the **Paragraph** group, click the **Bullets** button.

   The new list has the bullet character you selected for the previous list. This character will be the default until you change it.

5. Select the paragraphs under each of the bold headings, and then in the **Paragraph** group, click the **Bullets** button.

6. Scroll to the bottom of the page, select the four paragraphs under *The Sequence of Events*, and then in the **Paragraph** group, in the **Bullets Library**, click **None**.

   The bulleted paragraphs revert to normal paragraphs.

Numbering

7. With the paragraphs still selected, on the **Home** tab, in the **Paragraph** group, click the **Numbering** button.

   The selected paragraphs are reformatted as a numbered list.

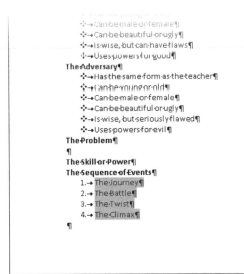

8. In the **Paragraph** group, click the **Numbering** arrow.

   The Numbering Library appears.

[Numbering gallery dialog]

Recently Used Number Formats

1. ——
2. ——
3. ——

Numbering Library

None	1. —— 2. —— 3. ——	1) —— 2) —— 3) ——
I. —— II. —— III. ——	A. —— B. —— C. ——	a) —— b) —— c) ——
a. —— b. —— c. ——	i. —— ii. —— iii. ——	

Document Number Formats

1. ——
2. ——
3. ——

⤼ Change List Level ▶
Define New Number Format...
⤼ Set Numbering Value...

9. In the gallery, click the **A. B. C.** box.

The numbers change to capital letters.

Decrease Indent

10. With the numbered paragraphs still selected, in the **Paragraph** group, click the **Decrease Indent** button.

The numbered list moves to the left margin.

Increase Indent

11. In the **Paragraph** group, click the **Increase Indent** button to move the list back to its original indent.

> **Tip** You can also adjust the indent level of a bulleted list by selecting its paragraphs, and on the horizontal ruler, dragging the Left Indent marker to the left or right. The First Line Indent and Hanging Indent markers move with the Left Indent marker. You can move just the Hanging Indent marker to adjust the space between the bullets and their text.

[A↓Z icon]
Sort

12. Scroll the document until you can see the bulleted list under *The Hero*, select the three bulleted paragraphs, and then on the **Home** tab, in the **Paragraph** group, click the **Sort** button.

The Sort Text dialog box opens.

13. With the **Ascending** option selected, click **OK**.

The order of the bulleted items changes to ascending alphabetical order.

Multilevel List

14. Click the blank paragraph under *The Ally*, and then on the **Home** tab, in the **Paragraph** group, click the **Multilevel List** button.

The List Library appears.

15. In the gallery, click the thumbnail under **Current List**.

The first item in the new numbered list will have a capital letter as its numbering style.

16. Type **Does not have to be human**, press ⎡Enter⎤, type **Is a stabilizing force**, press ⎡Enter⎤, and then press ⎡Tab⎤.

The new item is indented to the next level and assigned a different number style.

17. Type **A voice of conscience**, press ⎡Enter⎤, type **Not a "yes" person**, press ⎡Enter⎤, and then press ⎡Shift⎤ + ⎡Tab⎤.

18. Type **Embodies loyalty**.

Word takes care of all the formatting of the multilevel list.

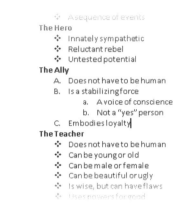

19. Under *The Problem*, click to the left of the blank paragraph mark, type * (an asterisk), press ⎡Tab⎤, type **A difficult choice**, and then press ⎡Enter⎤.

Word converts the asterisk into a bullet and formats the next paragraph as a bulleted item.

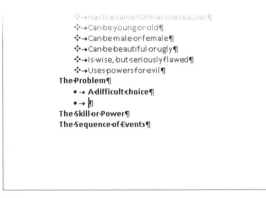

20. Type **An injustice**, press ⎡Enter⎤, and then type **A quest**.

> **CLOSE** the *04_Lists* document without saving your changes.

Formatting Text as You Type

The Word list formatting capabilities are just one example of the program's ability to intuit how you want to format an element based on what you type. You can learn more about these and other AutoFormatting options by exploring the AutoCorrect dialog box. To open this dialog box, click the Microsoft Office Button, click Word Options, click Proofing in the left pane of the Word Options window, and then click AutoCorrect Options in the right pane.

On the AutoFormat As You Type tab, you can see the options that Word implements by default, including bulleted and numbered lists. You can select and clear options to control Word's AutoFormatting behavior.

One interesting option is Border Lines. When this check box is selected, you can type three consecutive hyphens (-) and press Enter to have Word draw a single line across the page. Or you can type three consecutive equal signs (=) and press Enter to have Word draw a double line.

Key Points

- Quick Styles are a great way to apply combinations of formatting to give your documents a professional look.

- You can format characters with an almost limitless number of combinations of font, size, style, and effect—but for best results, resist the temptation to use more than a handful of combinations.

- You can change the look of paragraphs by varying their indentation, spacing, and alignment and by setting tab stops. Use these formatting options judiciously to create documents with a balanced, uncluttered look.

- Bulleted and numbered lists are a great way to present information in an easy to read, easy to understand format. If the built-in bulleted and numbered list styles don't provide what you need, you can define your own styles.

Chapter at a Glance

Change a document's
background, **page 96**

Change a document's
theme, **page 100**

Add headers
and footers,
page 113

Work with
templates,
page 104

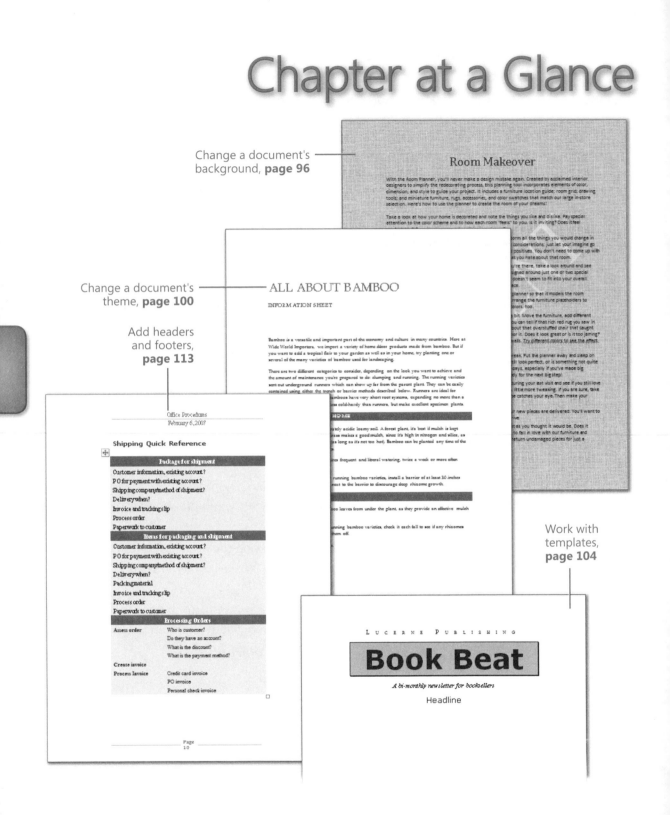

4 Changing the Look of a Document

In this chapter, you will learn to:
- ✔ Change a document's background.
- ✔ Change a document's theme.
- ✔ Work with templates.
- ✔ Add headers and footers.
- ✔ Control what appears on each page.

Microsoft Office Word 2007 comes with formatting tools that you can use to ensure the consistent presentation of an entire document. To give a document a polished look, you can specify a background for its pages and a theme for its major elements. You can control the look of a document by basing it on one of the predefined business or personal templates that are installed with Word or that are available for download from the Microsoft Office Online Web site. You can also create your own templates and use them as the basis for new documents.

Word gives you control of the layout of the pages in a document that will be printed. For example, if you want the same information to be repeated on every page, you can set up the information in headers and footers. You can control how the text in the document appears on each page by specifying page and section breaks.

In this chapter, you will apply a background pattern and color, and then you'll add a text watermark. You'll apply a theme to an existing document, change the colors and the fonts, and save a custom theme. You will use a predefined Word template to create a document, modify the document, and then save it as a new template. You will also create a custom template. Finally, you will add headers and footers to a document, and you'll learn how to use page and section breaks to keep information together in logical units.

See Also Do you need only a quick refresher on the topics in this chapter? See the Quick Reference entries on pages xxxix–lxiii.

> **Important**   Before you can use the practice files in this chapter, you need to install them from the book's companion CD to their default location. See "Using the Book's CD" on page xxv for more information.

> **Troubleshooting**   Graphics and operating system–related instructions in this book reflect the Windows Vista user interface. If your computer is running Microsoft Windows XP and you experience trouble following the instructions as written, please refer to the "Information for Readers Running Windows XP" section at the beginning of this book.

Changing a Document's Background

Whether you are creating a document that will be printed, viewed on a computer, or published on the Internet and viewed in a Web browser, you can make your document stand out by adding a background color or pattern.

See Also   For information about creating documents for the Web, see "Creating and Modifying a Web Document" in Chapter 11, "Creating Documents for Use Outside of Word."

There might be times when you want words or a graphic to appear behind the text of a printed or online document. For example, you might want the word *CONFIDENTIAL* to appear faintly behind the text in a contract, or you might want a graphic to appear faintly behind the text in a press release. These faint background images are called *watermarks*. Watermarks are visible in a document, but because they are faint, they don't interfere with the readers' ability to view the document's main text.

Background colors, patterns, and watermarks are applied by clicking buttons in the Page Background group on the Page Layout tab.

In this exercise, you will apply a background color and pattern, and then you'll add a text watermark.

> **USE**   the *01_Background* document. This practice file is located in the *Chapter04* subfolder under *SBS_Word2007*.
> **BE SURE TO**   start Word before beginning this exercise.
> **OPEN**   the *01_Background* document.

Page Color ▾ 1. On the **Page Layout** tab, in the **Page Background** group, click the **Page Color** button, and then under **Theme Colors**, click the second lightest green box (**Olive Green, Accent 3, Lighter 60%**).

The background of the document changes to the selected color.

2. In the **Page Background** group, click the **Page Color** button, and then click **Fill Effects**.

The Fill Effects dialog box opens.

3. Click the **Texture** tab.

4. Click the effect in the second column of the first row, and then click **OK**.

The background changes to display the effect rather than the color.

Watermark ▾ 5. On the **Page Layout** tab, in the **Page Background** group, click the **Watermark** button.

The Watermark gallery opens.

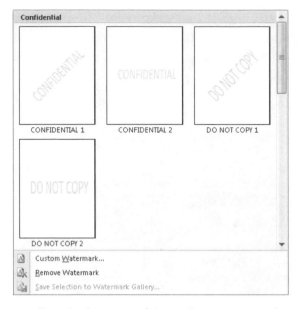

6. Scroll to the bottom of the gallery, noticing the available options.

   Clicking any of these options will insert the specified watermark in pale blue on every page of the current document.

7. Below the gallery, click **Custom Watermark**.

   The Printed Watermark dialog box opens. Notice that you can insert a picture or text as a watermark.

8. Select the **Text watermark** option, click the **Text** arrow, scroll down the list, and then click **URGENT**.

9. Click the **Color** arrow, and under **Theme Colors**, click the white box.

10. With the **Semitransparent** check box and **Diagonal** option selected, click **OK**.

   The specified text is inserted diagonally across the page.

11. At the right end of the status bar, click the **Zoom** button. Then in the **Zoom** dialog box, click **Whole Page**, and click **OK**.

   The document displays the texture and watermark you specified.

100%

Zoom

CLOSE the *01_Background* document without saving your changes.

> ## Using a Picture as a Watermark
>
> When you want to dress up the pages of your document without distracting attention from the main text, you might consider adding a graphic watermark.
>
> Here's how to add a graphic watermark to every page of a document:
>
> 1. On the **Page Layout** tab, in the **Page Background** group, click the **Watermark** button, and then click **Custom Watermark**.
>
> 2. In the **Printed Watermark** dialog box, select the **Picture watermark** option, and then click **Select Picture**.
>
> 3. In the **Insert Picture** dialog box, navigate to the folder where the picture you want to use is stored, and double-click the name of the picture.
>
> 4. Click the **Scale** arrow, and choose how big or small you want the watermark picture to appear in the document.
>
> 5. For a more vibrant picture, clear the **Washout** check box.
>
> 6. Click **OK**.
>
>   The picture is inserted as a watermark at the size you specified.

Changing a Document's Theme

You can enhance the look of a document by applying one of Word's pre-defined themes. A *theme* is a combination of colors, fonts, and effects that project a certain feeling or tone. For example, the Flow theme uses a palette of blues and greens, the Calabri and Constantia fonts, and understated effects.

You apply a theme to the entire document by clicking the Themes button in the Themes group on the Page Layout tab, and then making a selection from the Themes gallery. If you like the colors of one theme and the fonts of another, you can mix and match theme elements. First find the theme that most closely resembles the look you want, and then in the Themes group, change the colors by clicking the Theme Colors button or the fonts by clicking the Theme Fonts button.

If you create a combination of colors and fonts that you would like to be able to use with other documents, you can save the combination as a new theme. By saving the theme in the default *Document Themes* folder, you make the theme available in the Themes gallery. However, you don't have to store custom themes in the *Document Themes* folder; you can store them anywhere on your hard disk, on removable media, or in a network location. To use a theme that is stored in a different location, you can click the Themes button, and then click Browse For Themes at the bottom of the gallery. Locate the theme you want in the Choose Theme Or Themed Document dialog box, and then click Open to apply that theme to the current document.

> **Tip** Click Search Office Online at the bottom of the Themes gallery to display the Templates page of the Microsoft Office Online Web site, where you can find more information about themes and download themes and templates created by other people.

In this exercise, you'll apply a theme to an existing document and then change the colors and the fonts. You will then save the custom theme.

> **USE** the *02_Theme* document. This practice file is located in the *Chapter04* subfolder under *SBS_Word2007*.
> **OPEN** the *02_Theme* document.

1. On the **Page Layout** tab, in the **Themes** group, click the **Themes** button.

   The Themes gallery opens.

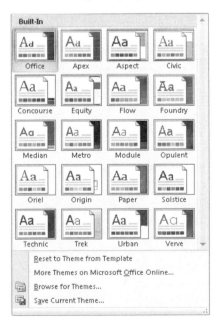

2. Hover over each thumbnail in turn to display a live preview of the theme.

3. In the **Themes** gallery, click **Aspect**.

   The colors and fonts change to those defined for the selected theme.

Theme Colors

4. In the **Themes** group, click the **Theme Colors** button.

   The Theme Colors gallery opens. The currently selected colors have a border around them.

Built-In	
	Office
	Grayscale
	Apex
	Aspect
	Civic
	Concourse
	Equity
	Flow
	Foundry
	Median
	Metro
	Module
	Opulent
	Oriel
	Origin
	Paper
	Solstice
	Technic
	Trek
	Urban
	Verve

Create New Theme Colors...

5. Display a live preview of any set of colors that interests you, and then in the gallery, click **Opulent**.

   The Opulent colors replace the Aspect colors, but nothing else in the document changes.

Theme Fonts

6. In the **Themes** group, click the **Theme Fonts** button.

   The Theme Fonts gallery opens. The currently selected fonts are highlighted. Each built-in option includes a set of two fonts—the first is used for headings and the second for text.

7. Display a live preview of any set of fonts that interests you, and then in the gallery, click **Apex**.

The Apex fonts replace the Aspect fonts, but the colors remain the same.

8. In the **Themes** group, click the **Themes** button, and then below the gallery, click **Save Current Theme**

The Save Current Theme dialog box opens, displaying the *Document Themes* folder in the Address bar. This dialog box resembles the Save As dialog box. The *Document Themes* folder is the default location for saving any new themes you create.

9. In the **File name** box, replace the suggested name with My Theme, and then click **Save**.

10. In the **Themes** group, click the **Themes** button to display the gallery.

Your new theme appears at the top of the gallery, under Custom. You can now apply this theme to any document.

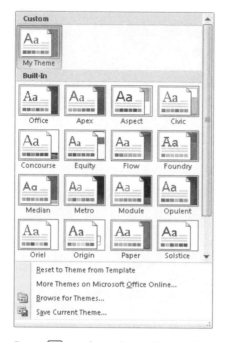

11. Press `Esc` to close the gallery without making a selection.

CLOSE the *02_Theme* document without saving your changes.

Working with Templates

When you want to quickly create an effective, visually attractive document, one of the most efficient methods is to leverage the design work of other people. With Word 2007, you have access to many ready made, professionally designed templates. A *template* is a file that stores text, character and paragraph styles, page formatting, and elements such as graphics for use as a pattern in creating other documents.

Unless you specify otherwise, all new documents are based on the Normal document template, which defines a few fairly plain styles, such as paragraph styles for regular text paragraphs, a title, and different levels of headings; and a few character styles that change the look of selected text. The styles from the Normal template appear in the

Styles gallery on the Home tab when you create a new blank document. If you create a document based on a different template, the styles defined in that template appear in the Styles gallery, and you can apply those styles to quickly format the text in the document.

> **Tip** Templates are stored with the .dotx file name extension.

See Also For more information about applying styles, see "Quickly Formatting Text and Paragraphs" in Chapter 3, "Changing the Look of Text."

In addition to the Normal document template, Word comes with a variety of templates for a variety of documents. To create a document based on one of these templates, you start by displaying the New Document window. Then in the left pane, under Templates, you click Installed Templates, and in the list that appears in the center pane, you click the template you want.

If none of the built-in templates meets your needs, you can look for templates on the Office Online Web site. To create a document based on one of these templates, you start by displaying the New Document window. Then in the left pane, under Microsoft Office Online, you click a category (such as Brochures or Newsletters), and in the list that appears in the center pane, you click first the subcategory and then the template you want.

Templates such as Normal contain only formatting information, which in addition to styles can include backgrounds, themes, and so on. These types of templates define the look of the document, and you add your own content. Templates can also contain content that you customize for your own purposes. For example, if you base a new document on a form template from Microsoft Office Online, the text of the form is already in place, and all you have to do is customize it for your organization.

Sometimes, a document based on a Word template displays formatted placeholders surrounded by square brackets—for example, *[Company Name]*. You replace a placeholder with your own text by clicking it and then typing the replacement. If you don't need a placeholder, you simply delete it. After you have entered all the text you need for the document, you save it in the usual way.

The changes you have made affect the document, not the template it is based on, which remains available to help create other documents.

In addition to using the templates that come with Word or that you download from Office Online, you can create your own templates. If you routinely create the same type of document, such as a monthly financial report, you can create and format the document once and then save it as a template on which to base future versions of that type of document. You can save your new template with text in it, which is handy if you create many documents with only slight variations. Or you can delete the text so that a document based on it will open as a new, blank document with the styles already defined and ready to apply to whatever content you enter.

> **Tip** If the designation *(Compatibility Mode)* appears in the title bar when you create a document based on a template, it indicates that the template was created in an earlier version of Word. Usually this will have no effect on your use of the template, but bear in mind that sometimes compatibility can have an impact on functionality.

To save even more time, you can create a document based on one of the Word templates, modify it—for example, by adding your own name and address—and then save the document as a new template with a different name. The next time you need to create this type of document, you can use your modified version of the template instead of the one provided by Word.

In this exercise, you will create a new template based on a predefined Word template, and then you'll create a new document based on the custom template. You will also convert a document to a template, and you'll modify the template by creating a new style. Finally, you'll create a document based on the template, and you'll apply the new style.

> **USE** the *03_Template* document. This practice file is located in the *Chapter04* subfolder under *SBS_Word2007*.
>
> **BE SURE TO** close all open documents before beginning this exercise.

Microsoft Office
Button

1. Click the **Microsoft Office Button**, click **New**, and then under **Templates** in the **New Document** window, click **Installed Templates**.

The center pane of the New Document window displays thumbnails of the installed templates.

2. In the center pane, scroll the **Installed Templates** list, and double click the **Oriel Fax** template.

Word opens a new fax cover document based on the selected template, with placeholders for the text you need to supply.

3. On the right side of the page, click the **[company name]** placeholder, and type Lucerne Publishing.

4. Click the **[address]** placeholder, type 4567 Oak Street, Seattle, WA 70110.

5. Scroll the page, click the **[phone number]** placeholder, type (505) 555-0145, and then click outside the placeholder.

6. Under **Judy Lew**, click the **[fax number]** placeholder, and then type (505) 555-0146.

7. Click the **[phone number]** placeholder, and then type (505) 555-0145.

8. On the right side of the page, click **Lucerne Publishing**, drag across it to select it, and then on the **Home** tab, in the **Styles** group, click the **Strong** style.

9. In turn, select the address and phone number, and apply the **Emphasis** style.

10. Click the **Microsoft Office Button**, and then click **Save As**.

    The Save As dialog box opens.

11. In the **File name** box, type My Fax Template.

12. Click the **Save as type** arrow, and then in the list, click **Word Template**.

> **Tip** If you want users who have older versions of Word to be able to use the template, click Word 97-2003 Template instead.

13. In the **Navigation Pane**, click **Templates**.

    Word displays your *Templates* folder.

> **Troubleshooting** Word expects templates to be stored in your default *Templates* folder. If you do not store the templates you create in this folder, Word will not display them in your My Templates list.

See Also For information about changing default file locations, see "Changing Default Program Options" in Chapter 12, "Customizing Word."

14. Click **Save**, and then close the template.

15. Display the **New Document** window, and under **Templates**, click **My templates**.

    The New dialog box opens.

16. On the **My Templates** tab, check that **My Fax Template** is highlighted, and then with the **Document** option selected under **Create New**, click **OK**.

    Word opens a new document based on the Lucerne Publishing fax cover template. The name on the From line is the name of your Windows user account.

17. Customize the fax cover page in any way you want, save it in the *Chapter04* folder with the name *My Fax*, and then close the document.

    > **Troubleshooting** Be sure to navigate to the *Documents\MSP\SBS_Word2007\Chapter04* folder before clicking **Save**.

18. Click the **Microsoft Office Button**, click **Open**, and then open the *03_Template* document from the *Chapter04* subfolder.

19. Display the **Save As** dialog box, and in the **File name** box, type *My Newsletter*. Change the **Save as type** setting to **Word Template**, change the save location to the **Templates** folder, and then click **Save**.

    Word saves the document as a template.

More

20. Click anywhere in the *Author Meet and Greet Update* heading, and then on the **Home** tab, in the **Styles** group, click the **More** button, and below the gallery, click **Save Selection as a New Quick Style**.

The Create New Style From Formatting dialog box opens. Notice that the style in the Paragraph Style Preview box reflects the formatting of the paragraph containing the insertion point.

Create New Style from Formatting
Name:
Style1
Paragraph style preview:
Style1
OK   Modify...   Cancel

21. In the **Name** box, replace **Style1** with Headline, and then click **Modify**.

The dialog box expands to display options for modifying the new style.

Create New Style from Formatting
Properties
Name: Headline
Style type: Linked (paragraph and character)
Style based on: ¶a Title
Style for following paragraph: ¶ Headline
Formatting
Verdana   18   B I U   Automatic

Previous Paragraph Previous Paragraph Previous Paragraph Previous Paragraph Previous Paragraph Previous Paragraph Previous Paragraph Previous Paragraph Previous Paragraph Previous Paragraph

Author Meet and Greet Update

Following Paragraph Following Paragraph Following Paragraph Following Paragraph Following Paragraph Following Paragraph Following Paragraph Following Paragraph Following Paragraph Following Paragraph Following Paragraph Following Paragraph Following Paragraph Following Paragraph Following Paragraph Following Paragraph Following Paragraph Following Paragraph Following Paragraph Following Paragraph

Font: Verdana, Space After: 12 pt, Style: Quick Style, Based on: Title

☑ Add to Quick Style list   ☐ Automatically update
◉ Only in this document   ○ New documents based on this template

Format ▾   OK   Cancel

22. At the bottom of the expanded dialog box, select the **New documents based on this template** option, and then click **OK**.

23. Back in the template, replace **Author Meet and Greet Update** with Headline, and then select all the text below the headline paragraph and press Backspace.

Save

24. On the **Quick Access Toolbar**, click the **Save** button, and then close the template.

25. Display the **New Document** window, click **My templates**, and from the **New** dialog box, create a new document based on the **My Newsletter** template.

    Word opens a new document with the template's title and headline already in place. First you need to customize the headline.

26. Select the word **Headline**, and type Fantasy Author Starts Book Tour.

    You can then add the text of the newsletter below the headline.

LUCERNE   PUBLISHING

Book Beat

A bi-monthly newsletter for booksellers

Fantasy Author Starts Book Tour

✕ **CLOSE** the document without saving your changes.

Tip If you want to change an existing template, you can open the template by displaying the Open dialog box, setting the file type to Word Templates, navigating to your *Templates* folder, and double-clicking the template.

Applying a Different Template to an Existing Document

A quick and easy way to change the look of an existing document is to apply a new template to it. For this to work smoothly, the new template must use the same paragraph and character style names as the existing template. For example, if the existing template uses the name Heading 1 for top-level headings, the new template must also use the name Heading 1. If the style names do not match, you can still apply a new template to a document and then use the Styles task pane to find all instances of each particular style and replace them with one of the new template's corresponding styles.

To apply a new template to an open document:

1. Click the **Microsoft Office Button**, click **Word Options**, and in the left pane, click **Add-Ins**.

2. At the bottom of the right pane, click the **Manage** arrow, and in the list, click **Templates**. Then click **Go**.

   The Templates And Add-ins dialog box opens.

3. Under **Document Template**, click **Attach**.

   The Attach Template dialog box opens.

4. Locate and double-click the template you want to attach.

5. In the **Templates and Add-ins** dialog box, select the **Automatically update document styles** check box, and then click **OK**.

   The new template is attached and the styles used in the document change to reflect their definitions in the new template.

To replace all instances of one style with another style:

1. On the **Home** tab, in the **Styles** group, click the **Styles** Dialog Box Launcher.

2. In the **Styles** list, point to a style you want to replace, click the arrow that appears, and then click **Select All Instance(s)**.

   Word selects all the text to which that style has been applied.

3. In the **Styles** list, click the style you want to apply.

4. Repeat Steps 2 and 3 for each style that needs to be replaced.

Adding Headers and Footers

You can display page numbers and other information on every page of your document by creating *headers* and *footers*—regions at the top and bottom of a page that can be created and formatted independently. You can have a different header and footer on the first page of a document, and you can have different headers and footers on odd and even pages.

> **Tip** If your document contains section breaks, each successive section inherits the headers and footers of the preceding section unless you break the link between the two sections. You can then create a different header and footer for the current section. For information about sections, see "Controlling What Appears on Each Page" later in this chapter.

When you create a header or footer, you can select the style you want from a gallery. Word applies the specified style to the document, indicates the header and footer areas by displaying dotted borders, and displays a contextual Design tab on the Ribbon. You can enter information in the header and footer areas the same way you enter ordinary text. You can use the buttons on the Design tab to enter and format items such as page numbers and to move from one header or footer to another.

In this exercise, you will add a header and footer to a document. You will then create a different header and footer for the first page.

> **USE** the *04_Header* document. This practice file is located in the *Chapter04* subfolder under *SBS_Word2007*.
> **OPEN** the *04_Header* document.

1. With the insertion point at the beginning of the document, on the **Insert** tab, in the **Header & Footer** group, click the **Header** button.

The Header gallery opens.

Built-In
Blank
[Type text]
Blank (Three Columns)
[Type text]   [Type text]   [Type text]
Alphabet
[Type the document title]
Annual
[Type the document title] [Year]

	Edit Header
	Remove Header
	Save Selection to Header Gallery...

2. Scroll through the gallery, noticing the variety of headers that are available, and then click **Motion (Even Page)**.

   Word displays a Header & Footer Tools contextual tab called *Design* on the Ribbon. It dims the text of the document, outlines the header area at the top of the first page, and adds the formatting defined for this header to the document.

1	[Type the document title]

   Header

   The Taguien Cycle

   A Series for Young Adults

   Judy Lew, Project Editor

   Rationale

3. On the **Design** tab, in the **Options** group, click the **Different First Page** check box.

   Word replaces the header area with an area labeled *First Page Header*.

4. On the **Design** tab, in the **Navigation** group, click the **Next Section** button.

   Word moves to Page 2 of the document, which still has the original header.

5. In the header, click the **[Type the document title]** placeholder, and then type The Taguien Cycle.

> **Tip** While the header or footer is active, you can edit and format its content just as you would ordinary text.

Go to Footer

6. On the **Design** tab, in the **Navigation** group, click the **Go To Footer** button.

Word displays the footer area at the bottom of the page.

Footer

7. In the **Header & Footer** group, click the **Footer** button, and then in the **Footer** gallery, click **Motion (Even Page)**.

Because the page number and document name are included in the header, you want only the date to appear in the footer.

Footer

[Pick the date]

8. Click the **Pick the date** placeholder, click the arrow to the right, and then in the date navigator, click today's date.

Word inserts the current date in the footer on Page 2.

9. In the **Navigation** group, click the **Previous Section** button.

Although you specified that Page 1 should be different, you do want the footer with the date to appear on this page.

10. In the **Header & Footer** group, click the **Footer** button, and then click **Motion (Even Page)** in the gallery.

The date is now shown on Page 1.

Close Header and Footer

11. On the **Design** tab, in the **Close** group, click the **Close Header and Footer** button.

12. At the right end of the status bar, click the **Zoom** button. In the **Zoom** dialog box, click **Whole page**, and then click **OK** to display the header and footer at the same time.

Two Pages

13. On the **View** tab, in the **Zoom** group, click the **Two Pages** button to display the headers and footers on both pages.

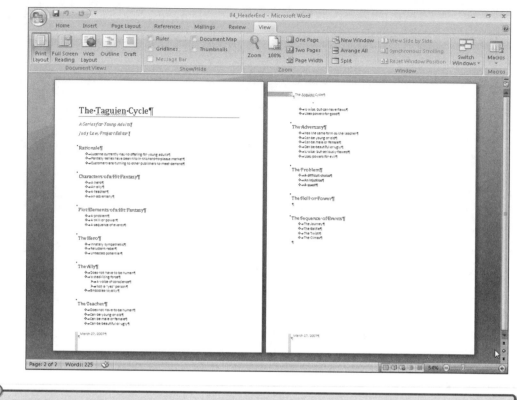

CLOSE the *04_Header* document without saving your changes.

Controlling What Appears on Each Page

When you add more content than will fit within the document's top and bottom margins, Word creates a new page by inserting a soft page break. A *soft page break* produces separate pages in Print Layout view and is displayed as a dotted line in Draft view.

If you want to control how pages break, you can insert a manual page break in one of three ways:

- Click Page Break in the Pages group on the Insert tab.
- Click Breaks in the Page Setup group on the Page Layout tab, and then click Page.
- Press Ctrl+Enter.

A *manual page break* produces separate pages in Print Layout view, and appears as a dotted line with the words *Page Break* in the middle in Draft view.

Inserting and Formatting Page Numbers

If the only information you want to appear in a header or footer is the page number, you can insert it by clicking the Page Number button in the Header & Footer group on the Insert tab. In the Page Number gallery, you can select a page number that is positioned at the top or bottom of the page and aligned in various ways with formatting that ranges from simple to fairly fancy. You can also position the page number in the margin at the side of the page.

If you want to change the style of existing page numbers, you can do so by clicking the Page Number button again and making a different selection from the Top Of Page, Bottom Of Page, or Page Margins options.

If you want to use a numbering scheme other than Arabic numerals, number pages by chapter, or control the starting number, you can do so by following these steps:

1. On the **Insert** tab, in the **Header & Footer** group, click the **Page Number** button, and then click **Format Page Numbers**.

   The Page Number Format dialog box opens.

2. Click the **Number format** arrow, and then in the list, click the number format you want.

3. Select any other options you want to apply, and then click **OK**.

Tip As you edit the text in a document, Word changes the location of the soft page breaks but not of any manual page breaks you might have inserted.

You can control whether page breaks leave widows and orphans—individual lines that appear on a different page from their paragraphs. A *widow* is the last line of a paragraph at the top of a page, and an *orphan* as the first line of a paragraph at the bottom of a page. These single lines of text can make a document hard to read, so by default Word specifies a two-line minimum. You can change the following options on the Line And Page Breaks tab of the Paragraph dialog box displayed when you click the Paragraph Dialog Box Launcher:

- **Widow/Orphan Control.** This option controls whether Word will break a page with the last line of a paragraph by itself at the top of a page or the first line of a paragraph by itself at the bottom of a page. This option is turned on by default for all new documents.

- **Keep With Next.** This option controls whether Word will break a page between the selected paragraph and the following paragraph.
- **Keep Lines Together.** This option controls whether Word will break a page within a paragraph.
- **Page Break Before.** This option controls whether Word will break a page before the selected paragraph.

> **Tip** You can apply the options in the Paragraph dialog box to individual paragraphs, or you can incorporate them into the styles you define for document elements such as headings. For more information about styles, see "Working with Templates" earlier in this chapter.

In addition to page breaks, you can insert section breaks in your documents. A *section break* identifies a part of the document to which you can apply page settings, such as orientation or margins, that are different from those of the rest of the document. For example, you might want to turn a large table sideways.

You insert a section break by clicking Breaks in the Page Setup group on the Page Layout tab. The following types of section breaks are available:

- **Next Page.** This break starts the following section on the next page.
- **Continuous.** This break creates a new section without affecting page breaks.
- **Even Page.** This break starts the following section on the next even-numbered page.
- **Odd Page.** This break starts the following section on the next odd-numbered page.

A section break is not displayed in Print Layout view unless non-printing characters are turned on, in which case it appears as a double-dotted line from the preceding paragraph mark to the margin. In Draft view, a section break appears as a double-dotted line across the page. In both cases, the words *Section Break* and the type of section break appear in the middle of the line.

> **Tip** To remove a page or section break, click to the left of the break and then press the Delete key.

In this exercise, you will insert page and section breaks, and ensure that the pages break in logical places.

> **USE** the *05_ControllingPage* document. This practice file is located in the *Chapter04* subfolder under *SBS_Word2007*.
> **OPEN** the *05_ControllingPage* document.

1. Scroll through the document, noticing any awkward page breaks, such as a section or list that starts close to the bottom of a page.

2. On the **Home** tab, in the **Editing** group, click the **Select** button, and then click **Select All**.

Dialog Box
Launcher

3. Click the **Paragraph** Dialog Box Launcher, and then in the **Paragraph** dialog box, click the **Line and Page Breaks** tab.

4. Select the **Widow/Orphan control** and **Keep lines together** check boxes.

5. Clear all the other check boxes by clicking them twice, and then click **OK**.

   These settings ensure that all the lines of text in each paragraph appear on the same page.

6. Scroll the document, and click to the left of the *Facilities* heading.

Page Break

7. On the **Insert** tab, in the **Pages** group, click the **Page Break** button.

   Word breaks the page and moves the *Facilities* heading and the following text to the next page.

8. Scroll down the document, select the **To use the intercom from the office** heading and the following two steps, and then on the **Home** tab, click the **Paragraph** Dialog Box Launcher.

9. On the **Line and Page Breaks** tab of the **Paragraph** dialog box, select the **Keep with next** check box, and then click **OK**.

   Word moves the procedure to the next page.

10. Click to the left of the *Shipping Quick Reference* heading toward the end of the document.

11. On the **Page Layout** tab, in the **Page Setup** group, click the **Breaks** button, and then under **Section Breaks**, click **Next Page**.

   A double dotted line with the words *Section Break (Next Page)* appears on the page before the section break.

12. Click anywhere in the heading of the newly defined section, and on the **Page Layout** tab, in the **Page Setup** group, click the **Margins** button. Then in the **Margins** gallery, click **Wide**.

   The text in the new section moves to the right between margins that are wider than the rest of the document.

13. On the **Insert** tab, in the **Header & Footer** group, click the **Header** button, and then click **Edit Header**.

   Because the Link To Previous and Different First Page options are turned on, the header for the first page of the new section is the same as the first page of the document.

14. On the **Design** tab, in the **Options** group, clear the **Different First Page** check box.

   Now the Link To Previous option causes the header text from Pages 2 through 9 of the document to be repeated for this section.

CLOSE the *05_ControllingPage* document without saving your changes.

Key Points

- A background color or pattern can really give a document pizzazz, but be careful that it doesn't overwhelm the text. The same is true for text or picture watermarks.

- The same document can look and feel very different depending on the theme applied to it. Colors, fonts, and effects can be combined to create just the look you want.

- Take the effort out of creating sophisticated documents by using one of Word's predefined templates as a starting point. You can also create your own templates.

- Headers and footers provide useful information and add a professional touch to any document that is longer than one page.

- You can control which elements should be kept together on a page, and you can divide a document into sections, each with its own margins and formatting.

Chapter at a Glance

Present information in columns, **page 124**

Present information in a table, **page 130**

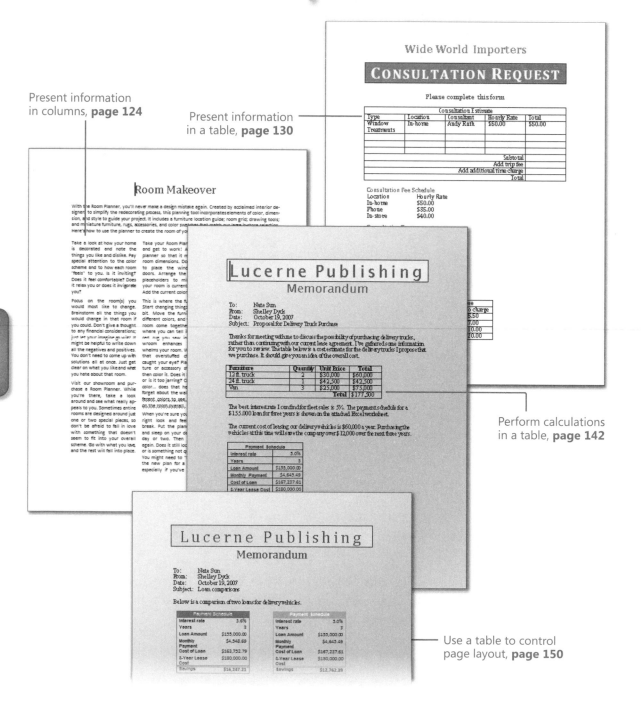

Perform calculations in a table, **page 142**

Use a table to control page layout, **page 150**

5 Presenting Information in Columns and Tables

In this chapter, you will learn to:

✔ Present information in columns.

✔ Create a tabular list.

✔ Present information in a table.

✔ Format table information.

✔ Perform calculations in a table.

✔ Use a table to control page layout.

When creating a Word document, you might find it useful to organize certain information into columns or tables. Flowing text in multiple columns is common practice in newsletters, flyers, and brochures. After you specify the number of columns, Word flows the text from one column to the next. You can also manually end one column and move subsequent text to the next column.

It is often more efficient to present numeric data in a table than to explain it in a paragraph of text. Tables make the data easier to read and understand. Small amounts of data can be displayed in simple columns separated by left, right, centered, or decimal tab stops to create a tabular list. Larger amounts or more complex data is better presented in a Word table that includes a structure of rows and columns, frequently with row and column headings.

A Word table is useful not only for presenting data but also for providing the structure for complex document layouts. For example, you can set up a table with two columns and two rows to present a set of four paragraphs, four bulleted lists, or four tables in a format in which they can be easily compared.

In this chapter, you will create and modify columns of text, create a simple tabular list, create tables from scratch and from existing text, format a table in various ways, and perform calculations within a table. You will copy and paste worksheet data, link to worksheet data, and create an Excel object. And finally, you will create a table for the purpose of displaying two other tables side by side.

See Also Do you need only a quick refresher on the topics in this chapter? See the Quick Reference entries on pages xxxix–lxiii.

Important Before you can use the practice files in this chapter, you need to install them from the book's companion CD to their default location. See "Using the Book's CD" on page xxv for more information.

Troubleshooting Graphics and operating system–related instructions in this book reflect the Windows Vista user interface. If your computer is running Microsoft Windows XP and you experience trouble following the instructions as written, please refer to the "Information for Readers Running Windows XP" section at the beginning of this book.

Presenting Information in Columns

By default, Word displays text in one *column*, but you can specify that text be displayed in two, three, or more columns to create layouts like those used in newspapers and magazines. When you format text to *flow* in columns, the text fills the first column and then moves to the top of the next column. You can insert a *column break* to move to the next column before the current column is full.

Word provides several standard options for dividing text into columns. You have the choice of one, two, or three equal columns, or two other two-column formats: one with a narrow left column and the other with a narrow right column. No matter how you set up the columns initially, you can change the layout or column widths at any time.

You can format the text in columns the same way you would any text. If you *justify* the columns for a neater look, you might want to have Word hyphenate the text to ensure that there are no large gaps between words.

In this exercise, you will divide part of a document into three columns. You will then justify the columns, change the column spacing, hyphenate the text, and indent a couple of paragraphs. You'll also break a column at a specific location instead of allowing the text to flow naturally from one column to the next.

1. Click just to the left of the paragraph that begins *Take a look* (do not click in the selection area). Then scroll the end of the document into view, hold down the `Shift` key, and click just to the right of the period after *credit cards*.

Word selects the text from the *Take a look* paragraph through the end of the document.

> **Tip** If you want to format an entire document with the same number of columns, you can simply click anywhere in the document—you don't have to select the text.

2. On the **Page Layout** tab, in the **Page Setup** group, click the **Columns** button, and then click **Three**.

3. Press `Ctrl`+`Home` to move to the top of the document.

Word has inserted a section break above the selection and formatted the text after the section break into three columns.

See Also For information about sections, see "Controlling What Appears on Each Page" in Chapter 4, "Changing the Look of a Document."

4. On the **Home** tab, in the **Editing** group, click the **Select** button, and then click **Select All**.

Justify

5. In the **Paragraph** group, click the **Justify** button.

The spacing of the text within the paragraphs changes so the right edge of the paragraph is straight.

Center

6. Press `Ctrl`+`Home` to deselect the text and move to the top of the document, and then in the **Paragraph** group, click the **Center** button to center the title.

7. At the right end of the status bar, click the **Zoom** button. Then in the **Zoom** dialog box, click **75%**, and click **OK**.

You can now see about two-thirds of the first page of the document.

8. Click anywhere in the first column.

On the horizontal ruler, Word indicates the margins of the columns.

9. On the **Page Layout** tab, in the **Page Setup** group, click the **Columns** button, and then click **More Columns**.

The Columns dialog box opens. Because the Equal Column Width check box is selected, you can adjust the width and spacing of only the first column.

10. Under **Width and spacing**, in the **Spacing** column, click the down arrow until the setting is **0.2"**.

Word changes the measurement in the box below and widens all the columns to reflect the new setting.

11. Click **OK**.

Word reflows the columns to fit their new margins.

12. Click immediately to the left of *Take a look*. Then in the **Page Setup** group, click the **Hyphenation** button, and click **Automatic**.

    Word hyphenates the text of the document, which fills in some of the large gaps between words.

13. Click anywhere in the *NOTE* paragraph in the third column.

14. On the horizontal ruler, in the third column, drag the **Hanging Indent** marker 0.25 inch (two marks) to the right.

    All the lines in the *NOTE* paragraph except the first are now indented, offsetting the note from the paragraphs above and below it.

15. Click just to the left of *Take your Room Planner home* at the bottom of the first column on Page 1. Then in the **Page Setup** group, click the **Breaks** button, and click **Column**.

    The text that follows the column break moves to the top of the second column.

Repeat

16. Click just to the left of *If you're not sure* at the bottom of the third column on Page 1, and then on the **Quick Access Toolbar**, click the **Repeat Insertion** button to insert another column break.

The text that follows the column break moves to the top of the first column on Page 2.

> **CLOSE** the *01_Columns* document without saving your changes.

Creating a Tabular List

If you have a relatively small amount of data to present in a table, you might choose to display it in a *tabular list*, which arranges text in simple columns separated by left, right, centered, or decimal tab stops.

See Also For more information about setting tab stops, see "Manually Changing the Look of Paragraphs" in Chapter 3, "Changing the Look of Text."

When entering text in a tabular list, people have a tendency to press the Tab key multiple times to align the columns of the list. If you do this, you have no control over the column widths. To be able to fine-tune the columns, you need to set custom tab stops rather than relying on the default ones. When you want to set up a tabular list, you should press Tab only once between the items that you want to appear in separate columns. You can then apply any necessary formatting and set the tabs in order from left to right so that you can see how everything lines up.

> **Tip** In addition to left, right, centered, and decimal tabs, you can set a bar tab. This type of tab does not align text like the others, but instead adds a vertical line to selected paragraphs. This bar can be used to further distinguish the columns in a tabular list.

In this exercise, you will create a tabular list. First you'll enter text separated by tabs, and then you'll format the text and set custom tab stops.

> **USE** the *02_TabularList* document. This practice file is located in the *Chapter05* subfolder under *SBS_Word2007*.
> **BE SURE TO** display the rulers and non-printing characters before starting this exercise.
> **OPEN** the *02_TabularList* document.

1. Scroll down to the bottom of the document, click to the left of the paragraph mark at the end of *The Skill or Power*, and then press [Enter].

2. Type Self, press `Tab`, type Other People, press `Tab`, type Nature, and then press `Enter`.

3. Add three more lines to the list by typing the following text. Press `Tab` once between each item in a line, and press `Enter` at the end of each line except the last.

Transformation `Tab` *Life/death* `Tab` *Weather*

Time travel `Tab` *Telepathy* `Tab` *Oceans*

Visible/invisible `Tab` *Mind control* `Tab` *Animals*

The tab characters push the items to the next default tab stop, but because some items are longer than others, they do not line up.

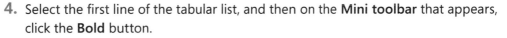

See Also For information about tab stops, see "Manually Changing the Look of Paragraphs" in Chapter 3, "Changing the Look of Text."

Bold

4. Select the first line of the tabular list, and then on the **Mini toolbar** that appears, click the **Bold** button.

> **Troubleshooting** If the Mini toolbar doesn't appear, click the Bold button in the Font group on the Home tab.

Increase Indent

5. Select all four lines of the tabular list, and then on the **Mini toolbar**, click the **Increase Indent** button.

6. With the lines still selected, on the **Page Layout** tab, in the **Paragraph** group, under **Spacing**, change the **After** setting to 0 pt.

Left Tab

7. Without changing the selection, verify that the **Tab** button at the junction of the horizontal and vertical rulers shows a Left Tab stop (an L), and then click the 2-inch mark on the horizontal ruler.

Word displays a Left Tab stop on the ruler, and the items in the second column of all the selected lines left-align themselves at that position.

8. Click the **Tab** button twice.

The icon on the button changes to a Right Tab stop (a backward L), indicating that clicking the ruler now will set a right-aligned tab.

9. Click the horizontal ruler at the 4-inch mark.

Word displays a Right Tab stop on the ruler, and the items in the third column of the selected lines jump to right-align themselves at that position.

10. On the Home tab, in the Paragraph group, click the Show/Hide ¶ button to hide non-printing characters. Then click away from the tabular list to see the results.

The tabular list resembles a simple table.

The Problem
❖ A difficult choice
❖ An injustice
❖ A quest

The Skill or Power

Self	Other People	Nature
Transformation	Life/death	Weather
Time travel	Telepathy	Oceans
Visible/invisible	Mind control	Animals

The Sequence of Events
❖ The Journey
❖ The Battle
❖ The Twist
❖ The Climax

> ✕ **CLOSE** the *02_TabularList* document without saving your changes.

Presenting Information in a Table

Creating a Word table is a simple matter of clicking the Table button and selecting the number of rows and columns you want from a grid. You can then enter text, numbers, and graphics into the table's *cells*, which are the boxes at the intersections of a row and a column. At any time, you can change the table's size; insert and delete columns, rows, and cells; and format individual entries or the entire table. You can sort the information in a logical order and perform calculations on the numbers in a column or row.

Clicking the Table button creates a table with the number of columns and rows you select from the grid, with all the cells of equal size. You can click Insert Table below the grid to open the Insert Table dialog box, where you can specify the number of rows and columns as well as their sizes. You can also create a table by drawing cells the size you want. If the text you want to appear in a table already exists in the document, you can convert the text to a table.

See Also For information about drawing tables, see "Using a Table to Control Page Layout" later in this chapter.

A new table appears in the document as a set of blank cells surrounded by *gridlines*. Each cell has an end-of-cell marker, and each row has an end-of-row marker. When the pointer is over the table, the table has a move handle in its upper-left corner and a size handle in its lower-right corner. While the insertion point is in the table, Word displays two Table Tools contextual tabs, Design and Layout.

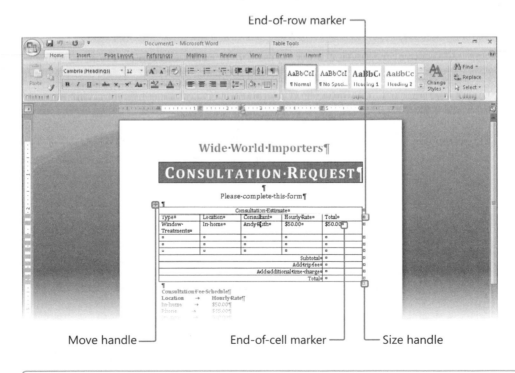

End-of-row marker

Move handle   End-of-cell marker   Size handle

Tip You cannot see the move handle and size handle in Draft view.

After you create a table, you can type text or numbers into cells and press the Tab key to move the insertion point from cell to cell. Pressing Tab when the insertion point is in the last cell in the last row adds a new row to the bottom of the table. In addition to the Tab key, you can use the Arrow keys to position the insertion point, or you can simply click any cell.

You can modify a table's structure at any time. To change the structure, you often need to select the entire table or specific rows or columns, by using the following methods:

- **Select a table.** Click anywhere in the table. Then on the Layout contextual tab, in the Table group, click the Select button, and click Select Table.
- **Select a column.** Point to the top border of the column. When the pointer changes to a black, down-pointing arrow, click once.
- **Select a row.** Point to the left border of the row. When the pointer changes to a white, right-pointing arrow, click once.
- **Select a cell.** Triple-click the cell or click its left border.
- **Select multiple cells.** Click the first cell, hold down the Shift key, and press the arrow keys to select adjacent cells in a column or row.

The basic methods for manipulating tables are as follows:

- **Insert a row or column.** Click anywhere in a row or column adjacent to where you want to make the insertion. Then on the Layout tab, in the Rows & Columns group, click the Insert Above, Insert Below, Insert Left, or Insert Right button. Selecting more than one row or column before you click an Insert button inserts that number of rows or columns in the table.

> **Tip** You can insert cells by clicking the Rows & Columns Dialog Box Launcher and specifying in the Insert Cells dialog box how adjacent cells should be moved to accommodate the new cells.

- **Delete a row or column.** Click anywhere in the row or column, and in the Rows & Columns group, click the Delete button. Then click Delete Cells, Delete Columns, Delete Rows, or Delete Table.
- **Size an entire table.** Drag the size handle.
- **Size a single column or row.** Drag a column's right border to the left or right. Drag a row's bottom border up or down.
- **Merge cells.** Create cells that span columns by selecting the cells you want to merge and clicking the Merge Cells button in the Merge group on the Layout tab. For example, to center a title in the first row of a table, you can create one merged cell that spans the table's width.

- **Split cells.** Divide a merged cell into its component cells by clicking Split Cells in the Merge group on the Layout tab.

- **Move a table.** Point to the table, and then drag the move handle that appears in its upper-left corner to a new location. Or use the Cut and Paste buttons in the Clipboard group on the Home tab to move the table.

- **Sort information.** Use the Sort button in the Data group on the Layout tab to sort the rows in ascending or descending order by the data in any column. For example, you can sort a table that has the column headings Name, Address, ZIP Code, and Phone Number on any one of those columns to arrange the information in alphabetical or numerical order.

In this exercise, you will work with two tables. First you'll create a table, enter text, align text in the cells, add rows, and merge cells. Then you'll create a second table by converting existing tabbed text, you'll size a column, and you'll size the entire table.

> **USE** the *03_Table* document. This practice file is located in the *Chapter05* subfolder under *SBS_Word2007*.
>
> **OPEN** the *03_Table* document.

1. Click in the second blank line below *Please complete this form.*

2. On the **Insert** tab, in the **Tables** group, click the **Table** button, point to the upper-left cell, and move the pointer across five columns and down five rows.

   Word highlights the cells as you drag across them and creates a temporary table in the document to show you what the selection will look like.

3. Click the lower-right cell in the selection.

Word creates a blank table with five columns and five rows. The insertion point is located in the first cell. Because the table is active, Word displays the Table Tools Design and Layout contextual tabs.

4. In the selection area, point to the first row, and then click to select the row.

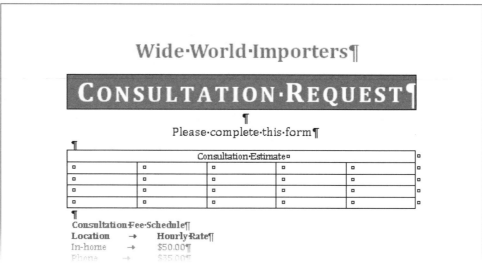

5. On the **Layout** contextual tab, in the **Merge** group, click the **Merge Cells** button.

Word combines the five cells in the first row into one cell.

6. With the merged cell selected, in the **Alignment** group, click the **Align Center** button.

The end-of-cell marker moves to the center of the merged cell to indicate that anything you type there will be centered.

7. Type **Consultation Estimate**.

The table now has a title.

8. Click the first cell in the second row, type **Type**, and then press [Tab].

9. Type **Location**, **Consultant**, **Hourly Rate**, and **Total**, pressing [Tab] after each entry.

The table now has a row of column headings. Pressing Tab after the *Total* heading moves the insertion point to the first cell of the third row.

10. Type **Window Treatments**, **In-home**, **Andy Ruth**, **$50.00**, and **$50.00**, pressing [Tab] after each entry.

You have entered a complete row of data.

Wide·World·Importers¶

CONSULTATION·REQUEST¶

¶
Please·complete·this·form¶

Consultation·Estimate□					□
Type□	Location□	Consultant□	Hourly·Rate□	Total□	□
Window·Treatments□	In-home□	Andy·Ruth□	$50.00□	$50.00□	□
□	□	□	□	□	□
□	□	□	□	□	□

¶
Consultation·Fee·Schedule¶
Location   →   Hourly·Rate¶
In-home   → $50.00¶

11. Select the last two rows, and then on the **Layout** tab, in the **Rows & Columns** group, click the **Insert Below** button.

Word adds two new rows and selects them.

12. In the last row, click the first cell, hold down the [⇧] key, and then press the [→] key four times to select the first four cells in the row.

13. In the **Merge** group, click the **Merge Cells** button.

Word combines the selected cells into one cell.

14. In the **Alignment** group, click the **Align Center Right** button.

Align Center Right

15. Type **Subtotal**, and then press [Tab] twice.

Word adds a new row with the same structure to the bottom of the table.

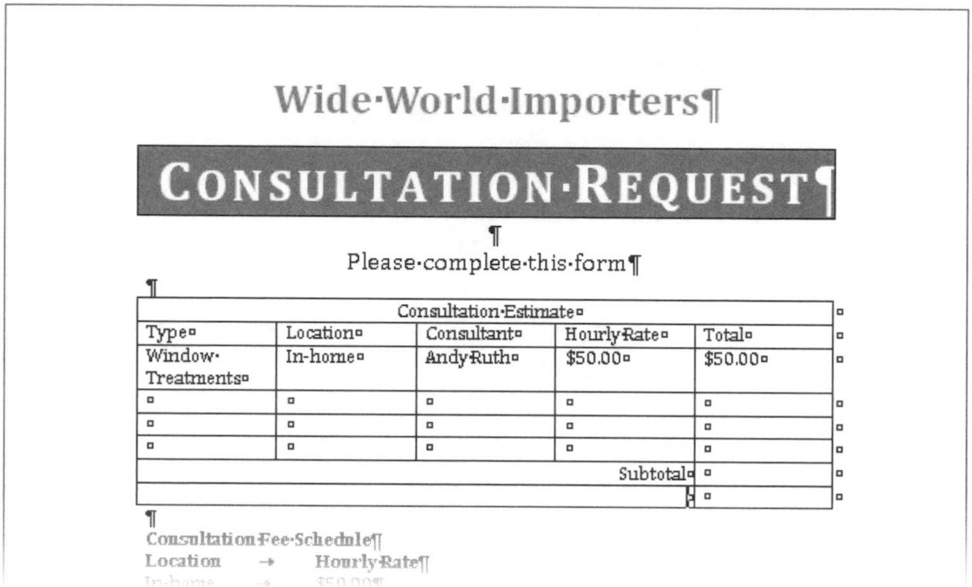

Wide·World·Importers¶

CONSULTATION·REQUEST¶

¶

Please·complete·this·form¶

Consultation·Estimate¤					¤
Type¤	Location¤	Consultant¤	Hourly·Rate¤	Total¤	¤
Window·Treatments¤	In-home¤	Andy·Ruth¤	$50.00¤	$50.00¤	¤
¤	¤	¤	¤	¤	¤
¤	¤	¤	¤	¤	¤
¤	¤	¤	¤	¤	¤
				Subtotal¤	¤
					¤

¶
Consultation·Fee·Schedule¶
Location   →   Hourly·Rate¶
In-home   → $50.00¶

16. Type Add trip fee, press [Tab] twice to add a new row, and then type Add additional time charge.

17. Press [Tab] twice to add a new row, and then type Total.

18. Scroll to the bottom of the document, and select the rows of the tabular list beginning with *Distance* and ending with *$20.00*.

19. On the **Insert** tab, in the **Tables** group, click the **Table** button, and then click **Convert Text to Table**.

    The Convert Text To Table dialog box opens.

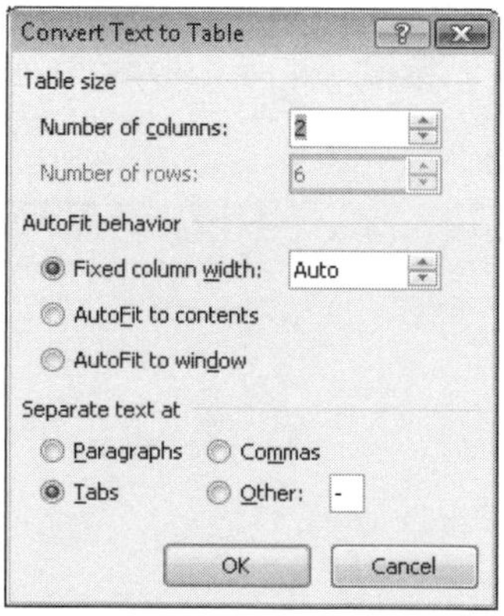

> **Tip** To convert a table to text, select the table, and then click the Convert To Text button in the Data group on the Layout tab.

20. Verify that the **Number of columns** box displays **2**, and then click **OK**.

The selected text appears in a table with two columns and six rows.

21. Click anywhere in the table to release the selection, and point to the right border of the table. When the pointer changes to two opposing arrows, double-click the right border.

Word adjusts the width of the right column so that it is exactly wide enough to contain its longest line of text.

Jo Berry¶
Andy Ruth¶
Carlos Caryallo¶

In-Home Trip Charge¶

Distance□	Fee□	□
0-5 miles□	No charge□	□
6-10 miles□	$5.50□	□
11-20 miles□	$7.00□	□
21-50 miles□	$10.00□	□
Over 50 miles□	$20.00□	□

¶

22. Point to the In-Home Trip Charge table.

Word displays the move handle in the upper-left corner and the size handle in the lower-right corner.

23. Drag the size handle to the right, releasing the mouse button when the right edge of the table aligns approximately with the 4-inch mark on the horizontal ruler.

CLOSE the *03_Table* document without saving your changes.

Other Layout Options

You can control many aspects of a table by clicking Properties in the Table group on the Layout tab to display the Table Properties dialog box. You can then set the following options:

- On the Table tab, you can specify the preferred width of the entire table, as well as the way it interacts with the surrounding text.

- On the Row tab, you can specify the height of each row, whether a row is allowed to break across pages, and whether a row of column headings should be repeated at the top of each page.

Tip The Repeat As Header Row option is available only if the insertion point is in the top row of the table.

- On the Column tab, you can set the width of each column.

- On the Cell tab, you can set the preferred width of cells and the vertical alignment of text within them.

Tip You can also control the widths of selected cells by using the buttons in the Cell Size group on the Layout contextual tab.

- You can control the margins of cells (how close text comes to the cell border) by clicking the Options button on either the Table or Cell tab.

Tip You can also control the margins by clicking the Cell Margins button in the Alignment group on the Layout contextual tab.

If the first row of your table has several long headings that make it difficult to fit the table on one page, you can turn the headings sideways. Simply select the heading row and click the Text Direction button in the Alignment group on the Layout tab.

Formatting Table Information

Formatting a table to best convey its data is often a process of trial and error. With Word 2007, you can quickly get started by creating a *quick table*, a preformatted table with sample data that you can customize. You can then apply one of the *table styles* available on the Design contextual tab, which include a variety of borders, colors, and other attributes to give the table a professional look.

To customize the appearance of a quick table or a table you have created from scratch, you can use the buttons on the Design and Layout contextual tabs. You can also use buttons in the Paragraph group on the Home tab to change alignment and spacing. You can format the text by using the buttons in the Font group, just as you would to format any text in a Word document. You can also apply character formatting from the Styles gallery.

In this exercise, you will create a quick table and then apply a table style to it. You will then change some of the text attributes and modify the borders and shading in various cells to make the formatting suit the table's data. There are no practice files for this exercise.

BE SURE TO display non-printing characters before starting this exercise.

OPEN a new, blank document.

Table

1. With the Zoom level at 100%, on the **Insert** tab, in the **Tables** group, click the **Table** button, and then point to **Quick Tables**.

   The Quick Tables gallery opens.

2. Scroll through the gallery, noticing the types of tables that are available, and then click **Matrix**.

   Word inserts the selected table and displays the Design contextual tab. Notice that the table data includes headings across the top and down the left column. Some of the cells are blank, and obviously have less importance than the cells that contain numbers. The table does not include summary data, such as totals.

City or Town¤	Point A¤	Point B¤	Point C¤	Point D¤	Point E¤	¤
Point A¤	—¤	¤	¤	¤	¤	¤
Point B¤	87¤	—¤	¤	¤	¤	¤
Point C¤	64¤	56¤	—¤	¤	¤	¤
Point D¤	37¤	32¤	91¤	—¤	¤	¤
Point E¤	93¤	35¤	54¤	43¤	—¤	¤

3. On the **Design** tab, in the **Table Style Options** group, clear the **Banded Rows** check box.

More

4. In the **Table Styles** group, point to each style in turn to see its live preview, and then click the **More** button to display the Table Styles gallery.

5. Explore all the styles in the gallery. When you finish exploring, click the **Medium Shading 2 – Accent 2** thumbnail.

You need to modify this style a bit, but it is a good starting point.

Borders ▾

6. Select all the white cells by dragging through them. Then in the **Table Styles** group, click the **Borders** arrow, and in the list, click **All Borders**.

7. Select all the cells in the last row (*Point E*) by clicking to its left, and in the **Table Styles** group, in the **Borders** list, click **Borders and Shading**.

The Borders And Shading dialog box opens, displaying the borders applied to the selected cells. The thick gray borders in the Preview area indicate that different borders are applied to different cells in the selection.

8. In the **Preview** area, click the bottom border of the diagram twice to remove all bottom borders.

9. Click the **Color** arrow, and then under **Theme Colors**, click the black box (**Black, Text 1**).

10. Click the **Width** arrow, and then in the list, click **2 1/4 pt**.

11. In the **Preview** area, click the bottom border of the diagram, and then click **OK**.

The table now has the same border at the top and bottom.

12. Select the empty cells in the *Point A* row. In the **Table Styles** group, click the **Shading** arrow, and then under **Theme Colors**, click the lightest burgundy box (**Red, Accent 2, Lighter 80%**).

13. Repeat Step 12 for all the remaining blank cells in the table.

B

Bold

14. Select the dash in the cell at the junction of the *Point A* column and the *Point A* row, hold down the ⌃ key, and select the other four dashes.

15. On the **Mini toolbar**, click the **Font Color** arrow, and then under **Standard Colors** in the palette, click the bright **Red** box.

> **Troubleshooting** If the Mini toolbar doesn't appear, click the Font Color arrow in the Font group on the Home tab.

Show/Hide ¶

16. Click outside the table to release the selection, and then in the **Paragraph** group, click the **Show/Hide ¶** button to hide non-printing characters.

You can now judge how well the table displays its data.

City or Town	Point A	Point B	Point C	Point D	Point E
Point A	—				
Point B	87	—			
Point C	64	56	—		
Point D	37	32	91	—	
Point E	93	35	54	43	—

CLOSE the document without saving your changes.

Performing Calculations in a Table

When you want to perform a calculation on numbers in a Word table, you can create a *formula* that uses a built-in mathematical function. You construct a formula by using the tools in the Formula dialog box, which you can access by clicking Formula in the Data group on the Layout contextual tab. A formula consists of an equal sign (=), followed by a function name (such as SUM), followed by parentheses containing the location of the cells on which you want to perform the calculation. For example, the formula =SUM(Left) totals the cells to the left of the cell containing the formula.

To use a function other than SUM in the Formula dialog box, you click the function you want in the Paste Function list. You can use built-in functions to perform a number of calculations, including averaging (AVERAGE) a set of values, counting (COUNT) the number of values in a column or row, or finding the maximum (MAX) or minimum (MIN) value in a series of cells.

Creating Table Styles

If none of the predefined table styles meets your needs, you can create your own styles for tables in much the same way you create styles for regular text.

To create a table style:

1. On the **Design** tab, in the **Table Styles** group, click the **More** button, and then click **New Table Style**.

   The Create New Style From Formatting dialog box opens.

2. In the **Name** box, type a name for the new style.

3. Click the **Apply formatting to** arrow, and in the list, select the table element for which you are creating the new style.

4. Select the formatting options you want, until the table shown in the Preview area looks the way you want it.

5. If you want the style to be available to tables in other documents based on this template, select that option, and then click **OK**.

To apply a custom table style:

1. Select the table element to which you want to apply the new style.

2. On the **Design** tab, in the **Table Styles** group, click the **More** button, and under **Custom**, click the thumbnail for your custom style.

Although formulas commonly refer to the cells above or to the left of the active cell, you can also use the contents of specified cells or constant values in formulas. To use the contents of a cell, you type the *cell address* in the parentheses following the function name. The cell address is a combination of the column letter and the row number—for example, A1 is the cell at the intersection of the first column and the first row. A series of cells in a row can be addressed as a range consisting of the first cell and the last cell separated by a colon, such as A1:D1. For example, the formula =SUM(A1:D1) totals the values in row 1 of columns A through D. A series of cells in a column can be addressed in the same way. For example, the formula =SUM(A1:A4) totals the values in column A of rows 1 through 4.

When the built-in functions don't meet your needs, you can insert a Microsoft Office Excel worksheet in a Word document. Part of the Microsoft Office system, Excel includes sophisticated functions for performing mathematical, accounting, and statistical calculations. For example, you can use an Excel worksheet to calculate loan payments at various interest rates. You can insert Excel worksheet data into a Word document in the following ways:

- **By copying and pasting.** You can open Excel, enter the data and formulas, and then copy and paste the data as a table in a Word document. The data is pasted as regular text, with the formulas converted to their results.

- **By linking.** While pasting Excel worksheet data into a Word document, you can link the version in the document to the original source worksheet. You can then double-click the linked object in the document to open the source worksheet in Excel for editing. After you edit and save the worksheet, you can return to the document, right-click the linked object, and then click Update Link to display the edited version of the data.

- **By embedding.** You can create an Excel worksheet directly in a Word document by clicking the Table button in the Tables group on the Insert tab, and then clicking Excel Spreadsheet. The worksheet is created as an object with Excel row and column headers, and the Excel tabs and groups replace those of Word so that you can enter data and manipulate it using Excel.

> **Tip** If you change a value in a Word table, you must recalculate formulas manually. If you change a value in an Excel worksheet, the formulas are automatically recalculated.

In this exercise, you will perform a few calculations in a Word table. Then you'll copy and paste worksheet data, link the same data, and enter the same data in an Excel object so that you can see the three different ways of working with Excel data.

> **USE** the *05_Calculations* document and the *05_LoanData* workbook. These practice files are located in the *Chapter05* subfolder under *SBS_Word2007.*
>
> **OPEN** the *05_LoanData* workbook in Excel, and then open the *05_Calculations* document in Word.

1. Save the practice file in the *Chapter05* folder with the name My Calculations.

fx Formula

2. In the table displayed in the document, click the cell below the *Total* column heading, and on the **Layout** contextual tab, in the **Data** group, click the **Formula** button.

   The Formula dialog box opens.

Formula

Formula:

`=SUM(LEFT)`

Number format:

Paste function:

Paste bookmark:

OK   Cancel

3. Select the contents of the **Formula** box, and then type =C2*B2.

4. Click the **Number format** arrow, and in the list, click **$#,##0.00;($#,##0.00)**.

5. In the **Number format** box, delete **.00** from both the positive and negative portions of the format, and then click **OK**.

You have told Word to multiply the first dollar amount under *Unit Price* by the quantity on the same row and to display the result as a whole dollar amount. Word enters the result, $60,000, in the cell containing the formula.

Memorandum

To: Nate Sun
From: Shelley Dyck
Date: October 19, 2007
Subject: Proposal for Delivery Truck Purchase

Thanks for meeting with me to discuss the possibility of purchasing delivery trucks, rather than continuing with our current lease agreement. I've gathered some information for you to review. The table below is a cost estimate for the delivery trucks I propose that we purchase. It should give you an idea of the overall cost.

Furniture	Quantity	Unit Price	Total
12 ft. truck	2	$30,000	$60,000
24 ft. truck	1	$45,000	
Van	2	$25,000	
		Total	

The best interest rate I can find for fleet sales is 5%. The payment schedule for a $155,000 loan for three years is shown on the attached Excel worksheet.

The current cost of leasing our delivery vehicles is $60,000 a year. Purchasing the

6. Repeat Steps 2 through 5 for the next two cells under *Total*, adjusting the cell addresses appropriately.

7. In cell **B4**, change **2** to **3**, right-click the formula in cell **D4**, and then click **Update Field**.

Word recalculates the formula and enters the new result, $75,000, in the cell.

8. Change the **Unit Price** of the **24 ft. truck** to $42,500, and then update the corresponding total.

9. Click cell **D5**, and in the **Data** group, click the **Formula** button.

10. With **=SUM(ABOVE)** in the **Formula** box, set the **Number format** to whole dollar amounts (following the method in Steps 3 and 4), and then click **OK**.

You have told Word to add the amounts in the *Total* column. Word enters the result, $177,500, in the cell containing the formula.

Memorandum

To: Nate Sun
From: Shelley Dyck
Date: October 19, 2007
Subject: Proposal for Delivery Truck Purchase

Thanks for meeting with me to discuss the possibility of purchasing delivery trucks, rather than continuing with our current lease agreement. I've gathered some information for you to review. The table below is a cost estimate for the delivery trucks I propose that we purchase. It should give you an idea of the overall cost.

Furniture	Quantity	Unit Price	Total
12 ft. truck	2	$30,000	$60,000
24 ft. truck	1	$42,500	$42,500
Van	3	$25,000	$75,000
		Total	$177,500

---

11. Press Ctrl + End to move to the end of the document, and then on the Windows taskbar, click the **Microsoft Excel** button.

> **Troubleshooting** If you have hidden your Windows taskbar, as we have, point to the bottom of the screen to make the taskbar appear so that you can click the Microsoft Excel button.

Copy

12. On **Sheet1** in the *05_LoanData* workbook, select cells **A1:B8** by dragging through them. Then on the **Home** tab, in the **Clipboard** group, click the **Copy** button.

The worksheet data is copied to the Clipboard. From there it can be pasted into any Microsoft Office program.

Paste

13. Redisplay the *My Calculations* document. Then on the **Home** tab, in the **Clipboard** group, click the **Paste** button.

Word pastes a copy of the worksheet data in the document as a table.

Furniture	Quantity	Unit Price	Total
12 ft. truck	2	$30,000	$60,000
24 ft. truck	1	$42,500	$42,500
Van	3	$25,000	$75,000
		Total	$177,500

The best interest rate I can find for fleet sales is 5%. The payment schedule for a $155,000 loan for three years is shown on the attached Excel worksheet.

The current cost of leasing our delivery vehicles is $60,000 a year. Purchasing the vehicles at this time will save the company over $12,000 over the next three years.

Payment Schedule	
Interest rate	5.0%
Years	3
Loan Amount	$155,000.00
Monthly Payment	$4,645.49
Cost of Loan	$167,237.61
3-Year Lease Cost	$180,000.00
Savings	$12,762.39

14. Press [Enter], and then in the **Clipboard** group, click the **Paste** arrow, and click **Paste Special**.

The Paste Special dialog box opens.

> **Paste Special**
>
> Source: Microsoft Office Excel Worksheet
> Sheet1!R1C1:R8C2
>
> As:
>
> ○ Paste:
> ○ Paste link:
>
> Microsoft Office Excel Worksheet Object
> Formatted Text (RTF)
> Unformatted Text
> Picture (Windows Metafile)
> Bitmap
> Picture (Enhanced Metafile)
> HTML Format
> Unformatted Unicode Text
>
> ☐ Display as icon
>
> Result
> Inserts the contents of the Clipboard as HTML Format.
>
> OK   Cancel

15. In the **As** list, click **Microsoft Office Excel Worksheet Object**, select the **Paste link** option, and then click **OK**.

Word pastes a second copy of the worksheet data as a linked table on a new page.

16. Double-click the new table.

The linked worksheet opens in Excel.

17. Click cell **B2**, type 6, and then press [Enter].

Troubleshooting If someone has already worked through this exercise using the practice files on your computer, 6.0% might already appear in cell B2. In that case, change the value to 5.0%.

Excel recalculates the formulas in the worksheet to reflect the new interest rate.

18. Save and close the workbook, and quit Excel.

19. In Word, right-click the linked table, and then click **Update Link**.

Word updates the table to reflect the change you made to the worksheet data.

20. Press [Ctrl]+[End] to move to the end of the document, press [Enter] twice to add some space, and then save the document.

21. On the **Insert** tab, in the **Tables** group, click the **Table** button, and then click **Excel Spreadsheet**.

Word inserts an Excel object in the document.

Payment Schedule	
Interest rate	6.0%
Years	3
Loan Amount	$155,000.00
Monthly Payment	$4,645.49
Cost of Loan	$167,237.61
3-Year Lease Cost	$180,000.00
Savings	$12,762.39

22. In row **1**, type Rate, press [Tab], and then type 5%.

23. Type the following in rows **2**, **3**, and **4**:

    2   Years [Tab] 3

    3   Amount [Tab] $155,000

    4   Payment [Tab]

24. With cell **B4** active, on the **Formulas** tab, in the **Function Library** group, click the **Financial** button, scroll the list, and then click **PMT**.

Excel enters =PMT() in cell B4 and then opens the Function Arguments dialog box so that you can enter the information needed to calculate the monthly payment on a loan of $155,000 at 5% interest for three years.

25. In the **Rate** box, type **B1/12** (the annual rate per month), in the **Nper** box, type **B2*12** (the number of years expressed as months), and in the **Pv** box, type **B3**. Then click **OK**.

Excel calculates the formula and enters the result, $4,645.49, expressed as a negative because it is money you are paying out.

> **Tip** To express the payment as a positive, you can insert a minus sign between the equal sign and PMT in the formula.

26. Drag the black handle in the lower-right corner of the Excel object up and to the left, until the frame of the object is just big enough to enclose the cells with data in them. Then click a blank area of the page to deactivate the object.

The object appears on the page as a table with barely visible borders around its cells.

Payment Schedule	
Interest rate	6.0%
Years	3
Loan Amount	$155,000.00
Monthly Payment	$4,645.49
Cost of Loan	$167,237.61
3-Year Lease Cost	$180,000.00
Savings	$12,762.39

Rate	5%
Years	3
Amount	$155,000
Payment	($4,645.49)

27. Double-click the object to activate it in Excel again, change the entry in cell **B1** to 7%, press ⌷Enter⌷, and then click a blank area of the page.

The object's formulas have updated the monthly payment to reflect the change.

CLOSE the *My Calculations* document without saving your changes.

Using a Table to Control Page Layout

Most people are accustomed to thinking of a table as a means of displaying data in a quick, easy-to-grasp format. But tables can also serve to organize your pages in creative ways. For example, suppose you want to display two tables next to each other. The simplest way to do this is to first create a table with one tall row and two wide columns and no gridlines. You can then insert one table in the first cell and the other table in the second cell. These *nested tables* then appear to be arranged side by side.

Memorandum

To: Nate Sun
From: Shelley Dyck
Date: October 19, 2007
Subject: Loan comparisons

Below is a comparison of two loans for delivery vehicles.

Payment Schedule	
Interest rate	3.6%
Years	3
Loan Amount	$155,000.00
Monthly Payment	$4,548.69
Cost of Loan	$163,752.79
3-Year Lease Cost	$180,000.00
Savings	$16,247.21

Payment Schedule	
Interest rate	5.0%
Years	3
Loan Amount	$155,000.00
Monthly Payment	$4,645.49
Cost of Loan	$167,237.61
3-Year Lease Cost	$180,000.00
Savings	$12,762.39

Deciding How to Insert Excel Data

To decide how to insert Excel data in a Word document, you need to understand how Microsoft Office system programs integrate data from outside sources. Understanding this will enable you to decide how to use information created in any other Office program, not just Excel.

If you don't need to maintain a connection with the source Excel worksheet and the data is simple enough to be edited in Word, you can copy and paste the data.

If you do need to maintain a connection with the source Excel worksheet, or if you need to be able to manipulate the data in Excel after it is incorporated into the Word document, you can use the Microsoft linking and embedding technology to insert an *object* (a file or part of a file) created in Excel into a document created in Word. The object is sometimes called the *source file*, and the document into which you are inserting the information is called the *destination file*. The difference between linking and embedding is the type of connection that is maintained between the source and destination files, as follows:

- A *linked object* is displayed in the destination file, but its data is stored in the source file. If you want to change the data, you do it in the source file. Then when you open the destination file, the linked object is updated to reflect the change.

- An *embedded object* is displayed in the destination file and its data is stored there. If you want to update the data, you do it in the destination file using the source program.

Whether an object should be linked or embedded depends on whether you need the information in the destination file to always be the same as the information in the source file. If you do, it is best to link the object so that you don't have to manually update the data in two places.

As with regular tables, you can create a nested table from scratch, by formatting existing information, or by inserting Excel data. And just like other tables, you can format a nested table either manually or using one of Word's ready-made table styles.

> **Tip** Tables can be used to organize a mixture of elements such as text, tables, charts, and diagrams. For more information, you might want to consult *Advanced Documents Inside Out* (Microsoft Press, 2007).

When creating a table to contain other elements, you might want to take advantage of the Word table-drawing feature. If you click Draw Table below the grid displayed when you click the Table button, the pointer changes to a pencil with which you can draw cells on the page. You can set up the container table visually, without having to fuss with dialog boxes and precise dimensions while you are designing the layout. Then after everything is set up the way you want it, you can use the Table Properties dialog box to fine-tune the table specifications.

In this exercise, you will draw a table to contain two other tables. You will then insert and format the nested tables.

USE the *06_Loan* workbook and the *06_Memo* and *06_TableAsLayout* documents. These practice files are located in the *Chapter05* subfolder under *SBS_Word2007*.

BE SURE TO display non-printing characters before starting this exercise.

OPEN the *06_Loan* workbook in Excel, and then open the *06_Memo* document and the *06_TableAsLayout* document in Word.

1. Before you begin, save a copy of the *06_TableAsLayout* document in the *Chapter05* subfolder as My Nested Tables.

    > **Troubleshooting** The operations you perform in this exercise use a lot of your computer's resources. You will have better results if you save the *My Nested Tables* document regularly.

2. In the *My Nested Tables* document, on the **Insert** tab, in the **Tables** group, click the **Table** button, and then click **Draw Table**.

    The pointer becomes a pencil.

3. Point below the last paragraph mark in the document, and drag across and down to create a cell about 3 inches wide and 1.5 inches tall.

    > **Tip** The location of the pencil is marked with guides on the horizontal and vertical rulers. You can use these guides to help you draw cells of specific dimensions.

4. Point to the upper-right corner of the cell (you don't have to be precise), and drag to create another cell about the same size as the first.

    When you release the mouse button, Word joins the two cells to create the structure of a table.

Switch
Windows

5. On the **View** tab, in the **Window** group, click the **Switch Windows** button, and then click *06_Memo*.

6. Scroll to the bottom of the page, click anywhere in the *Payment Schedule* table, and on the **Layout** tab, in the **Table** group, click **Select**, and then click **Select Table**.

Copy

7. On the **Home** tab, in the **Clipboard** group, click the **Copy** button.

8. Switch to the *My Nested Tables* document, right-click the first cell in the table, and then click **Paste as Nested Table**.

   Word inserts the table you copied into the cell and adjusts the size of the container table to fit the size of the nested table.

9. On the Windows taskbar, click the **Microsoft Excel** button to activate Sheet1 of the *06_Loan* workbook, select cells **A1:B8**, and then on the **Home** tab, in the **Clipboard** group, click the **Copy** button.

Paste

10. Switch back to the *My Nested Tables* document, click the second cell in the table, and then on the **Home** tab, in the **Clipboard** group, click the **Paste** button.

    Word inserts the worksheet data as a nested table in the cell.

> **Troubleshooting** If the pasted table doesn't appear in the container table, minimize the document window and then maximize it.

Memorandum

To: Nate Sun
From: Shelley Dyck
Date: October 19, 2007
Subject: Loan comparisons

Below is a comparison of two loans for delivery vehicles.

Payment Schedule	
Interest rate	3.6%
Years	3
Loan Amount	$155,000.00
Monthly Payment	$4,548.69
Cost of Loan	$163,752.79
3-Year Lease Cost	$180,000.00
Savings	$16,247.21

Payment Schedule	
Interest rate	5.0%
Years	3
Loan Amount	$155,000.00
Monthly Payment	$4,645.49
Cost of Loan	$167,237.61
3-Year Lease Cost	$180,000.00
Savings	$12,762.39

11. Move the pointer to the selection area adjacent to the container table, and then click to select its two cells.

Borders

12. On the **Home** tab, in the **Paragraph** group, click the **Borders** arrow, and then in the list, click **No Border**.

   Word removes the borders from the container cells.

13. Click anywhere in the left table, and on the **Design** contextual tab, in the **Table Style Options** group, select the **Header Row** and **Total Row** check boxes, and clear all the other check boxes.

14. In the **Table Styles** group, display the **Table Styles** gallery, and click the thumbnail of a table style that you want to apply to the nested table.

   We used Light List – Accent 4.

15. Repeat Steps 13 and 14 to format the right table, perhaps using a similar table style with a different color.

   We used Light List – Accent 6.

16. Turn off non-printing characters to see the results.

   The nested tables now look as shown at the beginning of this topic.

CLOSE the *My Nested Tables* document, saving your changes. Then close the *06_Memo* document, and if you are not proceeding directly to the next chapter, quit Word. Finally, close the *06_Loan* workbook without saving changes, and quit Excel.

Key Points

- To vary the layout of a document, you can divide text into columns.

- If your data is simple, you can create the look of a table by using tabs to set up the data as a tabular list.

- Word comes with quick tables that you can use as a starting point for creating professional, easy-to-read table formats.

- If you have already created a table, you can format it quickly by applying a table style. You can enhance the style by applying text attributes, borders, and shading.

- Formulas that perform simple calculations are easy to build in Word. For more complex calculations, you can create an Excel worksheet and then insert the worksheet data as a table in the Word document.

- Tables are great tools for organizing different types of information on the page. By using tables in creative ways, you can place information in non-linear arrangements for easy comparison or analysis.

Chapter at a Glance

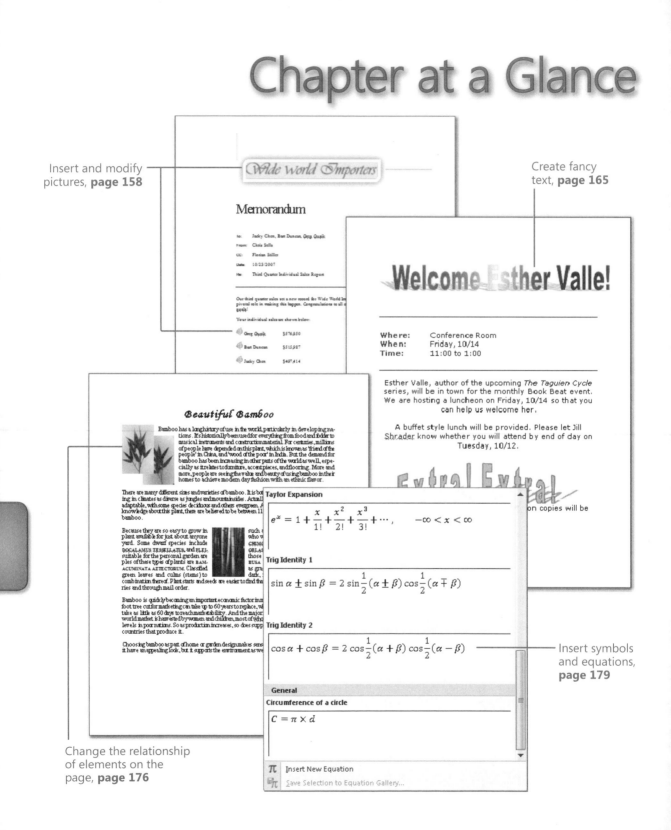

Insert and modify pictures, **page 158**

Create fancy text, **page 165**

Change the relationship of elements on the page, **page 176**

Insert symbols and equations, **page 179**

6 Working with Graphics, Symbols, and Equations

In this chapter, you will learn to:

- ✔ Insert and modify pictures.
- ✔ Create fancy text.
- ✔ Draw and modify shapes.
- ✔ Change the relationship of elements on the page.
- ✔ Insert symbols and equations.

Some documents are straightforward communications of information that require nothing more than words. Others might benefit from the addition of graphics, either to reinforce their concepts or to make them more attention grabbing or visually appealing.

Graphics can include a wide variety of images, including pictures and drawing objects. *Pictures* are graphics that have been created outside of Word—a scanned photograph, clip art, or a file created on a computer with a graphics program. *Drawing objects* are graphics that are created within Word—a shape, a diagram, a line, or WordArt text. You can use the buttons on the Insert tab to insert pictures and draw different kinds of objects. No matter what the origin of the graphic, you can change its position and how it relates to other elements on the page.

Like other graphics, symbols can add visual information or eye-appeal to a document. However, they are different from other graphics in that they are characters associated with a particular font. Equations are not graphics—they are accurately rendered mathematical formulas; however, they are similar to graphics in that they can be displayed inline with the surrounding text or in their own space with text above and below them.

In this chapter, you will insert and modify pictures, create WordArt objects, and draw shapes to create a simple picture. You will modify the text-wrapping, position, and stacking order of pictures in a document. Finally, you will also insert a symbol and build a simple equation.

See Also Do you need only a quick refresher on the topics in this chapter? See the Quick Reference entries on pages xxxix–lxiii.

> **Important** Before you can use the practice files in this chapter, you need to install them from the book's companion CD to their default location. See "Using the Book's CD" on page xxv for more information.

> **Troubleshooting** Graphics and operating system–related instructions in this book reflect the Windows Vista user interface. If your computer is running Microsoft Windows XP and you experience trouble following the instructions as written, please refer to the "Information for Readers Running Windows XP" section at the beginning of this book.

Inserting and Modifying Pictures

You can insert scanned photographs or pictures created in almost any program into a Word document. Two buttons in the Illustrations group on the Insert tab can be used to specify the source of the picture, as follows:

- **Picture.** Click this button to insert a picture from a file. If a digital camera is connected to your computer, you can also insert a picture directly from the camera.

- **Clip Art.** Click this button to insert one of the hundreds of clip art images that come with Word, such as photos and drawings of people, places, and things.

  See Also For information about organizing clip art, see the sidebar titled "Organizing Clips" later in this chapter.

After you insert a picture in a document, you can modify the image by using buttons on the Format contextual tab, which is displayed only when a picture or drawing object is selected. For example, you can use buttons in the Adjust group to change the picture's brightness and contrast, recolor it, and compress it to reduce the size of the document containing it. The Picture Styles group offers a wide range of picture styles that you can apply to a picture to change its shape and orientation, as well as add borders and picture effects. The Arrange group has buttons for moving and grouping pictures on the page. And finally, you can use the buttons in the Size group for cropping and resizing pictures.

In this exercise, you will insert and modify a picture. You will then insert, size, move, and copy a clip art image.

> **USE** the *01_Picture* document and the *01_Logo* graphic. These practice files are located in the *Chapter06* subfolder under *SBS_Word2007*.
>
> **BE SURE TO** start Word and display the rulers and non-printing characters before starting this exercise.
>
> **OPEN** the *01_Picture* document.

Picture

1. With the insertion point at the top of the page, on the **Insert** tab, in the **Illustrations** group, click the **Picture** button.

   The Insert Picture dialog box opens, displaying the contents of your *Pictures* folder.

2. In the **Favorite Links** pane, click **Documents**. Then double-click **MSP**, double-click **SBS_Word2007**, double-click **Chapter06**, and double-click *01_Logo*.

   Word inserts the picture at the insertion point and displays the Format contextual tab on the Ribbon.

3. On the lower-right corner of the graphic, point to the handle (the circle), and when it changes to a double arrow, click and drag up and to the left until the graphic's shadow frame is about at the 4.5-inch mark on the horizontal ruler.

Wide world Importers

Memorandum

To:	Jacky Chen, Bart Duncan, Greg Guzik
From:	Chris Sells
CC:	Florian Stiller
Date:	10/23/2007
Re:	Third Quarter Individual Sales Report

4. On the **Format** contextual tab, in the **Adjust** group, click the **Recolor** button.

5. In the **Recolor** gallery, under **Light Variations**, click the second thumbnail (**Accent color 1 Light**).

The picture's colors change.

6. In the **Adjust** group, click the **Brightness** button.

7. In the **Brightness** gallery, point to each option to preview its effect, and then click **+10%**.

8. In the **Adjust** group, click the **Contrast** button, and then in the **Contrast** gallery, click **-30%**.

> **Tip** You can fine-tune the brightness and contrast of a picture by clicking Picture Corrections Options at the bottom of either the Brightness or Contrast gallery. The Format Picture dialog box opens with the Picture page active. Drag the slider or change the percentage by clicking the up or down arrow. If you want to restore the original picture but don't remember what changes you made to it, click Reset Picture to discard any changes you made.

9. On the **Format** tab, in the **Picture Styles** group, click the **More** button.

The Picture Styles gallery opens.

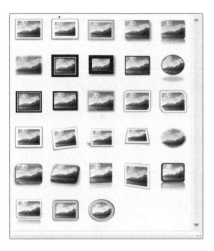

10. In the gallery, point to each thumbnail in turn to see its effects. Then click the fourth thumbnail in the third row (**Rounded Diagonal Corner, White**), and click away from the graphic.

    The logo now has a three-dimensional perspective.

Memorandum

To: Jacky Chen, Bart Duncan, Greg Guzik
From: Chris Sells
CC: Florian Stiller

11. Scroll down the document until you see the tabular list, and click at the end of the *Greg Guzik* paragraph.

12. On the **Insert** tab, in the **Illustrations** group, click the **Clip Art** button.

13. In the **Clip Art** task pane, select the current entry in the **Search for** box (or click in the box if there is no entry), type symbols, and then click **Go**.

> **Troubleshooting** If you see a message asking whether you want to search the clip art available from Microsoft Office Online, click No.

The task pane displays graphics representing common symbols.

Close

14. In the task pane, click the stylized dollar sign (**$**) to insert it in the document, and then click the task pane's **Close** button.

The inserted image is selected in the document, as indicated by the circular handles surrounding its frame.

15. Point to the lower-right handle of the image, and when the pointer changes to a double arrow, drag up and to the left until the image is about 0.25 inch square.

> **Tip** You can also change the size of a picture or clip art image by adjusting the Shape Height and Shape Width settings in the Size group on the Format tab.

16. Point to the dollar sign image, and when the pointer changes to a four-headed arrow, drag the image to the beginning of the *Greg Guzik* paragraph.

17. If the image is no longer selected, click it to select it.

> **Troubleshooting** If you have trouble selecting the image, press the Esc key, and then try again.

18. Point to the image, hold down the mouse button, hold down the ⌈Ctrl⌉ key, and drag a copy of the image to the left of *Bart Duncan*, releasing first the mouse button and then the ⌈Ctrl⌉ key.

A copy of the graphic is inserted in front of *Bart Duncan*.

> **Tip** If you release the Ctrl key first, Word will move the image from the second paragraph to the third instead of being copied.

19. Repeat Step 18 to drag a copy to the left of *Jacky Chen*.

The images preceding each paragraph resemble bullets.

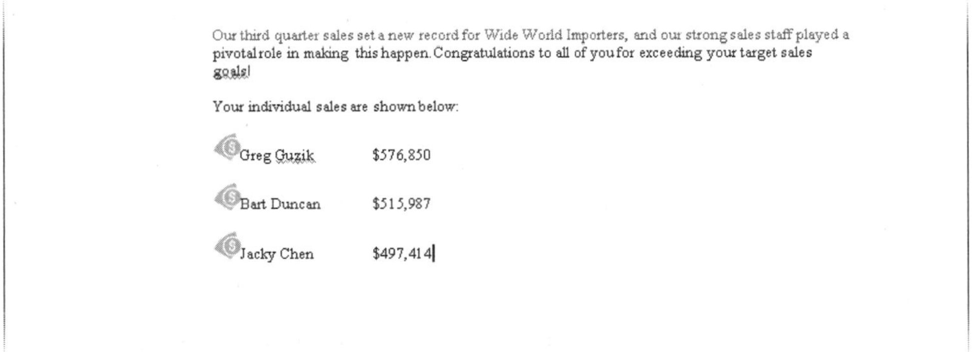

Our third quarter sales set a new record for Wide World Importers, and our strong sales staff played a pivotal role in making this happen. Congratulations to all of you for exceeding your target sales goals!

Your individual sales are shown below:

Greg Guzik $576,850

Bart Duncan $515,987

Jacky Chen $497,414

CLOSE the *01_Picture* document without saving your changes.

Organizing Clips

To make clip art images, pictures, sounds, and movie clips conveniently available regardless of where they are actually stored, you can use the *Microsoft Clip Organizer* to arrange them in collections. You can arrange clips from Microsoft Office, from the Web, or from other sources into existing collections or new ones.

To experiment with the Clip Organizer, follow these steps:

1. Display the **Clip Art** task pane, and at the bottom of the pane, click **Organize clips**.

   The Favorites - Microsoft Clip Organizer window opens.

2. In the **Collection List**, under **My Collections**, click **Favorites**.

3. On the window's **File** menu, point to **Add Clips to Organizer,** and then click **On My Own**.

   The Favorites - Add Clips To Organizer dialog box opens.

4. Navigate to the folder where the file you want to add to the Favorites collection is stored, click the file name, and then click **Add**.

   To place images in a different collection, click Add To in the Add To Clips Organizer dialog box. Then in the Import To Collection dialog box, select the collection, and click OK. (You can click New in the Import To Collection dialog box to create a new collection.)

5. Point to the thumbnail of the file you just added, click the arrow that appears, and then click **Edit Keywords**.

   The Keywords dialog box opens.

6. In the **Keyword** box, type the word or words that you want to associate with this file, and then click **Add**.

   The keyword is added to the Keywords For Current Clip list.

7. Click **OK** to close the **Edit Keywords** dialog box, and then close the **Microsoft Clip Organizer** window.

   You can now search for the file by that keyword in the Clip Art task pane.

To delete a clip from the Clip Organizer, in the Microsoft Clip Organizer window, click the clip's arrow, click Delete From Clip Organizer, and then click OK to confirm the deletion.

Creating Fancy Text

When you want a text banner that is fancier than one you can create by applying font attributes, you can use *WordArt*. WordArt text can swirl, grow bigger from one end to the other or in the middle, take on a three-dimensional shape, and change color from one letter to another.

To insert WordArt text, you click the WordArt button in the Text group on the Insert tab, and click a style in the WordArt gallery. Then in the Edit WordArt Text dialog box, you can enter the text. You can also adjust the font, font size, and font style. Clicking OK inserts the WordArt object in the document at the insertion point.

> **Tip** You can also select existing text before clicking the WordArt button to convert that text into a WordArt object.

Selecting a WordArt object displays the Format contextual tab, which you can use to edit and format a WordArt object to meet your needs. From the Format tab, you can add special effects such as shadows and 3-D effects; position the WordArt object on the page; change the fill color; and change the text spacing, alignment, and orientation.

In this exercise, you will insert a new WordArt object. Then you'll turn existing text into a WordArt object and modify the object to look the way you want it.

> **USE** the *02_WordArt* document. This practice file is located in the *Chapter06* subfolder under *SBS_Word2007*.
> **BE SURE TO** display non-printing characters before starting this exercise.
> **OPEN** the *02_WordArt* document.

1. Press the ⬇ key twice to move the insertion point to the third blank paragraph of the document.

2. On the **Insert** tab, in the **Text** group, click the **WordArt** button.

   The WordArt gallery opens, displaying a list of styles.

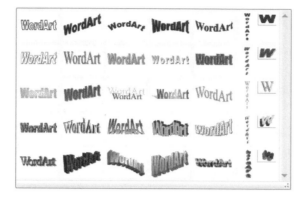

3. Click the fourth thumbnail in the third row (**WordArt style 16**).

The Edit WordArt Text dialog box opens, displaying the words *Your Text Here* as a placeholder.

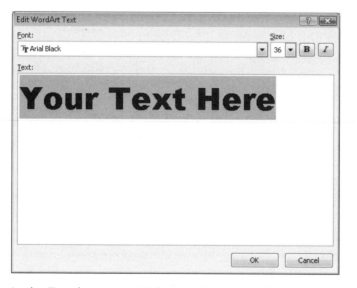

4. In the **Text** box, type Welcome Esther Valle!.

5. Click the **Size** arrow, and in the list, click **44**. Then click **OK**.

The text is inserted as an object at the insertion point, and the Format contextual tab appears on the Ribbon.

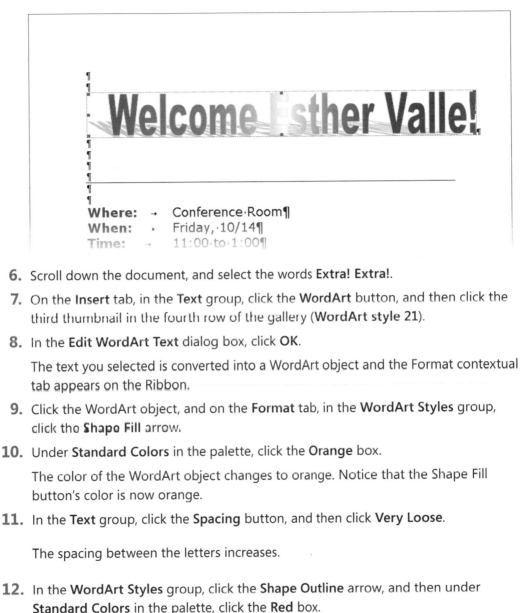

6. Scroll down the document, and select the words **Extra! Extra!**.

7. On the **Insert** tab, in the **Text** group, click the **WordArt** button, and then click the third thumbnail in the fourth row of the gallery (**WordArt style 21**).

8. In the **Edit WordArt Text** dialog box, click **OK**.

   The text you selected is converted into a WordArt object and the Format contextual tab appears on the Ribbon.

9. Click the WordArt object, and on the **Format** tab, in the **WordArt Styles** group, click the **Shape Fill** arrow.

10. Under **Standard Colors** in the palette, click the **Orange** box.

    The color of the WordArt object changes to orange. Notice that the Shape Fill button's color is now orange.

11. In the **Text** group, click the **Spacing** button, and then click **Very Loose**.

    The spacing between the letters increases.

12. In the **WordArt Styles** group, click the **Shape Outline** arrow, and then under **Standard Colors** in the palette, click the **Red** box.

    The letters are now outlined in red.

13. Point to the WordArt object's middle-right handle, and when the pointer changes to a double arrow, drag to the right for an inch or two to stretch the object's frame.

When you release the mouse button, the stretched object snaps to the horizontal center of the page.

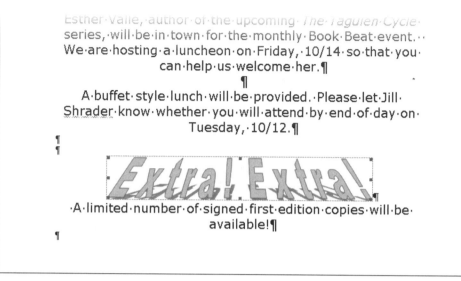

Esther Valle, author of the upcoming *The Taguien Cycle* series, will be in town for the monthly Book Beat event. We are hosting a luncheon on Friday, 10/14 so that you can help us welcome her.¶
¶
A buffet style lunch will be provided. Please let Jill Shrader know whether you will attend by end of day on Tuesday, 10/12.¶
¶
¶
Extra! Extra!¶
·A limited number of signed first edition copies will be available!¶
¶

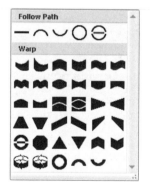
Change Shape

14. In the **WordArt Styles** group, click the **Change WordArt Shape** button.

    The Change Shape gallery opens.

15. In the gallery, click the first thumbnail in the third row (**Inflate Top**).

    The WordArt shape changes to an arch.

16. Drag the upper-middle handle upward to exaggerate the curve.

17. In the **Shadow Effects** group, click the **Shadow Effects** button, and in the **Shadow Effects** gallery, under **Perspective Shadow**, click the second thumbnail in the first row (**Shadow Style 7**).

The new shadow effect is applied to the letters.

18. On the **Format** tab, in the **3-D Effects** group, click the **3-D Effects** button.

> **Troubleshooting** If you see a 3-D Effects button but not a group, click the button to display the group, and then click the 3-D Effects button in the group to open the gallery.

19. In the **3-D Effects** gallery, point to each thumbnail in turn to observe its effects.

20. Press the [Esc] key to close the gallery without making a selection, and then if necessary, click [Esc] again to close the 3-D Effects group.

21. Turn off non-printing characters, and then click away from the WordArt object to see the results.

Esther Valle, author of the upcoming *The Tagmen Cycle* series, will be in town for the monthly Book Beat event. We are hosting a luncheon on Friday, 10/14 so that you can help us welcome her.

A buffet style lunch will be provided. Please let Jill Shrader know whether you will attend by end of day on Tuesday, 10/12.

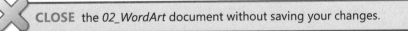

A limited number of signed first edition copies will be available!

CLOSE the *02_WordArt* document without saving your changes.

Formatting the First Letter of a Paragraph

Many books, magazines, and reports begin the first paragraph of a section or chapter by using an enlarged, decorative capital letter. Called a *dropped capital*, or simply a *drop cap*, this effect can be an easy way to give a document a finished, professional look.

To apply a drop cap, follow these steps:

1. Click anywhere in a paragraph of text, and then on the **Insert** tab, in the **Text** group, click the **Drop Cap** button.

   The Drop Cap gallery opens, providing two basic drop-cap styles: Dropped, which displaces some of the paragraph text, and In Margin, which hangs in the margin adjacent to the paragraph text. In either case, the drop cap is as tall as three lines of text and uses the same font as the rest of the paragraph.

2. Point to each thumbnail to display its live preview, and then click the one you want.

   Word converts the first letter of the paragraph into a graphic. If you selected Dropped, it wraps the text to the right of the graphic.

For more options, click Drop Cap Options at the bottom of the Drop Cap gallery to open the Drop Cap dialog box. There, you can choose a font for the drop cap that is different from the rest of the paragraph and make adjustments to the drop cap's height and distance from the text.

Drawing and Modifying Shapes

If you want to add visual interest and impact to a document but you don't need anything as fancy as a picture or a clip art image, you can draw a shape, also called a *drawing object*. Shapes can be simple, such as lines, circles, or squares, or more complex, such as stars, hearts, and arrows.

To draw a shape directly on the page (Word's default setting), you click the Shapes button in the Illustrations group on the Insert tab, click the shape you want in the Shapes gallery, and then do one of the following:

- Click the document where you want a drawing object of the default size and shape to be placed.

- Drag the pointer across the page to create a drawing object the size and shape you want.

If you want to assemble a group of shapes to create a drawing, you might want to draw the shapes on a drawing canvas instead of directly on the page. The drawing canvas keeps the parts of the drawing together, helps you position the drawing, and provides a frame-like boundary between your drawing and the text on the page. To open a drawing canvas, you click New Drawing Canvas at the bottom of the Shapes gallery. You can then draw shapes on the canvas in the usual ways. At any time, you can size and move the drawing canvas and the objects it contains as one unit.

> **Tip** If you prefer to always use the drawing canvas when creating drawing objects, click the Microsoft Office Button, click Word Options, and click Advanced. Then under Editing Options, select the Automatically Create Drawing Canvas When Inserting AutoShapes check box, and click OK.

> **Tip** To make a drawing canvas stand out on the page, but you can put a border around it and shade it. You can use the tools on the Format contextual tab to size and position it precisely and to specify how text should wrap around it.

When you finish drawing a shape, it is automatically selected. Later you can select the shape by clicking it. While the shape is selected, you can move and size it, and you can modify it by using the buttons on the Format contextual tab. The attributes you can change include the following:

- The fill color inside the object
- The color, thickness, and style of the border around the object
- The shadow effect behind the object
- The three-dimensional aspect, or perspective, from which you are observing the object
- The angle of rotation, or orientation, of the object
- The alignment of the object in relation to the page
- The way text wraps around the object
- The order of the object in a stack of objects
- The size of the object

You can also change the size and shape of an object by dragging its handles. You can reposition it by dragging it, or by pressing the Arrow keys on your keyboard to move the object in small increments.

> **Tip** If you change the attributes of a shape—for example, its fill color and border weight—and you want all the shapes you draw from now on in this document to have those attributes, right-click the shape, and then click Set AutoShape Defaults.

If you want to move or size more than one related graphic, you can ensure that they retain their positions in relation to each other by *grouping* them. They then act as one object. To break the bond, you can ungroup the objects.

In this exercise, you will draw and manipulate a few shapes on a drawing canvas, and you will then size and position the canvas.

USE the *03_Shapes* document. This practice file is located in the *Chapter06* subfolder under SBS_*Word2007.*

BE SURE TO display the rulers before starting this exercise.

OPEN the *03_Shapes* document.

1. Press Ctrl + End to position the insertion point at the end of the document.

2. On the **Insert** tab, in the **Illustrations** group, click the **Shapes** button, and then at the bottom of the **Shapes** gallery, click **New Drawing Canvas**.

   Word adds a page to the document, inserts a drawing canvas, and displays the Format contextual tab on the Ribbon.

3. On the **Format** contextual tab, in the **Insert Shapes** group, click the **Oval** button, and then move position the pointer in the upper-left corner of the drawing canvas.

4. Hold down the Shift key, and then drag down and to the right to draw a circle about 1.5 inches in diameter.

   > **Tip** To draw a shape with equal height and width, such as a square or circle, hold down the Shift key while you draw, and then release the mouse button before releasing the Shift key.

   When you finish drawing, the circle is selected, as indicated by the handles around it.

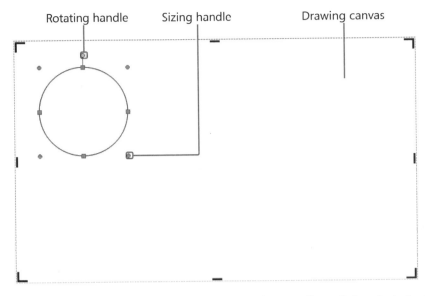

Rotating handle   Sizing handle   Drawing canvas

5. Hold down the ⌃Ctrl key, and drag the shadow outline of the circle to the upper middle of the drawing canvas. Be sure to release the mouse button before releasing the ⌃Ctrl key.

    Word creates a copy of the circle in the location where you release the mouse button.

6. Create a copy of the second circle in the upper-right corner of the drawing canvas.

7. Click the left circle. Then on the **Format** tab, in the **Shape Styles** group, click the **Shape Fill** arrow, and under **Standard Colors** in the palette, click the **Yellow** box.

8. Click the middle circle, and repeat Step 7 to fill it with the **Light Green** color.

9. Click the right circle, and repeat Step 7 to fill it with the **Purple** color.

    All the circles are now filled with color so that they resemble balloons.

10. In the **Insert Shapes** group, click the third button in the third row (**Curve**).

11. Point to the bottom of the left balloon, drag down and to the left about an inch, click the canvas, drag down and to the right about an inch, and then double-click the canvas.

    A curved line resembling a string appears below the left balloon.

12. Hold down ⌃Ctrl, point to the curved line, and drag a copy of it to the bottom of the middle balloon. Then drag another curved line to the bottom of the right balloon.

    All the balloons now have strings, and the one on the right is still selected.

Shape Fill

Curve

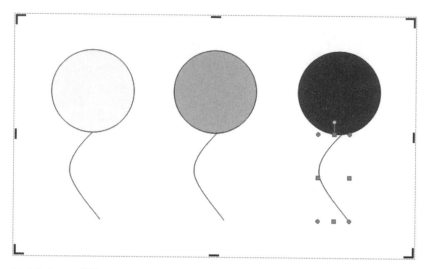

13. Hold down Ctrl, and click the purple balloon.

    Both the balloon and its string are selected.

Group

14. In the **Arrange** group, click the **Group** button, and then click **Group**.

    One set of handles now appears around the balloon and its string, indicating that the two shapes are grouped as one object.

Rotate

15. In the **Arrange** group, click the **Rotate** button, and then click **Flip Horizontal**.

    The balloon and its string are now facing the other way.

16. Press the ↑ key five times.

    The balloon and its string are now positioned slightly higher on the drawing canvas than the other two balloons.

17. Click a blank area of the drawing canvas to release the selection.

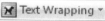

Shape Height

18. In the **Size** group, click the **Shape Height** down arrow until the height of the drawing canvas is **2"**.

    Word moves the drawing canvas to the bottom of the first page of the document, where it now fits. The balloons have shrunk in proportion to the canvas.

19. In the **Arrange** group, click the **Text Wrapping** button, and then click **In Front of Text**.

    You can now move the drawing canvas independently of the text around it.

    See Also For information about text wrapping, see "Changing the Relationships of Elements on the Page" later in this chapter.

Position

20. In the **Arrange** group, click the **Position** button.

    The Position gallery opens.

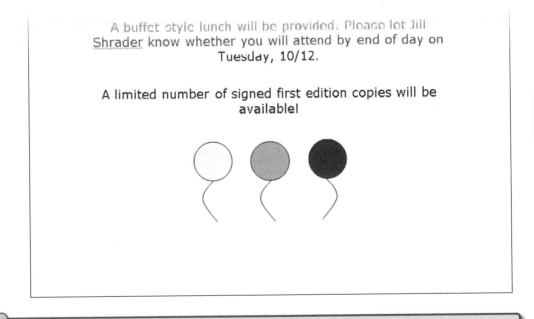

21. In the gallery, click the second thumbnail in the third row (**Position in Bottom Center with Square Text Wrapping**).

    The drawing canvas moves with the objects it contains to the center of the page, below the document's last paragraph.

22. Click outside of the drawing canvas.

    If non-printing characters are turned on, you might want to turn them off to get a better view of the results.

A buffet style lunch will be provided. Please let Jill Shrader know whether you will attend by end of day on Tuesday, 10/12.

A limited number of signed first edition copies will be available!

CLOSE the *03_Shapes* document without saving your changes.

Changing the Relationship of Elements on the Page

When you insert an object such as a picture into a document, it moves any associated text out of the way. You can change the way text wraps around objects and the relationship of overlapping objects by using the buttons in the Arrange group on the Format contextual tab.

When you choose any text wrapping option other than Behind Text or In Line With Text, you can specify that a picture be positioned in one of two ways:

- **Absolutely.** This option positions the picture at a distance you set from a margin, page, paragraph, or line.

- **Relatively.** This type of positioning is determined by the relationship of the picture to a margin or page.

After you position a picture, adding text might upset the arrangement of text and graphics on the page. You can specify whether a picture should remain anchored in its position on the page or should move with its related text. You can also specify whether the picture should be allowed to overlap text.

When graphics overlap each other, they are *stacked*. The stacking order (which graphic appears on top) is initially determined by the order in which you inserted the graphics. You can change the order by selecting a graphic and clicking the Bring To Front or Send To Back button in the Arrange group to move the graphic to the top or bottom of the stack. If you click either button's arrow and then click Bring Forward or Send Backward, the graphic moves forward or backward in the stack one position at a time.

In this exercise, you will modify the text-wrapping, position, and stacking order of pictures that have already been inserted into a document.

> **USE** the *04_Relationships* document. This practice file is located in the *Chapter06* subfolder under *SBS_Word2007*.
> **BE SURE TO** display non-printing characters before starting this exercise.
> **OPEN** the *04_Relationships* document.

1. Scroll to the bottom of the first page, and drag the picture of a bamboo grove up to the beginning of the word *TESSELLATUS* in the middle of the paragraph that begins *Because they are so easy*.

   The picture is positioned wherever you dropped it, and the surrounding text is moved to make room.

2. On the **Format** contextual tab, in the **Arrange** group, click the **Text Wrapping**

button, and then click **More Layout Options**.

The Advanced Layout dialog box opens, with the In Line With Text option selected.

3. Click the **Square** wrapping style, and in the **Wrap text** area, select the **Both sides** option. Then click the **Picture Position** tab.

The options on this tab control the location of the picture on the page and whether it moves when you make changes to the text.

4. Under **Horizontal**, select the **Alignment** option, click the **Alignment** arrow, and then click **Centered**. Then under **Vertical**, change the **Absolute position** setting to 0".

5. Click **OK**.

The picture is repositioned so that it is aligned with the top and center of the paragraph, with the paragraph text wrapped on either side.

6. Click to the left of the word *Because* at the beginning of the paragraph, and press Enter .

The picture moves with the paragraph.

There are many different sizes and varieties of bamboo. It is both tropical and subtropical, growing in climates as diverse as jungles and mountainsides. Actually giant, woody grasses, it is very adaptable, with some species deciduous and others evergreen. Although there isn't yet a complete knowledge about this plant, there are believed to be between 1100 and 1500 different species of bamboo.

Because they are so easy to grow in such a variety of climates, there is a plant available for just about anyone who wishes to grow one in their back-yard. Some dwarf species include CHIMONOBAMBUSA MARMOREA, IN-DOCALAMUS TESSELLATUS, and PLEI-OBLASTUS CHINO VAGINATUS. Also suitable for the personal garden are those categorized as mid size. Exam-ples of these types of plants are BAM-BUSA GLAUCOPHYLLA and OTATEA ACUMINATA AZTECTORUM. Classified as grasses, the color range is from light green leaves and culms (stems) to dark, rich shades of green or some combination thereof. Plant starts and seeds are easier to find than ever, being available at nurse-ries and through mail order.

Bamboo is quickly becoming an important economic factor in many developing nations. A sixty foot tree cut for marketing can take up to 60 years to replace, whereas a sixty foot bamboo can take as little as 60 days to reach marketability. And the majority of bamboo destined for the

7. On the **Quick Access Toolbar**, click the **Undo** button to remove the extra blank paragraph.

Undo

8. Scroll to the next page, and change the text wrapping style of the two pictures on that page from **In line with text** to **Tight**.

The relationship of the pictures with the text is broken, and because they are now essentially floating over the text, they both move to the first page.

9. Scroll to the top of the document, and drag the selected picture down and to the right, releasing the mouse button while the pictures are still overlapped.

10. In the **Arrange** group, click the **Text Wrapping** button, and then click **More Layout Options**.

11. In the **Advanced Layout** dialog box, on the **Text Wrapping** tab, under **Wrap text**, select the **Right only** option, and then click **OK**.

12. On the **Format** tab, in the **Arrange** group, click the **Send to Back** button.

Send to Back The lower picture moves behind the upper picture.

13. Hold down [Shift], and click the upper picture to add it to the selection. Then press the [↓] key to nudge the pictures down until the text is neatly aligned to the right of the pictures.

14. Click a blank area of the page to release the selection.

CLOSE the *04_Relationships* document without saving your changes.

Inserting Symbols and Equations

Some documents require characters not found on a standard keyboard. These characters might include the copyright (©) or registered trademark (®) symbols, currency symbols (such as € or £), Greek letters, or letters with accent marks. Or you might want to add arrows (such as ↗ or ↖) or graphic icons (such as ☎ or ✈). Word gives you easy access to a huge array of symbols that you can easily insert into any document.

> **Tip** You can insert some common symbols by typing a keyboard combination. For example, if you type two consecutive dashes followed by a word and a space, Word changes the two dashes to a professional-looking em-dash—like this one. (This symbol gets its name from the fact that it was originally the width of the character *m*.) To use these features, click the Microsoft Office Button, click Word Options, and in the Proofing panel, click AutoCorrect Options. On the AutoCorrect tab of the AutoCorrect dialog box, make sure the Replace Text As You Type check box is selected, and select any check boxes you like on the AutoFormat As You Type tab.

You can insert mathematical symbols such as π (pi) or ∑ (sigma, or summation) the same way you would insert any other symbol. But you can also create entire mathematical equations in a document. You can drop some equations, including the Quadratic Formula, the Binomial Theorem, and the Pythagorean Theorem, into a document with a few clicks. If you need something other than the standard equations that are pre-defined in Word, you can build your own equations using a library of mathematical symbols.

The buttons for inserting symbols and equations are in the Symbols group on the Insert tab:

- Clicking the Symbol button displays a Symbol gallery of commonly used symbols. From this gallery, you can also open the Symbol dialog box, where you can select from hundreds of symbols and special characters in a variety of fonts.

- Clicking the Equation arrow displays the Equation gallery of commonly used equations that you can click to insert in your document.

- Clicking the Equation button inserts a blank area where you can type an equation and also adds the Design contextual tab to the Ribbon. This tab provides access to mathematical symbols, structures such as fractions and radicals, and the Equation Options dialog box. After building your equation, you can add it to the Equation gallery so that it is readily available the next time you need it.

An equation appears in the document as a field. It resembles a graphic in that you can choose whether to display it inline with the surrounding text or displayed in its own space, with the surrounding text flowing above and below it.

In this exercise, you will insert a graphical icon into a document, and then you will build a simple equation and add it to the Equation gallery.

> **USE** the *05_Symbols* document. This practice file is located in the *Chapter06* subfolder under *SBS_Word2007.*
>
> **OPEN** the *05_Symbols* document.

Ω Symbol ▾

1. With the insertion point to the left of the document's title, on the **Insert** tab, in the **Symbols** group, click the **Symbol** button, and then click **More Symbols**.

   The Symbol dialog box opens.

2. On the **Symbols** tab of the dialog box, click the **Font** arrow, and then in the list, click **Webdings**.

3. In the list of symbols, click the ninth icon in the third row (the house), click **Insert**, and then click **Close**.

   Word inserts the house icon at the insertion point.

4. Press [End], and in the **Symbols** group, click the **Symbol** button.

   The Symbol gallery opens, with the icon you just inserted at the top.

5. Click the house icon.

   The house icon now appears at both ends of the title.

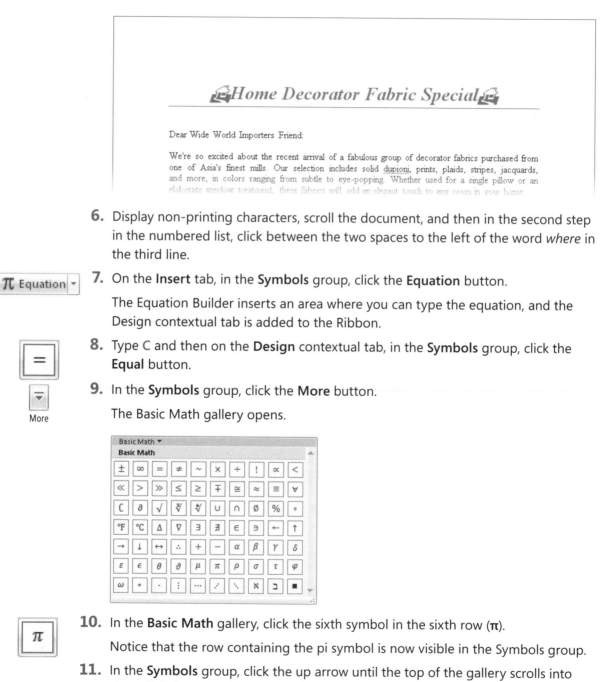

6. Display non-printing characters, scroll the document, and then in the second step in the numbered list, click between the two spaces to the left of the word *where* in the third line.

7. On the **Insert** tab, in the **Symbols** group, click the **Equation** button.

The Equation Builder inserts an area where you can type the equation, and the Design contextual tab is added to the Ribbon.

8. Type C and then on the **Design** contextual tab, in the **Symbols** group, click the **Equal** button.

9. In the **Symbols** group, click the **More** button.

The Basic Math gallery opens.

10. In the **Basic Math** gallery, click the sixth symbol in the sixth row (π).

Notice that the row containing the pi symbol is now visible in the Symbols group.

11. In the **Symbols** group, click the up arrow until the top of the gallery scrolls into view, click the **Multiplication Sign** button, and then type d.

As you add to the equation, the Equation Builder adjusts the spacing and formatting of the formula.

12. Click outside the equation to see how it looks.

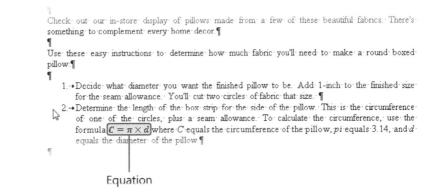

Check out our in-store display of pillows made from a few of these beautiful fabrics. There's something to complement every home decor.¶

¶

Use these easy instructions to determine how much fabric you'll need to make a round boxed pillow.¶

¶

    1.→Decide what diameter you want the finished pillow to be. Add 1-inch to the finished size for the seam allowance. You'll cut two circles of fabric that size. ¶

    2.→Determine the length of the box strip for the side of the pillow. This is the circumference of one of the circles, plus a seam allowance. To calculate the circumference, use the formula $C = \pi \times d$ where C equals the circumference of the pillow, pi equals 3.14, and d equals the diameter of the pillow ¶

¶

Equation

13. Click the equation, click the arrow that appears to the right, and then click **Save as New Equation**.

The Create New Building Block dialog box opens.

See Also For more information about building blocks, see "Inserting Ready-Made Document Parts" in Chapter 8, "Working with Longer Documents."

14. In the **Name** box, type Circumference of a circle, and then click **OK**.

15. Press the ⊥ to release the selection. Then on the **Insert** tab, in the **Symbols** group, click the **Equation** arrow, and scroll the **Equation** gallery.

Your custom equation is now available in the Equation gallery.

Taylor Expansion

$$e^x = 1 + \frac{x}{1!} + \frac{x^2}{2!} + \frac{x^3}{3!} + \cdots, \qquad -\infty < x < \infty$$

Trig Identity 1

$$\sin \alpha \pm \sin \beta = 2 \sin \frac{1}{2}(\alpha \pm \beta) \cos \frac{1}{2}(\alpha \mp \beta)$$

Trig Identity 2

$$\cos \alpha + \cos \beta = 2 \cos \frac{1}{2}(\alpha + \beta) \cos \frac{1}{2}(\alpha - \beta)$$

General

Circumference of a circle

$$C = \pi \times d$$

π   Insert New Equation

π   Save Selection to Equation Gallery...

16. Press the [Esc] key to close the gallery without making a selection.

17. Click the equation, click its arrow, and then click **Change to Display**.

    Word inserts a line break before and after the equation and positions it in the center of the page.

18. Click the equation's arrow, point to **Justification**, and then click **Left**.

19. Click the equation's arrow, click **Change to Inline**, and then click a blank area of the document.

CLOSE the *05_Symbols* document without saving your changes, and if you are not continuing directly on to the next chapter, quit Word.

Important When you quit Word, you will be asked whether you want to save the addition you have made to the Building Blocks template. Click No if you want to discard the equation you added in this exercise.

Key Points

- You can insert artwork created with most graphics programs, as well as scanned photographs and images, into a Word document.

- When character formatting doesn't produce the dramatic effect you need for a document, create fancy text banners for your documents by using WordArt.

- You can dress up a document with simple shapes. You can also group shapes on a drawing canvas to create simple pictures.

- You can position a graphic in relation to the text that surrounds it or to other objects in the document.

- The Symbols dialog box provides access not only to the kinds of symbols you might need in a professional document but also to little icons that add pizzazz.

- The Equation Builder can help construct and display complex formulas.

Chapter at a Glance

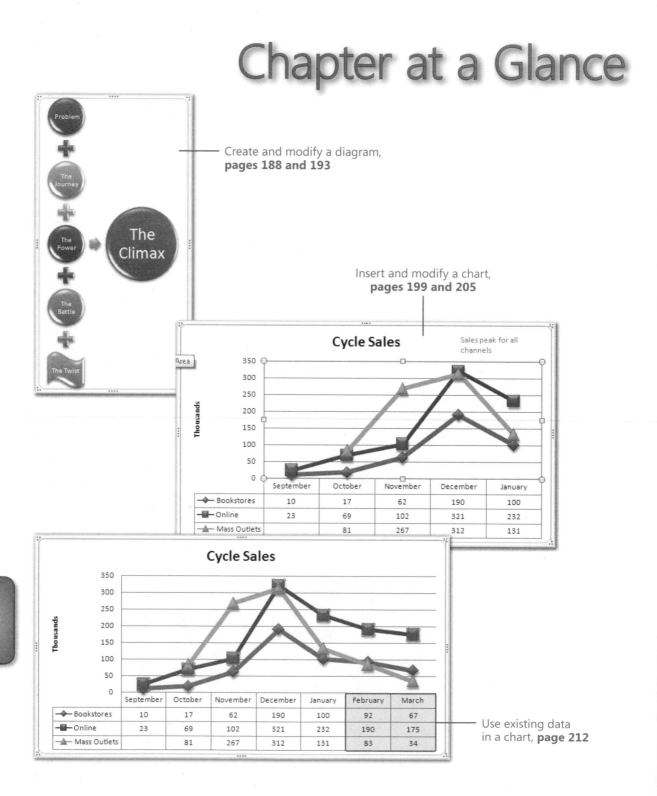

Create and modify a diagram,
pages 188 and 193

Insert and modify a chart,
pages 199 and 205

Cycle Sales

Sales peak for all channels

Thousands

	September	October	November	December	January
Bookstores	10	17	62	190	100
Online	23	69	102	321	232
Mass Outlets		81	267	312	131

Cycle Sales

Thousands

	September	October	November	December	January	February	March
Bookstores	10	17	62	190	100	92	67
Online	23	69	102	321	232	190	175
Mass Outlets		81	267	312	131	83	34

Use existing data
in a chart, **page 212**

7 Working with Diagrams and Charts

In this chapter, you will learn to:

✔ Create a diagram.

✔ Modify a diagram.

✔ Insert a chart.

✔ Modify a chart.

✔ Use existing data in a chart.

You will often find it helpful to reinforce the argument you are making in a document with facts and figures that are best presented in a diagram or chart. These graphic objects serve the following purposes:

● *Diagrams.* These objects depict hierarchies or processes.

● *Charts.* These objects present numerical information in visual ways when it is more important for your audience to understand trends than identify precise values.

In this chapter, you will add a diagram to a document and specify the position of the diagram in relation to the document text and margins. You will add shapes to the diagram, edit and add text, and change the layout, visual style, and color theme. Then you will add a chart to a document and modify its appearance by changing its chart type, style, and layout as well as the color of various elements. Finally, you will create a chart from data stored in a Microsoft Office Excel worksheet.

See Also Do you need only a quick refresher on the topics in this chapter? See the Quick Reference entries on pages xxxix–lxiii.

Important Before you can use the practice files in this chapter, you need to install them from the book's companion CD to their default location. See "Using the Book's CD" on page xxv for more information.

> **Troubleshooting**   Graphics and operating system–related instructions in this book reflect the Windows Vista user interface. If your computer is running Microsoft Windows XP and you experience trouble following the instructions as written, please refer to the "Information for Readers Running Windows XP" section at the beginning of this book.

Creating a Diagram

When you need your document to clearly illustrate a concept such as a process, cycle, hierarchy, or relationship, you can create a dynamic, visually appealing diagram by using *SmartArt graphics*, a powerful new tool available in Microsoft Office Word 2007, Microsoft Office PowerPoint 2007, and Microsoft Office Outlook 2007. By using predefined sets of sophisticated formatting, you can almost effortlessly put together any of the following diagrams:

- *List diagrams*. These diagrams visually represent lists of related or independent information—for example, a list of items needed to complete a task, including pictures of the items.

- *Process diagrams*. These diagrams visually describe the ordered set of steps required to complete a task—for example, the steps you take to process an order.

- *Cycle diagrams*. These diagrams represent a circular sequence of steps, tasks, or events; or the relationship of a set of steps, tasks, or events to a central, core element—for example, the importance of introducing the basic elements of a story in order to build up to an exciting ending.

- *Hierarchy diagrams*. These diagrams illustrate the structure of an organization or entity—for example, the top-level management structure of a company.

- *Relationship diagrams*. These diagrams show convergent, divergent, overlapping, merging, or containment elements—for example, how using similar methods to organize your e-mail, calendar, and contacts can improve your productivity.

- *Matrix diagrams*. These diagrams show the relationship of components to a whole—for example, the product teams in a department.

- *Pyramid diagrams*. These diagrams illustrate proportional or interconnected relationships—for example, the amount of time that should ideally be spent on different phases of a project.

The categories are not mutually exclusive, meaning that some diagrams appear in more than one category.

You create a diagram by clicking the SmartArt button in the Illustrations group on the Insert tab. Then you select the type of diagram you want to create and insert it into the document. You add text to the diagram either directly or from its text pane.

In this exercise, you will add a diagram to a document, add text to the diagram, and then specify the position of the diagram in relation to the document text and page margins.

> **USE** the *01_Diagram* document. This practice file is located in the *Chapter07* subfolder under *SBS_Word2007*.
>
> **BE SURE TO** start Word before beginning this exercise.
>
> **OPEN** the *01_Diagram* document.

SmartArt

1. Click at the end of the third bulleted item under *Rationale*, press ⟨Enter⟩, and then on the **Insert** tab, in the **Illustrations** group, click the **SmartArt** button.

   The Choose A SmartArt Graphic dialog box opens, displaying all the available graphics.

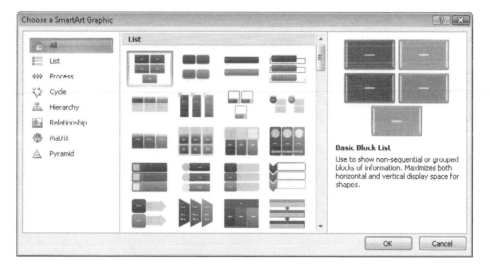

2. In the left pane, click each diagram category in turn to display only the available layouts of that type in the center pane.

3. In the left pane, click **Process**. Then in the center pane, click each process diagram layout in turn to view an example, along with a description of what the diagram best conveys, in the right pane.

4. When you finish exploring, click the first thumbnail in the fourth row (**Vertical Process**), and then click **OK**.

The process diagram is inserted at the insertion point. Text placeholders appear in the diagram shapes and in the adjacent text pane, where they are formatted as a bulleted list. The Design and Format contextual tabs appear on the Ribbon.

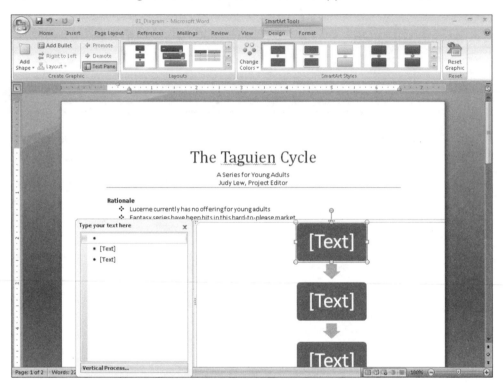

> **Troubleshooting** If the text pane is not visible, click the tab on the left side of the diagram's frame. You can also display the text pane by clicking the Text Pane button in the Create Graphic group on the Design contextual tab.

5. With the first bullet selected in the text pane, type The Journey, and then press the ↓ key to move the insertion point to the next placeholder.

As you type in the text pane, the words also appear in the shapes of the diagram.

6. Repeat Step 5 for the remaining two placeholders, entering The Battle and The Twist.

7. With the insertion point at the end of the third bulleted item in the text pane, press Enter to extend the bulleted list and add a new box to the chart. Then type The Climax.

The Taguien Cycle

A Series for Young Adults
Judy Lew, Project Editor

Rationale
❖ Lucerne currently has no offering for young adults
❖ Fantasy series have been hits in this hard-to-please market

Type your text here   ✕

• The Journey
• The Battle
• The Twist
• The Climax

Vertical Process...

The Journey

The Battle

The Twist

The Climax

Page: 1 of 2   Words: 2   100%

Close

8. In the text pane, click the **Close** button.

9. Drag the left center *sizing handle* of the diagram pane to the right until the pane is approximately as wide as the shapes within the diagram.

> **Troubleshooting** Be sure to point to the set of dots (the sizing handle) on the diagram's frame, not to a blank part of the frame.

You can ignore the diagram while you drag. When you release the mouse button, the diagram pane moves to the left margin of the document, with the diagram centered within it.

> **Tip** You can precisely resize the diagram pane by clicking the Size button on the Format contextual tab and then adjusting the Shape Height or Shape Width setting.

10. On the **Format** contextual tab, in the **Arrange** group, click the **Text Wrapping** button, and then in the list, click **More Layout Options**.

Text
Wrapping ▾

> **Troubleshooting** Depending on your window size and screen resolution, you might need to click the Arrange button to display the Arrange group.

The Advanced Layout dialog box opens, with the Text Wrapping tab active.

See Also For more information about text wrapping, see "Changing the Relationship of Elements on the Page" in Chapter 6, "Working with Graphics, Symbols, and Equations."

11. Under **Wrapping style**, click **Tight**, and under **Wrap text**, select the **Both sides** option.

12. Click the **Picture Position** tab.

    On this tab are options for controlling where the diagram appears relative to other elements of the document.

13. Under **Horizontal**, select the **Alignment** option.

14. Click the **Alignment** arrow, and then in the list, click **Right**.

15. Click the **relative to** arrow, and then in the list, click **Margin**.

16. Under **Vertical**, with the **Absolute position** option selected, click the **below** arrow, and then in the list, click **Page**.

17. Click **OK**. Then click a blank area of the document to see the results of your changes.

    Instead of sitting at the left margin with text before and after it, the diagram now sits to the right of the text, without interrupting its flow.

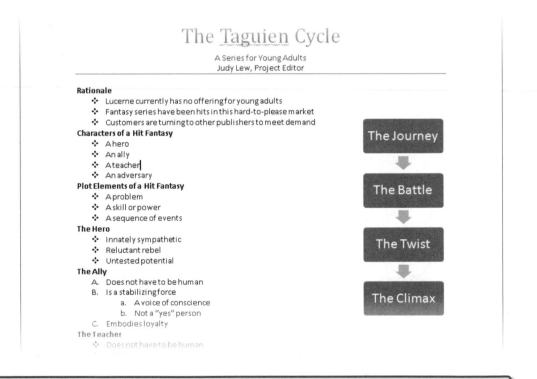

CLOSE the *01_Diagram* document without saving your changes.

Modifying a Diagram

After you create a diagram, you can add and remove shapes and edit its text by making changes in the text pane. If you scroll the document while the text pane is open, the text pane remains visible so that you can easily copy text from the document into the text pane rather than retyping it.

You can also customize a diagram by using the options on the SmartArt Tools contextual tabs. You can make changes such as the following by using the buttons on the Design contextual tab:

- Switch to a different layout of the same type or of a different type.

> **Tip** If you have entered more text than will fit in the new layout, the text is not shown, but it is retained so that you don't have to retype it if you switch the layout again.

- Add shading and three-dimensional effects to all the shapes in a diagram.
- Change the color scheme.
- Add and change the hierarchy of shapes.

> **Tip** You can remove a shape by selecting it and then pressing the Delete key. You can also rearrange shapes by dragging them.

You can customize individual shapes in the following ways by using the buttons on the Format contextual tab:

- Change an individual shape—for example, you can change a square into a star to make it stand out.
- Apply a built-in shape style.
- Change the color, outline, or effect of a shape.

> **Tip** You can use live preview to display the effects of these changes before you apply them. If you apply a change and then decide you preferred the original version, you can click the Reset Graphic button in the Reset group on the Design tab.

In this exercise, you will add shapes to a diagram; add and edit text; and then change the diagram layout, its visual style and color theme, and the shape of one of its elements.

> **USE** the *02_ModifyingDiagram* document. This practice file is located in the *Chapter07* subfolder under *SBS_Word2007*.
>
> **OPEN** the *02_ModifyingDiagram* document.

1. Click the diagram to activate it, and then click the **Text Pane** tab to open the text pane.

   Note that the type of layout used for the diagram (Vertical Process) is described at the bottom of the text pane.

2. Position the insertion point to the left of *The Journey*, and then press [Enter].

   A blank placeholder is added at the beginning of the bulleted list, and a new shape is added to the top of the diagram.

3. Press the [↑] key to move to the new bullet, type The Problem, and then close the text pane.

Add Shape ▾

4. Click the second shape in the diagram (*The Journey*). Then on the **Design** contextual tab, in the **Create Graphic** group, click the **Add Shape** arrow, and in the list, click **Add Shape After**.

   A new shape is added and selected.

5. With the new shape selected, type The Power.

6. Double-click the word *The* in the first shape.

   A box appears around the selection, and the Mini toolbar appears.

7. Press the [Del] key, and then remove *The* from the remaining shapes in the diagram.

   After you remove the word from the final shape, all the shapes in the diagram become narrower.

8. Click a blank area inside the diagram pane to activate the diagram as a whole.

> **Troubleshooting** If any of the shapes in the diagram is surrounded by a dotted line and white handles, that shape is selected instead of the diagram as a whole.

More

9. On the **Design** contextual tab, in the **Layouts** group, click the **More** button.

   The Layouts gallery opens.

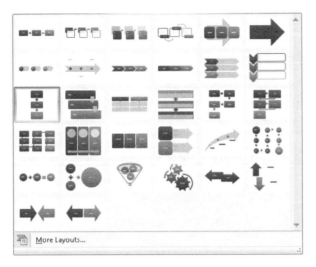

10. In the **Layouts** gallery, point to other diagram options to preview the diagram with those layouts.

    Because changing the layout does not change the width of the diagram, the horizontal layouts create a very small diagram.

11. In the **Layouts** gallery, click the second thumbnail in the fifth row (**Vertical Equation**).

    The diagram changes to a series of circles arranged in an equation.

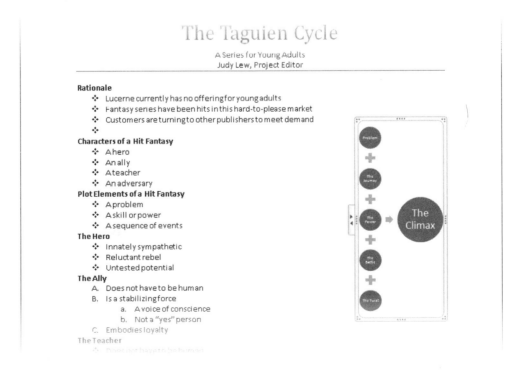

12. Point to the diagram's frame, and when the pointer changes to a four-headed arrow, drag the frame down until its top edge is aligned with the third heading (*Plot Elements of a Hit Fantasy*).

> **Troubleshooting** Be sure to point to a blank part of the frame, not to the sizing handles (the sets of dots on the diagram's frame).

13. Scroll the document, and then drag the sizing handle in the lower-left corner of the diagram's frame drag down and to the left until the frame is about an inch wider and an inch taller than its original size.

When you release the mouse button, the shapes in the diagram expand to fill the resized frame.

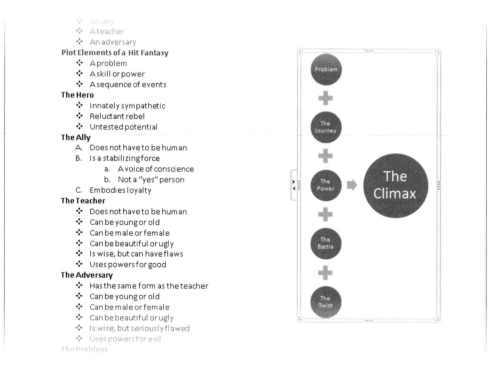

14. On the **Design** contextual tab, in the **SmartArt Styles** group, click the **More** button.

The SmartArt Styles gallery opens.

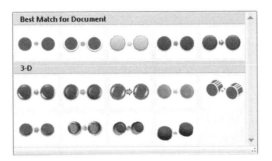

15. In the gallery, point to each style, noticing the changes to your diagram. Then under **3-D**, click the first thumbnail in the first row (**Polished**).

> **Troubleshooting** The live preview from this gallery might be slower than from other galleries. Just be patient; you will soon see the effects of the style on your diagram.

The diagram takes on the effects of the new style.

16. In the **SmartArt Styles** group, click the **Change Colors** button.

The Theme Colors gallery opens.

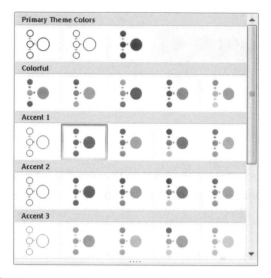

17. Display the live preview of a few color combinations, and then under **Colorful**, click the first thumbnail (**Colorful – Accent Colors**).

18. On the left side of the diagram, click the bottom shape (*Twist*), and then on the **Format** contextual tab, in the **Shapes** group, click the **Change Shape** button.

19. Under **Stars and Banners**, click the seventh shape in the second row (**Wave**).

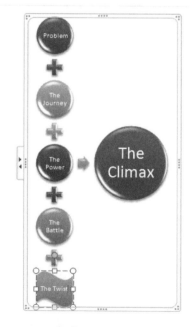

CLOSE the *02_ModifyingDiagram* document without saving your changes.

Inserting a Chart

When you add a chart to a document created in Word 2007, a sample chart is embedded in the document. The data used to plot the sample chart is stored in an Excel 2007 worksheet that is incorporated into the Word file. (You don't have to maintain a separate Excel file.)

> **Tip** You can't see charts in Draft or Outline view.

To customize the chart, you replace the sample data in the Excel worksheet with your own data, in much the same way you would enter information in a table. Because the Excel worksheet is linked to the chart, when you change the values in the worksheet, the chart changes as well.

The Excel worksheet is composed of rows and columns of cells that contain values, or *data points*, that make up a *data series*. To enter data in an individual cell—the intersection of a row and column—you click the cell to select it, and start typing. You can select an entire column by clicking the *column heading*—the shaded box containing a letter at the top of each column—and an entire row by clicking the *row heading*—the shaded box containing a number to the left of each row. You can select the entire worksheet by clicking the Select All button—the darker box at the junction of the column headings and row headings.

> **Tip** If you create a chart and later want to edit its data, you can open the associated work-sheet by clicking the chart and then clicking the Edit Data button in the Data group on the Design contextual tab.

In this exercise, you will add a chart to a document and then replace the sample data in the worksheet with your own data.

> **Troubleshooting** If you open a document created in Word 2003 in Word 2007 and then add a chart to it, Word uses Microsoft Graph to create the chart. This Word 2003 charting technology has been retained to maintain compatibility with earlier versions of the program. The steps in this exercise will work only with a document created in Word 2007.

> **USE** the *03_Chart* document. This practice file is located in the *Chapter07* subfolder under *SBS_Word2007*.
>
> **OPEN** the *03_Chart* document.

1. Press Ctrl + End to move the insertion point to the end of the document.

Chart

2. On the **Insert** tab, in the **Illustrations** group, click the **Chart** button.

   The Insert Chart dialog box opens.

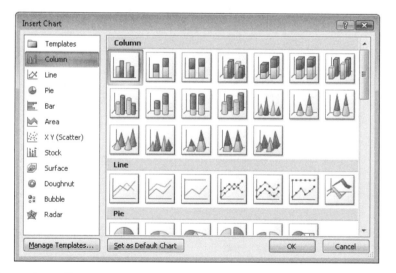

3. In the gallery on the right, under **Column**, click the fourth thumbnail in the first row (**3-D Clustered Column**). Then click **OK**.

   A sample column chart is inserted in the document on the left and an Excel work-sheet containing the plotted sample data opens on the right.

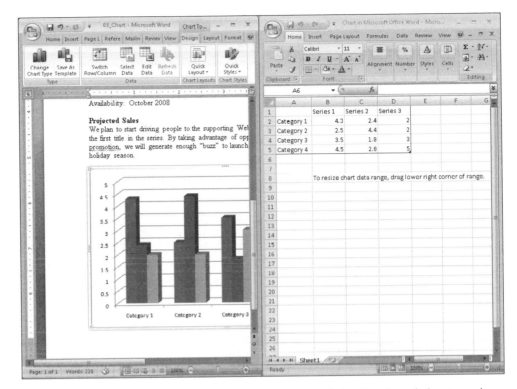

4. Click the **Select All** button in the upper-left corner of the Excel worksheet, and then press the ⌈Del⌉ key.

   The sample data in the worksheet is deleted, leaving a blank worksheet. The columns in the sample chart in the document disappear, leaving a blank chart area.

5. In the first cell in row 1 (cell **A1**), type Period, and then press the ⌈Tab⌉ key.

   > **Tip** As with Word tables, each worksheet cell is identified by an address consisting of its column letter and row number—for example, A2. A range of cells is identified by the address of the cell in the upper-left corner and the address of the cell in the lower-right corner, separated by a colon—for example, A2:D5.

   Excel enters the heading and activates the next cell in the same row.

6. In cells **B1** through **D1**, type Bookstores, Online, and Mass Outlets, pressing ⌈Tab⌉ after each to move to the next cell.

7. Point to the border between any two columns, and when the pointer changes to a double-headed arrow, double-click.

   Excel adjusts the width of the columns to fit their entries.

8. In cells **A2** through **C2**, type September, 10, and 23. (There is no data in D2.)

> **Tip** You can use the keyboard to move around the worksheet. Press Enter to move down in the same column or Shift+Enter to move up; and press Tab to move to the right in the same row or Shift+Tab to move to the left. You can also press the Arrow keys to move up, down, left, or right one cell at a time.

9. Type the following data into the cells of the Excel worksheet:

	A	B	C	D
3	October	17	69	81
4	November	62	102	167
5	December	190	321	312
6	January	100	232	131

As you enter data, the chart changes to reflect what you type. (We've scrolled the Word window to display more of the chart.)

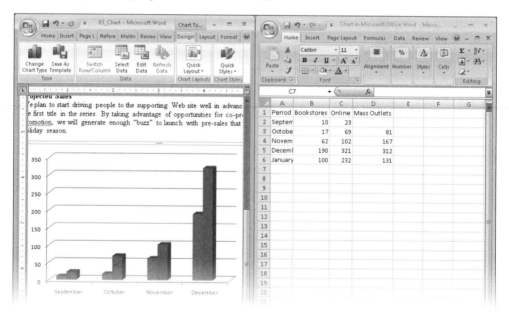

Something is wrong. You entered data for September through January, but January is not shown. This is because the original sample chart plotted only the cells in the range A1:D5, and you have entered data in A1:D6. You need to specify the new range.

10. In the Word document, click the chart to activate it. Then on the **Design** contextual tab, in the **Data** group, click the **Select Data** button.

Select
Data

In the Excel worksheet, the plotted data range is surrounded by a blinking dotted border, and the Select Data Source dialog box opens so that you can make any necessary adjustments.

11. At the right end of the **Chart data range** box, click the **Collapse Dialog** button to shrink the **Select Data Source** dialog box.

Collapse

12. In the Excel worksheet, point to cell **A1**, and drag down and to the right to cell **D6**. Then in the **Select Data Source** dialog box, click the **Expand Dialog** button.

Expand

In the Select Data Source dialog box, the Chart Data Range box now contains the new range and the Horizontal (Category) Axis Labels list now includes January.

The following table shows the data in the worksheet:

A	B	C	D	E	F	G
Period	Bookstores	Online	Mass Outlets			
Septem	10	23				
Octobe	17	69	81			
Novem	62	102	167			
Deceml	190	321	312			
January	100	232	131			

Select Data Source

Chart data range: =Sheet1!$A$1:$D$6

Switch Row/Column

Legend Entries (Series)

Add   Edit   Remove

Bookstores
Online
Mass Outlets

Horizontal (Category) Axis Labels

Edit

September
October
November
December
January

Hidden and Empty Cells   OK   Cancel

13. Click **OK** to close the dialog box, and then in the upper-right corner of the Excel window, click the **Close** button to close the worksheet.

Close

The Word window expands to fill the screen. The data for January now appears in the chart. Suppose you realize that you made an error when typing the data for mass outlets.

14. On the **Design** tab, in the **Data** group, click the **Edit Data** button to open the Excel worksheet.

Edit
Data

15. In the Excel worksheet, click cell **D4**, type 267 to change the data, press [Enter], and then close the Excel window.

In the chart, the Mass Outlets column for November becomes taller to represent the new value.

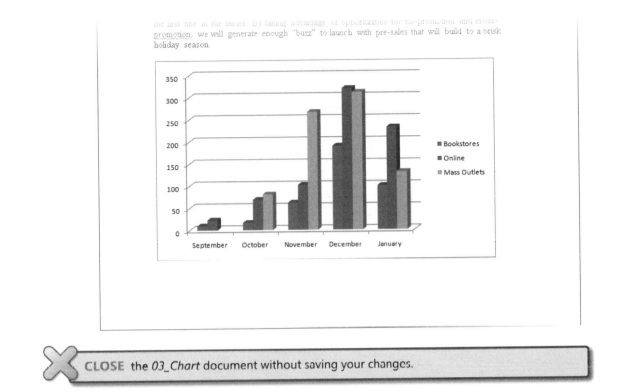

the first title in the series. By taking advantage of opportunities for co-promotion and cross-promotion, we will generate enough "buzz" to launch with pre-sales that will build to a brisk holiday season.

CLOSE the *03_Chart* document without saving your changes.

Modifying a Chart

If you decide that the chart you created doesn't adequately depict the most important characteristics of your data, you can change the chart type at any time. Word provides 11 types of charts, each with two-dimensional and three-dimensional variations. Common chart types include the following:

- *Column charts.* These are good for showing how values change over time.
- *Bar charts.* These are good for showing the values of several items at a single point in time.
- *Line graphs.* These are good for showing erratic changes in values over time.
- *Pie charts.* These are good for showing how parts relate to the whole.

Having settled on the most appropriate chart type, you can modify the chart as a whole or any of its elements, which include the following:

- *Chart area.* This is the entire area within the frame displayed when you click a chart.
- *Plot area.* This is the rectangular area bordered by the axes.

- *X-axis* **and** *y-axis*. The data is plotted against an x-axis—also called the *category axis*—and a y-axis—also called the *value axis*. (Three-dimensional charts also have a *z-axis*.)

- *Tick-mark labels*. Along each axis are labels that identify the data.

- *Data markers*. Each data point in a data series is represented graphically in the chart by a *data marker*.

- *Legend*. This key identifies the data series.

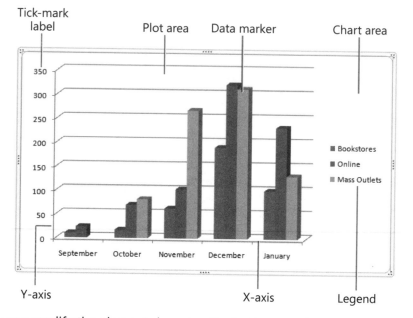

You can modify the elements by using the buttons on the Layout contextual tab. To modify a specific element, you first select it by clicking it, or by clicking its name in the Chart Elements box in the Current Selection group on the Format contextual tab. You can then use the buttons on the Format contextual tab. If you make extensive modifications, you might want to save the customized chart as a template so that you can use it for plotting similar data in the future without having to repeat all the changes.

In this exercise, you will modify the appearance of a chart by changing its chart type and style. You will change the color of the plot area and the color and weight of a data series. You will then hide gridlines and change the layout to display titles and a datasheet. After adding an annotation in a text box, you will save the chart as a template.

USE the *04_ModifyingChart* document. This practice file is located in the *Chapter07* subfolder under *SBS_Word2007*.

OPEN the *04_ModifyingChart* presentation.

1. Scroll the document to display the chart, and click anywhere in the chart to activate it.

   Word displays the Design, Layout, and Format. contextual tabs.

Change
Chart Type

2. On the **Design** contextual tab, in the **Type** group, click the **Change Chart Type** button.

   The Change Chart Type dialog box opens.

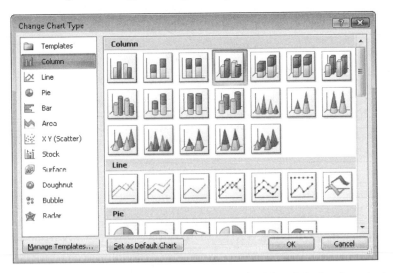

3. In the gallery on the right, under **Line**, double-click the fourth thumbnail (**Line with Markers**).

   The column chart changes to a line chart, which depicts data by using colored lines instead of columns.

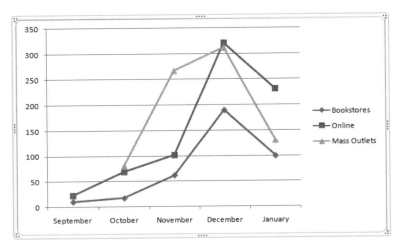

More

4. On the **Design** tab, in the **Chart Styles** group, click the **More** button.

The **Chart Styles** gallery opens.

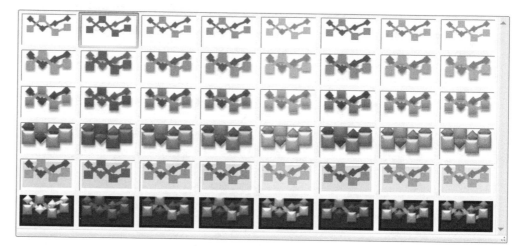

5. In the gallery, click the second thumbnail in the fourth row (**Style 26**).

The lines are now thicker, and the data points are three-dimentional.

6. Click the plot area—the area of the chart containing the data markers—to select it, and then click the **Format** contextual tab.

The Chart Elements box in the Current Selection group on the Format tab displays the name of the selected chart element.

Shape Fill

7. On the **Format** tab, in the **Shape Styles** group, click the **Shape Fill** button, and then in the list, click **More Fill Colors**.

The Colors dialog box opens.

8. On the **Standard** tab of the **Colors** dialog box, click the color to the lower left of the center (the palest yellow), and then click **OK**.

The plot area is now shaded a pale yellow to distinguish it from the rest of the chart.

> **Tip** To change several aspects of the plot area, right-click the area and then click Format Plot Area to open the Format Plot Area dialog box. You can then change the fill, border, shadow, and 3-D format in one location.

9. In the **Current Selection** group, click the **Chart Elements** arrow, and then in the list, click **Series "Online"**.

Small blue circles appear around the data points of the selected series.

10. In the **Current Selection** group, click the **Format Selection** button.

The Format Data Series dialog box opens.

11. In the left pane, click **Line Color**. Then on the **Line Color** page, select the **Solid Line** option, click the **Color** button that appears, and under **Standard Colors**, click the **Purple** box.

12. In the left pane, click **Line Style**. Then on the **Line Style** page, in the **Width** box, type or select **3 pt**. Then click **Close**.

The Online data series is now represented by a thin purple line.

13. On the **Layout** contextual tab, in the **Axes** group, click the **Gridlines** button, point to **Primary Horizontal Gridlines**, and then click **None** to remove the horizontal gridlines from the chart.

14. On the **Design** contextual tab, in the **Chart Layouts** group, click the **More** button.

The Chart Layouts gallery opens.

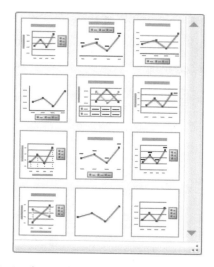

15. In the gallery, click the second thumbnail in the second row (**Layout 5**).

The legend now appears below the chart with a datasheet, gridlines have been turned back on, and placeholders for a chart title and axis title have been added to the top of the chart.

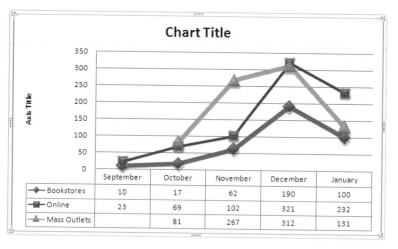

16. In the chart, replace the **Chart Title** placeholder at the top with Cycle Sales and the **Axis Title** placeholder on the left with Thousands.

17. On the **Layout** contextual tab, in the **Insert** group, click the **Draw Text Box** button.

Draw Text Box

18. In the chart, point to a spot above the December peak sales, and then drag diagonally down and to the right until the text box fills the space to the right of the title.

19. Type Sales peak for all channels. Then select the text, and on the **Home** tab, in the **Font** group, change the size to **10** points and the color to **Red**.

20. Click outside the chart to see the results of your changes.

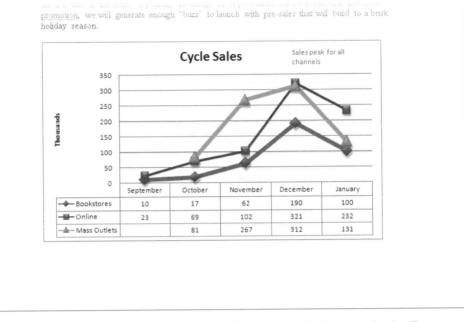

Save As
Template

21. Click the chart area to activate the chart. Then on the **Design** tab, in the **Type** group, click the **Save As Template** button.

The Save Chart Template dialog box opens and displays the contents of your *Charts* folder, which is a subfolder of your *Templates* folder.

> **Troubleshooting** If the *Charts* folder is not displayed in the Address bar, navigate to the *AppData\Roaming\Microsoft\Templates\Charts* folder under your user profile.

22. With the *Charts* folder displayed in the Address bar, type My Sales Chart in the **File name** box, and then click **Save**.

23. In the **Type** group, click the **Change Chart Type** button, and then in the left pane of the **Change Chart Type** dialog box, click **Templates**.

The folder contains an unidentified template with a line chart icon.

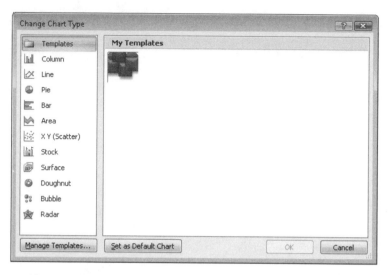

24. Verify that this template is the one you just saved by pointing to it to view the ScreenTip, and then click **Cancel** to close the dialog box.

CLOSE the *04_ModifyingChart* document without saving your changes.

Using Existing Data in a Chart

If the data you want to plot as a chart already exists in a Microsoft Office Access database, an Excel worksheet, or a Word table, you don't have to retype it in the chart's worksheet. You can copy the data from its source program and paste it into the worksheet.

In this exercise, you will copy data stored in a range of cells in an Excel worksheet into a chart's worksheet and then expand the plotted data range so that the new data appears in the chart.

USE the *05_ExistingData* document and the *05_Sales* workbook. These practice files are located in the *Chapter07* subfolder under *SBS_Word2007*.
OPEN the *05_ExistingData* document.

1. Press Ctrl + End to move to the end of the document, right-click the chart, and then click **Edit Data** to open the associated Excel worksheet.

2. In the Excel window, click the **Microsoft Office Button**, and then click **Open**. In the **Open** dialog box, navigate to your *Documents\MSP\SBS_Word2007\Chapter07* folder, and double-click the *05_Sales* workbook.

Microsoft Office Button

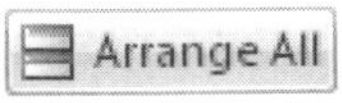

Arrange All

3. On the Excel **View** tab, in the **Window** group, click the **Arrange All** button.

4. In the **Arrange Windows** dialog box, click the **Horizontal** option, and click **OK**.

   Excel arranges one of the open worksheets above the other, so that both are visible at the same time.

5. Scroll the *05_Sales* worksheet, point to cell **A10**, and drag down and to the right to select the range **A10:D11**.

Copy

6. On the Excel **Home** tab, in the **Clipboard** group, click the **Copy** button.

Paste

7. Click the **Chart in Microsoft Office Word** worksheet to activate it, click cell **A7**, and then on the Excel **Home** tab, in the **Clipboard** group, click the **Paste** button.

   The data from the *05_Sales* worksheet is pasted into the chart's worksheet.

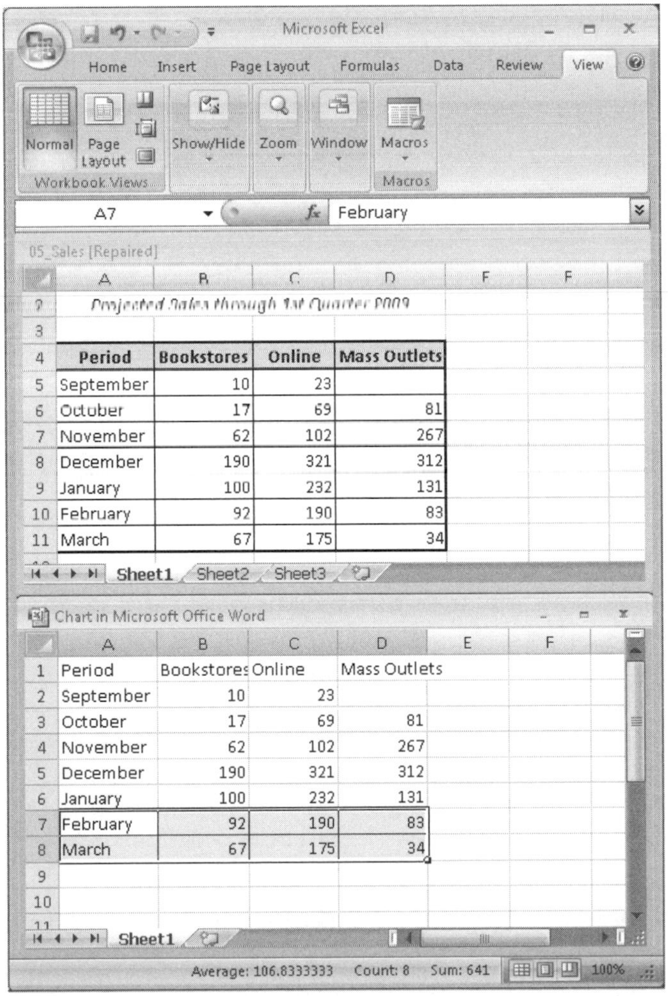

8. Close the *05_Sales* workbook.

   The top window closes, but the bottom window does not expand to take its place.

Maximize

9. Click the chart worksheet's **Maximize** button.

   Now you need to specify that the new data should be included in the chart.

Select Data

10. Click the chart in the document to activate it, and then on the **Design** contextual tab, in the **Data** group, click the **Select Data** button.

    The Select Data Source dialog box opens.

11. Move the dialog box so that all of the data in the Excel window is visible.

12. Click at the right end of the **Chart data range** box, change the cell range to read =Sheet1!$A$1:$D$8, and then click **OK**.

13. Close the Excel window.

    The chart now contains two more months of data.

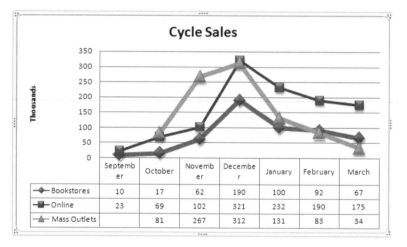

14. Click *Sales peak for all channels*, click the border of the text box, and then press Del.

15. In the middle of the frame's right border, drag the dotted handle to the right until all the month labels in the datasheet appear on one line.

CLOSE the *05_ExistingData* document without saving your changes.

Tip You can also import data into your chart from a text file, Web page, or other external source, such as Microsoft SQL Server. To import data, first activate the linked Excel worksheet. Then on the Excel Data tab, in the Get External Data group, click the button for your data source, and navigate to the source. For more information see Microsoft Office Online Help.

Key Points

- You can easily create a sophisticated diagram to convey a process or the relationship between hierarchical elements.

- Diagrams are dynamic illustrations that you can customize to produce precisely the effect you are looking for.

- A chart is often the most efficient way to present numeric data with at-a-glance clarity.

- You can select the type of chart and change the appearance of its component elements until it clearly conveys key information.

- Existing data in a Word table, Excel workbook, Access database, or other structured source can easily be copied and pasted into a chart's worksheet, eliminating time-consuming typing.

Chapter at a Glance

Create and modify a
table of contents, **page 226**

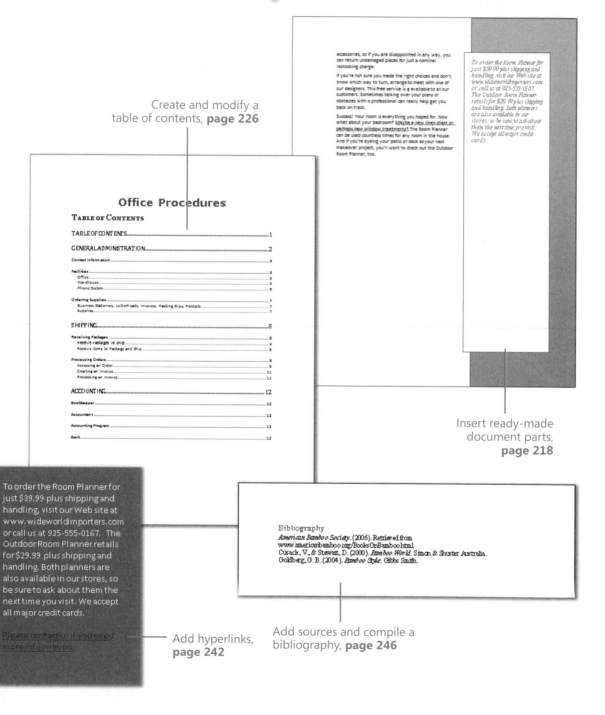

Office Procedures

accessories, so if you are disappointed in any way, you can return undamaged pieces for just a nominal restocking charge.

If you're not sure you made the right choices and don't know which way to turn, arrange to meet with one of our designers. This free service is available to all our customers. Sometimes talking over your plans or obstacles with a professional can really help get you back on track.

Success! Your room is everything you hoped for. Now what about your bedroom? Maybe a new linen chest or perhaps new window treatments? The Room Planner can be used countless times for any room in the house. And if you're eyeing your patio or deck as your next makeover project, you'll want to check out the Outdoor Room Planner, too.

To order the Room Planner for just $39.99 plus shipping and handling, visit our Web site at www.wideworldimporters.com or call us at 925-555-0167. The Outdoor Room Planner retails for $29.99 plus shipping and handling. Both planners are also available in our stores, so be sure to ask about them the next time you visit. We accept all major credit cards.

Insert ready-made
document parts,
page 218

To order the Room Planner for just $39.99 plus shipping and handling, visit our Web site at www.wideworldimporters.com or call us at 925-555-0167. The Outdoor Room Planner retails for $29.99 plus shipping and handling. Both planners are also available in our stores, so be sure to ask about them the next time you visit. We accept all major credit cards.

Please contact us if you need more information.

Add hyperlinks,
page 242

Bibliography
American Bamboo Society. (2006). Retrieved from www.americanbamboo.org/BooksOnBamboo.html
Cusack, V., & Stewart, D. (2000). *Bamboo World*. Simon & Shuster Australia.
Goldberg, G. B. (2004). *Bamboo Style*. Gibbs Smith.

Add sources and compile a
bibliography, **page 246**

8 Working with Longer Documents

In this chapter, you will learn to:

- ✔ Insert ready-made document parts.
- ✔ Create and modify a table of contents.
- ✔ Create and modify an index.
- ✔ Add bookmarks and cross-references.
- ✔ Add hyperlinks.
- ✔ Add sources and compile a bibliography.

If you create long, complex documents and are concerned about helping your readers find the information they are looking for, you can rely on the following Microsoft Office Word 2007 tools to do the job:

- **Building blocks.** You can draw attention to specific information and add visual interest to a document by incorporating these preformatted document parts (such as cover pages, pull quotes, and sidebars) into a document. You can choose from a variety of elements and formatting styles, as well as create your own building blocks.

- **Table of contents.** You can provide an overview of the information contained in a document and help readers locate topics by compiling a table of contents from the document headings. Depending on the intended delivery format (printed or electronic) you can choose to include page numbers or hyperlinks to each heading.

- **Index.** You can help readers locate specific information by inserting index entry fields within a document and compiling an index of keywords and concepts that directs the reader to the corresponding page numbers.

- **Bookmarks.** You can quickly return to a specific location in a document by inserting a bookmark (also called an *anchor*). You can go to a bookmarked location by selecting it from the Bookmarks dialog box; you can also help readers find information by inserting hyperlinks or cross-references to bookmarks.

- **Cross-references.** To help a reader move to a related location in a document, you can insert a cross-reference.

- **Hyperlinks.** To help a reader move to a location in the same file, in another file, or on a Web page, you can add links from text or graphics to the target location.

- **Information sources and a bibliography.** You can appropriately attribute information to its source by inserting citations within a document; Word will compile a professional bibliography from the citations.

In this chapter, you will insert several preformatted building blocks in a document, and save an element of the document as a custom building block. After creating and updating both a table of contents and an index, you will experiment with bookmarks, cross-references, and hyperlinks. Finally, you will use the Source Manager to enter source information, insert a few citations, and compile a bibliography.

See Also Do you need only a quick refresher on the topics in this chapter? See the Quick Reference entries on pages xxxix–lxiii.

Important Before you can use the practice files in this chapter, you need to install them from the book's companion CD to their default location. See "Using the Book's CD" on page xxv for more information.

Troubleshooting Graphics and operating system–related instructions in this book reflect the Windows Vista user interface. If your computer is running Microsoft Windows XP and you experience trouble following the instructions as written, please refer to the "Information for Readers Running Windows XP" section at the beginning of this book.

Inserting Ready-Made Document Parts

Longer documents typically include elements such as a cover page and headers and footers to provide identifying and organizing information. To reinforce key concepts and also alleviate the monotony of page after page of plain text, they might also include elements such as sidebars and quotations pulled from the text.

To simplify the creation of professional visual text elements, Word 2007 introduces *building blocks*, which are available from the Building Blocks Organizer.

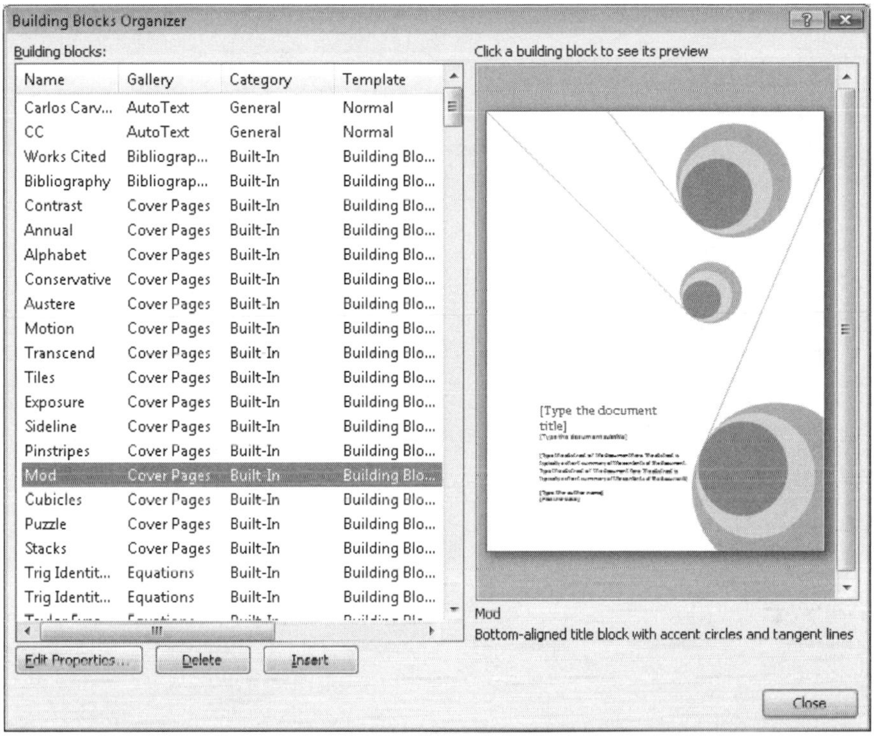

The names of the building blocks that come with Word indicate the graphic theme of the element—in most cases, an entire family of building blocks is available in a theme, including page elements such as:

- Cover pages
- Page headers
- Page footers
- Page numbers
- Quotes
- Sidebars

Other page elements, such as bibliographies, tables, equations, and watermarks, aren't specific to a theme.

The Gallery column indicates the page element created by the building block. More information about each building block is available by scrolling the Building Blocks list to the right.

The Behavior column indicates whether Word inserts the building block in the existing text, in its own paragraph, or on its own page. The Description column includes information about the building block, and in some cases, recommendations for its use.

> **Tip** You can display the entire contents of a column by pointing to the right column header border and then, when the pointer changes to a double-headed arrow, dragging to the right, into the preview pane. (In the case of the Description column, you drag into the preview pane.

Some building blocks are also available from the Ribbon—for example, you can add headers and footers from the Header & Footer group on the Insert tab. If you frequently use a specific element in your documents, such as a formatted title-subtitle-author arrangement at the beginning of reports, you can define it as a custom building block. It is then available from the Building Blocks Organizer.

In this exercise, you will insert several ready-made building blocks in a document. You will also save an element of the document as a custom building block.

> **USE** the *01_Parts* document. This practice file is located in the *Chapter08* subfolder under *SBS_Word2007*.
> **OPEN** the *01_Parts* document.

Quick Parts ▾

1. With the insertion point at the beginning of the document, on the **Insert** tab, in the **Text** group, click the **Quick Parts** button, and then click **Building Blocks Organizer**.

> **Troubleshooting** If you or your organization have made custom building blocks available from your computer, clicking the Quick Parts button displays them in the Quick Parts gallery. If no custom building blocks are available, clicking the Quick Parts button displays a list of building block-related commands.

The Building Blocks Organizer opens. The left pane displays a complete list of all the building blocks available on your computer; clicking a building block in the left pane displays a preview in the right pane.

> **Tip** The Building Blocks list you see on your computer includes AutoText entries for your user name and initials. To change either of these entries, click the Microsoft Office Button, click Word Options, and then on the Popular page of the Word Options window, update your information and click OK.

2. Scroll through the **Building blocks** list, and preview a few of the building blocks.

Notice that page elements of the same theme are coordinated and that page elements with different themes contain similar information.

3. If the **Gallery** column of the **Building blocks** list is not sorted alphabetically, double-click the **Gallery** column heading. Then in the list of **Cover Pages**, click the **Pinstripes** cover page, and click **Insert**.

Word inserts the cover page at the beginning of the document, adds the title, company name, and user name that are attached as properties to the document, and indicates with placeholders where you should type the subtitle and date.

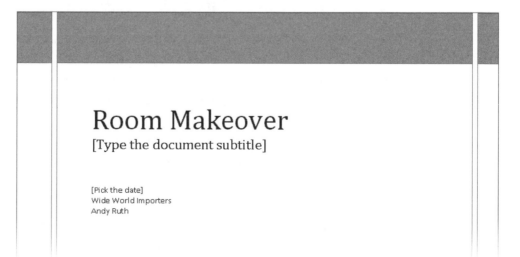

Room Makeover
[Type the document subtitle]

[Pick the date]
Wide World Importers
Andy Ruth

4. Click anywhere in the subtitle placeholder, and type Information Sheet. Then click the date placeholder, click the arrow that appears, and in the calendar, click today's date (indicated by a red box).

5. Move to Page 2 (which was originally the first page of the document), and click anywhere on the page. Then display the **Building Blocks Organizer**, scroll to the list of **Text Boxes**, click **Pinstripes Quote**, and click **Insert**.

Word inserts the quote box half way down the right side of the page. Placeholder text in the quote box tells you how to insert your own text and format the block.

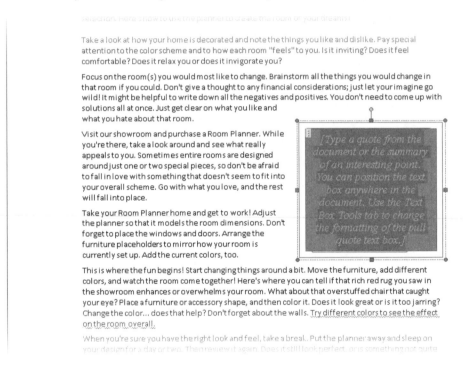

6. Select and copy the last sentence of the fourth paragraph (*Go with what you love...*), and then click the quote box to select the placeholder text.

7. On the **Home** tab, in the **Clipboard** group, click the **Paste** arrow, and in the list, click **Paste Special**. Then in the **Paste Special** dialog box, click **Unformatted Text**, and click **OK**.

The copied text replaces the placeholder, and because it was pasted as unformatted text, it retains the formatting of the placeholder text. The quote box automatically resizes to fit its new contents.

> **Tip** You can reposition the quote box by dragging it to another location in the document. You can change the outline and fill colors by using the commands in the Text Box Styles group on the Format contextual tab.

8. Move to Page **3**, and click anywhere on the page. Then display the **Building Blocks Organizer**, scroll to the list of **Text Boxes**, click **Pinstripes Sidebar**, and then click **Insert**.

    Word inserts the sidebar on the right third of the page.

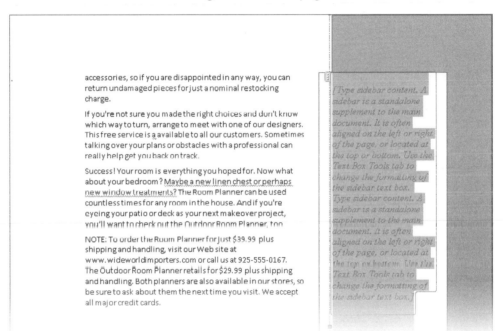

9. Delete **NOTE:** (including the colon and following space) from the beginning of the last paragraph of the document, select the paragraph, and then in the **Clipboard** group, click the **Cut** button.

10. Click the sidebar to select the placeholder text, and then in the **Clipboard** group, click the **Paste** arrow, and in the list, click **Paste Special**. Then in the **Paste Special** dialog box, click **Unformatted Text**, and click **OK**.

    The sidebar is too narrow to completely hold the Web site address, so you need to widen it.

Cut

accessories, so if you are disappointed in any way, you can return undamaged pieces for just a nominal restocking charge.

If you're not sure you made the right choices and don't know which way to turn, arrange to meet with one of our designers. This free service is available to all our customers. Sometimes talking over your plans or obstacles with a professional can really help get you back on track.

Success! Your room is everything you hoped for. Now what about your bedroom? Maybe a new linen chest or perhaps new window treatments? The Room Planner can be used countless times for any room in the house. And if you're eyeing your patio or deck as your next makeover project, you'll want to check out the Outdoor Room Planner, too.

To order the Room Planner for just $39.99 plus shipping and handling, visit our Web site at www.wideworldimporters. com or call us at 925-555-0167. The Outdoor Room Planner retails for $29.99 plus shipping and handling. Both planners are also available in our stores, so be sure to ask about them the next time you visit. We accept all major credit cards.

11. Drag the blue handle on the left edge of the white sidebar placeholder to the left, until it sits slightly to the left of the frame of the text block.

12. On the **Insert** tab, in the **Text** group, click the **Quick Parts** button, and then click **Save Selection to Quick Part Gallery**.

> **Troubleshooting** If you click the text in the sidebar or elsewhere in the document after resizing the sidebar, it will no longer be selected and the Save Selection To Quick Part Gallery command will not be available. If this happens, click the sidebar's sizing handle to reselect the sidebar, and then repeat Step 12.

The Create New Building Block dialog box opens.

Create New Building Block	
Name:	To order the
Gallery:	Quick Parts
Category:	General
Description:	
Save in:	Building Blocks
Options:	Insert content only

The options in this dialog box correspond to the columns of information displayed in the Building Blocks Organizer. You can save this building block in the Building Blocks template or the Normal template.

13. Replace the text in the **Name** box with Order Sidebar, and then click **OK**.

You can now insert this custom sidebar from the Quick Parts gallery into other documents.

14. In the **Text** group, click the **Quick Parts** button.

The Order Sidebar custom building block appears at the top of the Quick Parts gallery.

15. Display the **Building Blocks Organizer**, and click the **Category** column heading to sort the **Building blocks** list by that column. Then scroll to the **General** category.

The General category includes your custom building block and the AutoText entries.

16. In the list, click **Order Sidebar** once.

In the preview pane, Word displays the building block you just created.

> **Tip** To delete a building block from your computer, select it in the Building Blocks Organizer, and then click Delete.

17. Close the **Building Blocks Organizer** dialog box.

CLOSE the *01_Parts* document without saving your changes.

> **Important** When you quit Word after saving a custom building block, you will be asked whether you want to save changes to the template in which you stored the building block. If you want the building block to be available for future documents, click Yes; otherwise, click No.

Creating and Modifying a Table of Contents

If you create a long document with headings and subheadings, such as an annual report or a catalog that has several sections, you might want to add a *table of contents* to the beginning of the document to give your readers an overview of and the document's contents and to help them navigate to specific sections. In a document that will be printed, you can indicate with a page number the starting page of each section; if the document will be distributed electronically, you can link each heading and subheading in the table of contents to the section in the document, so that readers can jump directly there with a click of the mouse.

By default, Word expects to create a table of contents based on paragraphs within the document that you have formatted with the standard heading styles (Heading 1, Heading 2, and so on). (Word can also create a table of contents based on outline levels or on fields that you have inserted in the document.) When you tell Word to create the table, Word identifies the table of contents entries and inserts the table at the insertion point as a single field. You can modify the elements on which Word bases the table at any time.

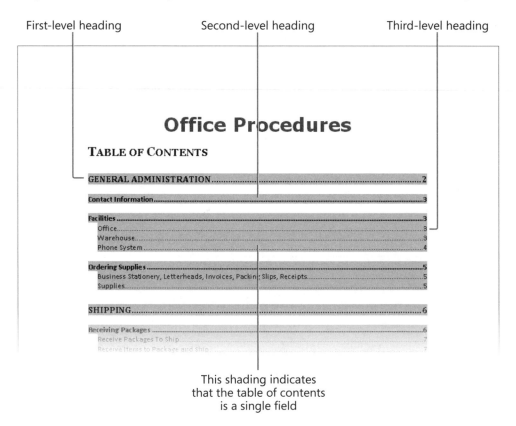

First-level heading   Second-level heading   Third-level heading

This shading indicates that the table of contents is a single field

See Also For information about applying styles, see "Working with Templates" in Chapter 4, "Changing the Look of a Document."

The Table Of Contents gallery (available from the References tab) offers three standard table options:

- **Automatic Table 1.** This option inserts a table of contents with the heading Contents.
- **Automatic Table 2.** This option inserts a table of contents with the heading Table of Contents.
- **Manual Table.** This option inserts a table of contents with placeholders that you replace manually.

The formatting of the entries in a table of contents is controlled by nine levels of built-in TOC styles (TOC 1, TOC 2, and so on). By default, Word uses the styles that are assigned in the template attached to the document. If you want to use a different style, instead of clicking one of the standard options in the Table Of Contents gallery, you can click Insert Table Of Contents below the gallery to display the Table Of Contents dialog box, where you can choose from several variations, such as Classic, Fancy, and Simple.

> **Tip** If you create a table of contents based on the document's template, you can customize the TOC styles during the creation process. On the References tab, in the Table Of Contents group, click the Tables Of Contents button, and then in the list, click Insert Table Of Contents. In the Table Of Contents dialog box, click Modify. The Style dialog box opens, displaying the nine TOC styles. You can modify the font, paragraph, tabs, border, and other formatting of these styles the same way you change any other style.

After you create a table of contents, you can format it manually by selecting text and then applying character or paragraph formatting or styles.

You can edit the text of a table of contents, but it is much easier to click the Update Table button and have Word do the work for you. You have the option of updating only the page numbers, or if you have changed, added, or deleted headings, you can update (re-create) the entire table.

In this exercise, you will create a table of contents for a document based on heading styles. Then you will alter the document by inserting page breaks, and update the table of contents to reflect your changes.

> **USE** the *02_Contents* document. This practice file is located in the *Chapter08* subfolder under *SBS_Word2007*.
>
> **OPEN** the *02_Contents* document.

1. Position the insertion point to the left of *GENERAL ADMINISTRATION*, and then on the **References** tab, in the **Table of Contents** group, click the **Table of Contents** button.

2. In the **Table of Contents** gallery, click **Automatic Table 1**. Then press ⌈Ctrl⌉ + ⌈Home⌉ to return to the beginning of the document.

Word inserts a table of contents with predefined styles at the insertion point.

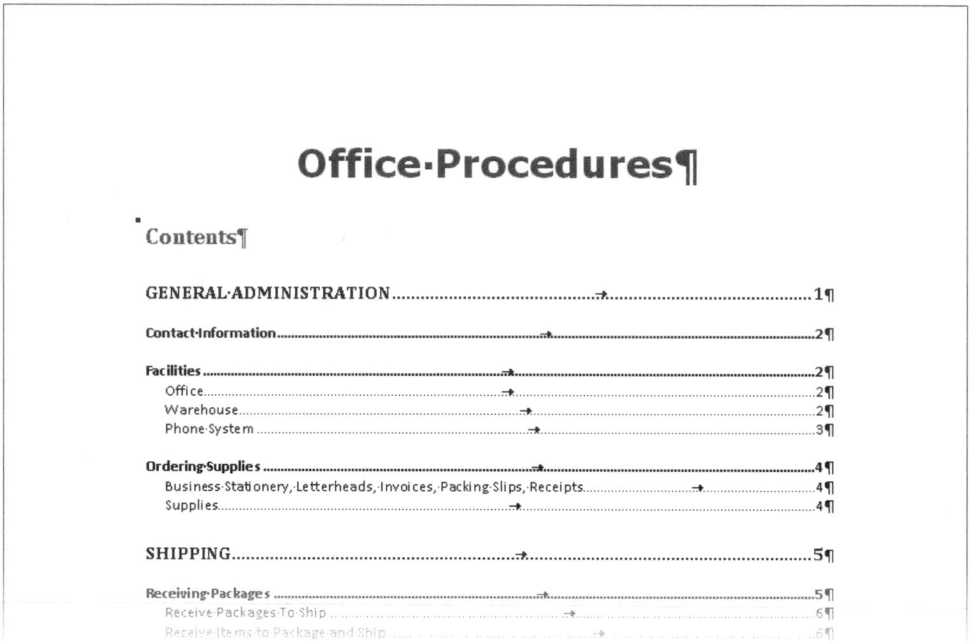

Office·Procedures¶

Contents¶

3. In the **Table of Contents** group, click the **Table of Contents** button, and then below the gallery, click **Remove Table of Contents**.

▐ Page Break

4. Position the insertion point to the left of *GENERAL ADMINISTRATION*, type Table of Contents, press the ⌈Enter⌉ key, and then on the **Insert** tab, in the **Pages** group, click the **Page Break** button.

5. Press the ⌈↑⌉ key to position the insertion point in the empty page break paragraph.

> **Tip** If you want to see this paragraph, display non-printing characters.

6. On the **References** tab, in the **Table of Contents** group, click the **Table of Contents** button, and then below the gallery, click **Insert Table of Contents**.

The Table Of Contents dialog box opens.

7. On the **Table of Contents** tab, under **General**, click the **Formats** arrow, and then in the list, click **Classic**.

   Examples of the Classic table of contents format appears in the preview boxes.

8. Click the **Tab leader** arrow, and then in the list, click the dotted line.

   The Print Preview box changes to display dotted tab leaders.

9. Click **OK** to insert the table of contents, and then press [Ctrl]+[Home] to return to the beginning of the document.

10. Point to any entry in the table.

    A ScreenTip appears, notifying you that you can hold down the Ctrl key and click any entry in the table of contents to jump to that heading in the document.

11. Click anywhere in the table.

    The entire table is selected, because it consists of only one field.

12. Move to the top of the third page, click at the beginning of the *Contact Information* heading, and then press [Ctrl]+[Enter] to insert a page break.

    The *Contact Information* heading is now on Page 4.

13. Scroll down to the *Ordering Supplies* heading, and insert a page break before that heading.

14. On the **References** tab, in the **Table of Contents** group, click the **Update Table** button.

    The Update Table Of Contents dialog box opens.

15. Select the **Update entire table** option, and click **OK**. Then press Ctrl + Home .

Word has updated the table of contents to reflect the new page numbers.

CLOSE the *02_Contents* document without saving your changes.

Creating Other Types of Tables

If a document includes figures or tables that have descriptions, or *captions*, you can tell Word to create a *table of figures*. If a legal document contains items such as regulations, cases, and statutes that are identified as legal citations, you can tell Word to create a *table of authorities*. Word uses the captions or citations to create these types of tables the same way it uses headings to create a table of contents.

To insert a caption:

1. Position the insertion point where you want the caption to appear (usually directly after the figure), and then on the **References** tab, in the **Captions** group, click the **Insert Caption** button.

   The Caption dialog box opens.

2. If you want to change the designator shown in the **Caption** box (the default is *Figure*), click **New Label**, type the caption you want, and then click **OK**.

3. In the **Caption** box, click to the right of the default text and number, press Space , type the caption, and then click **OK**.

   Word adds the caption to the document.

To create a table of figures:

1. Position the insertion point where you want to insert the table of figures, and then on the **References** tab, in the **Captions** group, click **Insert Table of Figures**.

   The Table Of Figures dialog box opens.

2. If you want to change the default type of caption to be included in the table, under **General**, click the **Caption label** arrow, and then in the list, click the type of caption you want.

3. If you want to change the default table format, click the **Formats** arrow, and then in the list, click the format you want.

4. Select any additional options you want, and then click **OK**.

   Word inserts the table in the specified format above the insertion point.

To insert a legal citation:

1. Select the first legal reference that you want to mark with a citation.

2. On the **References** tab, in the **Table of Authorities** group, click the **Mark Citation** button.

   The Mark Citation dialog box opens.

3. In the **Selected text** box and the **Short citation** box, edit the citation to reflect the way you want it to appear in the table.

4. If you want to change the category, click the **Category** arrow, and then in the list, click the category that applies to the citation.

5. To mark a single citation, click **Mark**. To mark all citations that match the selected citation, click **Mark All**.

To create a table of authorities:

1. Position the insertion point where you want the table of authorities to appear, and then on the **References** tab, in the **Table of Authorities** group, click the **Insert Table of Authorities** button.

   The Table Of Authorities dialog box opens.

2. In the **Category** list, click the category of citations that you want to appear in the table, or click **All** to include all categories.

3. Select formatting options for the table, and then click **OK**.

   Word inserts the table in the specified format before the insertion point.

Creating and Modifying an Index

To help readers find specific concepts and terms that might not be readily located by looking at a table of contents, you can include an *index* at the end of a document. Word creates an index by compiling an alphabetical listing with page numbers based on *index entry fields* that you have marked in the document. As with a table of contents, an index is inserted at the insertion point as a single field.

> **Tip** You don't need to create indexes for documents that will be distributed electronically because readers can use the Find feature or Windows Desktop Search to go directly to search terms.

In the index, an *index entry* might apply to a word or phrase that appears on a single page or is discussed for several pages. The entry might have related *subentries*. For example, the main index entry *shipping* might have below it the subentries *supplies*, *procedures*, and *packing*. An index might also include *cross-reference entries* that direct readers to related entries. For example, the main index entry *shipping* might have below it a cross-reference to *warehouse*.

To insert an index entry field in the document, you select the text you want to mark, and click Mark Entry in the Index group on the References tab to open the Mark Index Entry dialog box, where you can do the following:

- Use the selected text as is, modify the entry, and add a subentry.
- Format the entry—for example, to make it appear bold or italic in the index—by right-clicking it, clicking Font, and selecting the options you want.
- Designate the entry as a cross-reference, a single-page entry, or a page-range entry.

> **Tip** Cross-references appear in the index in the format
>
> intercom. *See* phones
>
> In this manner, you can direct readers to index terms they might not think of when looking for specific information.

● Specify the formatting of this entry's page number.

After you have set the options in the dialog box the way you want them, you can insert an index entry field adjacent to the selected text by clicking Mark, or adjacent to every occurrence of the selected text in the document by clicking Mark All. The Mark Index Entry dialog box remains open to simplify the process of inserting multiple index entry fields—you don't have to click the Mark Entry button for each new entry. You can move the dialog box off to the side so that it doesn't block the text you're working with.

> **Tip** When building an index, you should choose the text you mark carefully, bearing in mind what terms readers are likely to look up. One reader might expect to find information about *cell phones* by looking under *cell*, whereas another might look under *mobile*, another under *phones*, and another under *telephones*. A good index will include all four entries.

Index entry fields are formatted as hidden; you cannot see them unless you click the Show/Hide ¶ button in the Paragraph group on the Home tab. When the field is visible, it appears in the document enclosed in quotation marks within a set of braces, with the designator XE and a dotted underline.

Hidden index entry field
with main entry and subentry

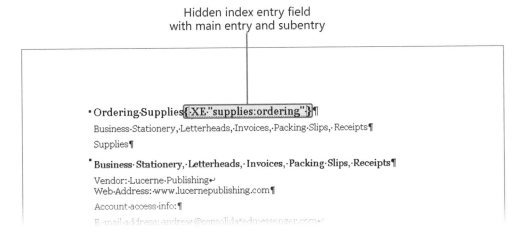

> **Tip** You can hide any text in a document by selecting it, clicking the Font Dialog Box Launcher on the Home tab, selecting the Hidden check box, and clicking OK. When you print the document, Word will not include the hidden text unless you click Options in the Print dialog box and then under Printing Options, select the Print Hidden Text check box.

You can change the text of an index entry by editing the text within the quotation marks in the index entry field as you would any other. (You could also edit the text in the inserted index, but that change would not be permanent; regenerating the index or pulling index entry fields for another purpose would restore the original entry.) To delete an index entry, you select the entire hidden field and then press the Delete key. You can also move and copy index entries using the techniques you would use for regular text.

> **Tip** Dragging through any part of an index entry field that includes one of the enclosing braces selects the entire field.

To create an index based on its index entries, you position the insertion point where you want the index to appear and then click the Insert Index button in the Index group on the Reference tab to open the Index dialog box, where you can specify the following:

- Whether the index formatting should use styles from the current template or be based on one of six predefined formats that you can preview in the Print Preview box.
- Whether page numbers should be right-aligned, and if so whether they should have dotted, dashed, or solid tab leaders.
- Whether the index should be indented, with each subentry on a separate line below the main entries, or run-in, with subentries on the same line as the main entries.

When you click OK in the Index dialog box, Word calculates the page numbers of all the entries and subentries, consolidates them, and inserts the index as a single field in the specified format at the specified location in the document. If you make changes to the document that affect its index entries or page numbering, you can update the index by clicking it and then clicking the Update Index button in the Index group on the References tab.

> **Tip** You can also update the index by right-clicking it and then clicking Update Field.

In this exercise, you will first mark a few index entries and a cross-reference entry. Then you'll create and format an index, delete an index entry from the document, and update the index.

USE the *03_Index* document. This practice file is located in the *Chapter08* subfolder under *SBS_Word2007*.

BE SURE TO display non-printing characters before starting this exercise.

OPEN the *03_Index* document.

1. In the table of contents, point to the **Warehouse** heading, hold down the ⌃Ctrl key, and then click the heading to move to the bottom of Page 3.

2. In the paragraph below the heading, select the word **Receiving**. Then on the **References** tab, in the **Index** group, click the **Mark Entry** button.

Mark Entry

The Mark Index Entry dialog box opens.

> **Mark Index Entry**
>
> Index
>
> Main entry: Receiving
>
> Subentry:
>
> Options
>
> ○ Cross-reference: See
>
> ● Current page
>
> ○ Page range
>
> Bookmark:
>
> Page number format
>
> ☐ Bold
>
> ☐ Italic
>
> This dialog box stays open so that you can mark multiple index entries.
>
> Mark   Mark All   Cancel

3. In the **Main entry** box, change *Receiving* to *receiving* (with a lowercase *r*).

> **Tip** Index entries will appear in the index exactly as they appear in the Mark Index Entry dialog box. For consistency, make all entries lowercase except those for proper nouns.

4. Click **Mark All**.

Word inserts hidden index entry fields adjacent to every occurrence of the word *Receiving* in the document.

> **Tip** If this document contained instances of the word *receiving*, those would not be marked because their capitalization does not match the selected word.

5. In the same paragraph, select the word **Shipping**, and click the title bar of the **Mark Index Entry** dialog box to activate it and enter the selected text. Then change the first letter in the **Main entry** box from uppercase to lowercase, and click **Mark All**.

6. Repeat Step 5 for the words **Packaging** and **Inventory** in the same paragraph.

> **Troubleshooting** You might have to move the dialog box to see and select the words you want to mark.

7. On the next page, in the paragraph under the *Phone System* heading, select the word **phone**, and then in the **Mark Index Entry** dialog box, change the entry to phones, and click **Mark All**.

8. In the same paragraph, select the word **intercom**, and then in the **Mark Index Entry** dialog box, under **Options**, select the **Cross-reference** option.

   The insertion point moves to the space after the word *See* in the adjacent box.

9. Without moving the insertion point, type phones, and then click **Mark**.

   A cross-reference to the *phones* index entry appears adjacent to the word *intercom*.

10. Move to Page **5**, and select the word **Supplies** in *Ordering Supplies*. Then in the **Mark Index Entry** dialog box, change word in the **Main entry** box to supplies, type ordering in the **Subentry** box, and click **Mark**.

11. Move to the bottom of Page **6**, and select the word **Packages** in the second *Receiving Packages* heading. Then in the **Mark Index Entry** dialog box, replace the word *Packages* in the **Main entry** box with supplies, type receiving in the **Subentry** box, and click **Mark**.

12. Close the **Mark Index Entry** dialog box.

13. Press ⌃Ctrl + End to move to the end of the document, and then press ⌃Ctrl + Enter to insert a page break.

    The insertion point moves to the top of the new page.

14. Type Index, press Enter , apply the **Heading 1** style to the new heading, press Ctrl + Enter , and then press Enter again.

15. On the **Home** tab, in the **Paragraph** group, click the **Show/Hide ¶** button to hide non-printing characters.

¶

Show/Hide ¶

> **Troubleshooting** When hidden text is visible, the document might not be paginated correctly. Always turn off the display of non-printing characters before creating an index.

16. On the **References** tab, in the **Index** group, click the **Insert Index** button.

Insert Index

    The Index dialog box opens.

17. In the **Columns** box, change the setting to **1**.

18. Click the **Formats** arrow, and in the list, click **Formal**.

19. Clear the **Right align page numbers** check box. Then click **OK**.

   Word compiles a short index based on the few index entries you just marked. The index is formatted in one column with the page numbers adjacent to their index entries.

20. Display non-printing characters so that you can see the index entry fields in the document, and move to the *Phone System* heading on Page **4**.

21. Select the entire cross-reference entry following *intercom*, and press the ⌷Del⌷ key.

> **Troubleshooting** If you find it hard to select just this entry, try pointing to the right of the closing brace (}) and dragging slightly to the left.

The cross-reference entry is deleted from the document.

22. Press [Ctrl]+[End] to move to the end of the document, and click anywhere in the index to select it.

23. Hide the non-printing characters. Then on the **References** tab, in the **Index** group, [Update Index] click the **Update Index** button.

The index is updated to reflect that you have deleted the cross-reference.

> ✖ **CLOSE** the *03_Index* document without saving your changes.

Adding Bookmarks and Cross-References

Word provides several tools for navigating long documents, two of which—bookmarks and cross-references—enable you to jump easily to designated places within the same document. Both tools require you to mark locations in the document and name them.

See Also For information about using hyperlinks to jump to other locations, see "Adding Hyperlinks" later in this chapter. For information about using the Document Map to jump to any paragraph styled as a heading, see "Displaying Different Views of a Document" in Chapter 1, "Exploring Word 2007."

Whether the document you are reading was created by you or by someone else, you can insert bookmarks to flag information to which you might want to return later. Like a physical bookmark, a Word bookmark marks a specific place in a document. After inserting a bookmark, you can quickly jump to it by displaying the Bookmark dialog box, clicking the bookmark you want to locate, and then clicking Go To.

> **Tip** Alternatively, you can display the Go To tab of the Find And Replace dialog box, click Bookmark in the Go To What list, and then select the bookmark you want from the Enter Bookmark Name list.

If you are developing a long document, you can create cross-references to quickly move readers to associated information elsewhere in the document. You can create cross-references to two types of elements:

- Headings, figures, and tables, for which Word automatically creates pointers
- Manually created bookmarks

If you later delete an item you have designated as the target of a cross-reference, you will need to update the cross-reference.

In this exercise, you will insert a bookmark and then jump to it. You will also create a cross-reference, edit the referenced item, and then update the cross-reference.

> **USE** the *04_Bookmarks* document. This practice file is located in the *Chapter08* subfolder under *SBS_Word2007*.
>
> **OPEN** the *04_Bookmarks* document.

Find

1. On the **Home** tab, in the **Editing** group, click the **Find** arrow, and in the list, click **Go To**. The Find And Replace dialog box opens, with the Go To tab active.

2. With **Page** selected in the **Go to what** list, in the **Enter page number** box, type 8. Then click **Go To**, and click **Close**.

Bookmark

3. On Page 8, position the insertion point to the left of the *Checking the credit of new customers* heading, and then on the **Insert** tab, in the **Links** group, click the **Bookmark** button.

The Bookmark dialog box opens.

4. Move the dialog box to the right side of the screen, and then scroll the list of pre-defined bookmarks.

Word has already created bookmarks for headings down to the fourth level by re-moving articles (*a* and *the*), spaces, and punctuation and initial capping words. For example, notice the *DoesCustomerAlreadyHaveAccount* bookmark for the fourth-level *Does the customer already have an account?* heading on this page.

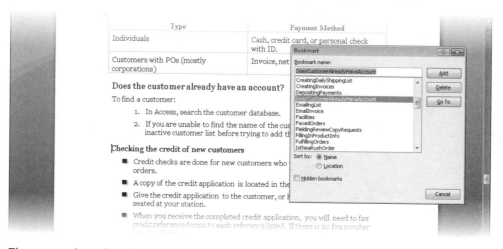

The name that already appears in the Bookmark Name box is the name of the bookmark selected in the list below, not a suggested name for your new book-mark. Replacing it will not delete that existing bookmark.

5. In the **Bookmark name** box, type **CreditCheck**, and then click **Add**.

> **Troubleshooting** Bookmark names cannot contain spaces. If you enter a space and then type a character, the Add button becomes inactive. To name bookmarks with multiple words, either run the words together and capitalize each word or re-place the spaces with underscores for readability.

The Bookmark dialog box closes, and although you can't see it, a bookmark named CreditCheck is inserted into the document.

> **Tip** To know whether a document contains bookmarks, display the Bookmark dialog box. You can sort the bookmarks alphabetically or in the order in which they are located.

6. Press [Ctrl]+[Home] to move to the beginning of the document. Then on the **Home** tab, in the **Editing** group, click the **Find** arrow, and click **Go To**.

7. In the **Find and Replace** dialog box, in the **Go to what** list, click **Bookmark**.

The dialog box changes so that you can specify the bookmark you want to jump to.

8. Click the **Enter bookmark name** arrow, click **CreditCheck** in the list, and then click **Go To**.

The insertion point moves to the location of the bookmark. The dialog box remains open in case you want to move somewhere else.

9. Close the **Find and Replace** dialog box.

> **Tip** To delete a bookmark, click Bookmark in the Links group on the Insert tab, click the bookmark's name, and then click Delete.

10. At the top of Page **7**, position the insertion point at the right end of the Step 1 paragraph, press ⎵Space⎵, type For more information, see, and then press ⎵Space⎵ again.

11. On the **Insert** tab, in the **Links** group, click the **Cross-reference** button.

⊡ Cross-reference   The Cross-Reference dialog box opens.

12. Click the **Reference type** arrow, and in the list, click **Heading**. Then with **Heading text** selected in the **Insert reference to** box, scroll the **For which heading** list, and click **Does the customer already have an account?**.

13. Click **Insert**, and then click **Close**.

   The text *Does the customer already have an account?* appears in the document at the insertion point. Although it is not obvious, the text is inserted as a single field and formatted as a cross-reference.

14. Hold down the `Ctrl` key, and then click the cross-reference to move to that heading.

15. In the heading, click to position the insertion point after the word *account* (before the question mark), press `Space`, and then type **with us**.

16. Move back to the top of Page 7, and at the end of the Step 1 paragraph, click **Does the customer have an account?** to select the cross-reference field.

> **Troubleshooting** Don't select the *For more information, see* introductory text.

17. Right-click the selected cross-reference, and then click **Update Field**.

   Word inserts the words *with us* at the end of the cross-reference to reflect the change you made to the heading.

18. Hold down `Ctrl`, and click the cross-reference to return to the associated heading.

> ✕ **CLOSE** the *04_Bookmarks* document without saving your changes.

Adding Hyperlinks

Like Web pages, Word documents can include hyperlinks that provide a quick way to perform tasks such as opening another document, downloading a file, or sending an e-mail message. You insert hyperlinks into a Word document by displaying the Insert Hyperlink dialog box, specifying the type of link you want to create, and then entering an appropriate target for that type of link.

While creating a hyperlink to a target in the same document, in another document, or on a Web page, you can specify whether the target information should appear in the same window or frame as the document or in a new window or frame. You can also make a particular setting the default for all hyperlinks.

> **Tip** When the target is a Web page, you specify its location by using its *Uniform Resource Locator (URL)*, such as *www.microsoft.com*.

Within a document, hyperlinks appear underlined and in the color specified for hyperlinks by the document's theme. You can jump to the target of the hyperlink by holding down the Ctrl key and clicking the link. After you click the hyperlink, it appears in the color specified for followed hyperlinks.

To edit or remove a hyperlink, you can select it and click Hyperlink in the Links group on the Insert tab or you can right-click the selection and then click the appropriate command.

In this exercise, you will insert, test, and modify a hyperlink.

> **USE** the *05_Hyperlinks* and *05_OtherLogos* documents. These practice files are located in the *Chapter08* subfolder under *SBS_Word2007*.
>
> **OPEN** the *05_Hyperlinks* document.

Hyperlink

1. Click the **Wide World Importers** logo graphic at the top of the page. Then on the **Insert** tab, in the **Links** group, click the **Hyperlink** button.

   The Insert Hyperlink dialog box opens. On the Link To bar, Existing File Or Web Page is selected, and the dialog box shows the contents of the *Chapter08* practice file folder.

> **Troubleshooting** If you don't see the contents of the *Chapter08* folder, click Existing File Or Web Page on the Link To bar, and then navigate to your *Documents\ MSP\SBS_Word 2007\Chapter08 folder*.

2. In the list of file names, click (don't double-click) the *05_OtherLogos* document, and then click **Target Frame**.

The Set Target Frame dialog box opens with Page Default (none) selected as the frame in which the document will open.

3. Click the **Select the frame** arrow, and in the list, click **New window**. Then click **OK**.

4. Click **OK** to insert a hyperlink from the logo graphic to the specified document, and then click a blank area of the document to release the selection.

> **Troubleshooting** When a hyperlinked word or object (such as the logo) is selected, the hyperlink might not work correctly.

5. Point to the logo.

Word displays a ScreenTip that shows the path to the *05_OtherLogos* document and instructions for following the link.

6. Hold down [Ctrl], and then click the logo.

Word opens the *05_OtherLogos* document in a new window.

7. On the **View** tab, in the **Window** group, click the **Switch Windows** button, and then click *05_Hyperlinks*.

8. Move to Page 2, click at the end of the paragraph in the sidebar, and press [Enter] twice.

9. Type Please contact us if you need more information, and then select the text.

10. On the **Insert** tab, in the **Links** group, click the **Hyperlink** button, and then on the **Link to** bar of the **Insert Hyperlink** dialog box, click **E-mail Address**.

The dialog box changes so that you can enter the information appropriate for an e-mail hyperlink.

11. In the **E-mail address** box, type Kelly@wideworldimporters.com.

> **Tip** When you begin typing the e-mail address, Word inserts *mailto:* in front of it.

When a person clicks the link, Word will start his or her default e-mail program and open a new e-mail message window.

12. In the **Subject** box, type Room Planner inquiry.

This text will be automatically entered in the Subject box of the new message.

13. Click **OK**.

The hyperlinked text is indicated by an underline and its assigned theme color. Pointing to it displays a ScreenTip with the hyperlink's target.

14. Right-click the **Please contact us** hyperlink, and then click **Edit Hyperlink**.

The Edit Hyperlink dialog box opens with the current destination for this link in the E-Mail Address box.

15. In the upper-right corner of the dialog box, click **ScreenTip**.

The Set Hyperlink ScreenTip dialog box opens.

16. In the **ScreenTip text** box, type Send e-mail message to Wide World Importers, and then click **OK**.

17. In the **E-mail address** box, replace *Kelly* with Carlos, and click **OK**.

18. Point to the hyperlink to see the new ScreenTip. Then hold down ⌖Ctrl⌕, and click the hyperlink.

Your e-mail program opens, with the specified e-mail address in the To box and the specified description in the Subject box.

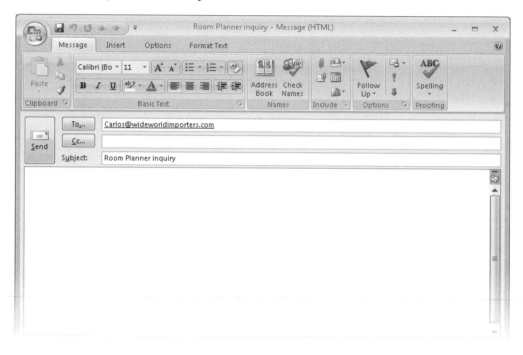

19. Close the message window, clicking **No** when asked whether you want to save the changes.

The hyperlinked text is now displayed in the color assigned to followed hyperlinks.

> **CLOSE** the *05_OtherLogos* and *05_Hyperlinks* documents without saving your changes.

Adding Sources and Compiling a Bibliography

Word 2007 includes the new Source Manager feature, which keeps track of the sources you use while researching a document and helps you reference them in the proper format. Whether your sources are books, periodicals, Web pages, or interviews, you can record details about them and then select a common style guide, such as the *Chicago Manual of Style*, to have Word automatically list your sources in that style guide's standard format.

Adding Footnotes and Endnotes

When you want to make a comment about a statement in a document—for example, to explain an assumption or cite the source for a different opinion—you can enter the comment as a footnote or an endnote. Doing so inserts a number or symbol called a *reference mark*, and your associated comment appears with the same number or symbol either as a *footnote* at the bottom of the page or as an *endnote* at the end of the document or document section. In most views, footnotes or endnotes are divided from the main text by a *note separator* line.

To create a footnote or endnote:

1. With the insertion point where you want the reference mark to appear, on the **References** tab, in the **Footnotes** group, click either the **Insert Footnote** or the **Insert Endnote** button.

   Word inserts the reference mark in the document and creates a linked area at the bottom of the page or end of the section.

2. Type the note text.

Word applies default styles to the reference marks for footnotes and endnotes. By default, footnote reference marks use the 1, 2, 3 format, and endnote reference marks use the i, ii, iii style. To change the number format of existing footnotes or endnotes:

1. On the **References** tab, click the **Footnotes** Dialog Box Launcher.

2. In the Footnote and Endnote dialog box, select the **Footnotes** or **Endnotes** option.

3. Under **Format**, click the **Number format** arrow, and then in the list, click the number format you want.

4. With **Whole document** shown in the **Apply changes to** box, click **Apply**.

   All footnotes or endnotes change to the new number format.

To change the formatting applied to footnote or endnote reference marks:

1. In the document text, select the reference mark for any footnote or endnote.

2. On the **Home** tab, in the **Editing** group, click the **Select** button, and then click **Select Text with Similar Formatting**.

   All the footnote or endnote reference marks are selected.

3. On the **Home** tab, apply the character formatting you want the reference marks to have.

   All the reference marks in the body of the document now appear with the character formatting you applied.

There are two ways to enter a new source:

- You can open the Source Manager dialog box and enter all the sources you know you will need to cite in the document.

- You can open the Create Source dialog box and enter the information for one specific source. When you click OK, the citation is entered in parentheses at the insertion point.

No matter which method you use to enter the source information, Word stores the sources in a separate file on your computer's hard disk so that you can cite them in any document you create. You can view this Master List and select which sources are available to the current document from the Source Manager dialog box. After you copy a source from the Master List to the Current List, you can cite it anywhere in the current document.

After you enter sources, you can easily compile them into a bibliography or list of works cited. The Bibliography gallery (available from the Citations & Bibliography group on the References tab) includes two options:

- **Bibliography.** This option builds the source list at the insertion point with a Bibliography heading.

- **Works Cited.** This option builds the source list at the insertion point with a Works Cited heading.

You can also click Insert Bibliography at the bottom of the gallery to insert a list of sources without a heading.

When you compile a bibliography, Word inserts it at the insertion point as a single field. You can edit the text of a bibliography, but if the source information might change, it is much easier to update it in the same way you would a table of contents or index.

> **Tip** You can update a bibliography by clicking the bibliography, and then clicking the Update Citations and Bibliography button that appears above the field. If you used the Insert Bibliography command to compile the source list, the Update Citations and Bibliography button does not appear when you click the field. In that case, you can update the bibliography by right-clicking anywhere in the field and then clicking Update Field.

In this exercise, you will enter information for a couple of sources, insert citations for existing sources, add a new source, compile a bibliography, and then change its format.

> **USE** the *06_Bibliography1* and *06_Bibliography2* documents. These practice files are located in the *Chapter08* subfolder under *SBS_Word2007*.
> **OPEN** the *06_Bibliography1* document.

1. On the **References** tab, in the **Citations & Bibliography** group, click the **Style** arrow, and then click **Chicago**.

Any sources you create and citations you insert will be formatted according to the *Chicago Manual of Style* rules.

2. In the **Citations & Bibliography** group, click the **Manage Sources** button.

The Source Manager dialog box opens.

> **Troubleshooting** Don't worry if your dialog box already contains sources. If other documents on your hard disk contain citations, their source information might appear.

3. In the **Source Manager** dialog box, click **New**.

The Create Source dialog box opens.

4. With **Book** selected in the **Type of Source** list, under **Bibliography Fields for Chicago**, type Goldberg, Gale Beth in the **Author** box, Bamboo in the **Title** box, 2004 in the **Year** box, Gibbs Smith in the **Publisher** box, and then click **OK**.

The new source is added not only to the Master List but also to the Current List, which is the list of sources that can be used in this document.

5. In the **Source Manager** dialog box, click **New**, and then in the **Create Source** dialog box, click **Edit**.

The Edit Name dialog box opens.

6. Under **Add name**, type Cusack in the **Last** box, type Victor in the **First** box, and then click **Add**.

Cusack, Victor appears in the Names box.

The new source is added not only to the Master List but also to the Current List, which is the list of sources that can be used in this document.

7. To enter a second author for the same book, type Stewart in the **Last** box, type Deirdre in the **First** box, click **Add**, and then click **OK**.

8. In the **Create Source** dialog box, type Bamboo World in the **Title** box, 2000 in the **Year** box, and Simon & Schuster Australia in the **Publisher** box. Then click **OK**.

9. Close the **Source Manager** dialog box.

10. Open the *06_Bibliography2* document, and then open the **Source Manager** dialog box.

The two sources you just entered appear in the Master List but not in the Current List, meaning they are not available for use in this document.

11. With the **Cusack** source selected in the **Master List** box, click **Copy** to make that source available in this document. Then copy the **Goldberg** source to the **Current List** box, and click **Close**.

12. In the document, position the insertion point to the right of *Bamboo Style* on the last line of the first paragraph. Then on the **References** tab, in the **Citations & Bibliography** group, click the **Insert Citation** button, and in the list of citations, click **Goldberg, Gale Beth**.

Word inserts the source in parentheses.

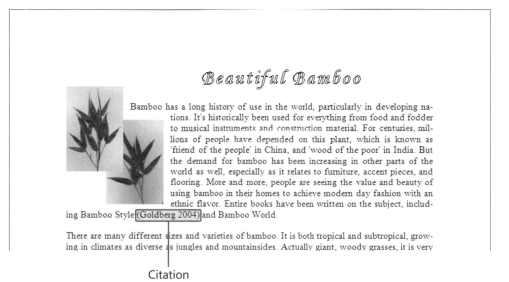

Citation

13. Insert a **Cusack, Victor** citation to the right of *Bamboo World* (but before the period) at the end of the same paragraph.

14. Position the insertion point to the right of *Entire books*, and then in the **Citations & Bibliography** group, click the **Insert Citation** button, and in the list, click **Add New Source**.

15. In the **Create Source** dialog box, click the **Type of Source** arrow, and then click **Web site**. Then type American Bamboo Society in the **Name of Web Page** box, 2006 in the **Year** box, and www.americanbamboo.org/BooksOnBamboo.html in the **URL** box, and click **OK**.

Word inserts the source in parentheses at the insertion point.

16. In the **Citations & Bibliography** group, click the **Manage Sources** button.

In the Source Manager dialog box, the new citation appears in both the Master List and the Current List. Because the sources in the Current List are actually cited in the document, they have a check mark beside them.

17. Close the **Source Manager** dialog box, and then press Ctrl + End to move to the end of the document.

18. In the **Citations & Bibliography** group, click **Bibliography**, and then in the gallery, click **Bibliography**.

Word inserts a bibliography of all the citations in the document in alphabetical order and formatted according to the *Chicago* style.

Bibliography

American Bamboo Society. 2006. www.americanbamboo.org/BooksOnBamboo.html.
Cusack, Victor, and Deirdre Stewart. *Bamboo World.* Simon & Shuster Australia, 2000.
Goldberg, Gale Beth. *Bamboo Style.* Gibbs Smith, 2004.

19. In the **Citations & Bibliography** group, click the **Style** arrow, and in the list, click **APA**.

> **Tip** You don't have to select the bibliography to apply this change; you can do it from anywhere in the document.

The format of the bibliography and of the citations changes to bring it in line with the *Associated Press* style.

> **CLOSE** the *06_Bibliography1* and *06_Bibliography2* documents without saving your changes.

Key Points

- Word comes with predefined building blocks you can use to quickly create a specific type of document or to add an element to an existing document.

- You can quickly navigate to specific points in a document by using bookmarks to flag information you might want to look up later, and cross-references to quickly jump to related information.

- A table of contents provides an overview of the topics covered in a document and lets readers navigate quickly to a topic. You can format the table of contents by selecting a predefined format or by changing individual table of content styles.

- After marking index entries for key concepts, words, and phrases, you can use the Insert Index command to tell Word to compile the index.

- Documents can contain hyperlinks to Web pages, files, bookmarks, or e-mail addresses.

Chapter at a Glance

	A	B	C	D	E	F	G	H
1	FirstName	LastName	Address1	City	State	PostalCode		
2	Linda	Martin	7899 38th St.	Tucker	NJ	90025		
3	Garth	Fort	5678 Ford Ave.	Planter	WA	10002		
4	Dan	Wilson	1234 Editorial Way	Harvest	WA	10004		
5	Mike	Tiano	456 South Rd.	Harvest	WA	10004		
6	John	Rodman	987 Hard Rock Way	Poter				
7								
8								
9								

Prepare data for mail merge, **page 257**

Prepare a form letter, **page 263**

Wide World Importers

3456 ELM STREET, SAN FRANCISCO, CA 10012

February 18, 2007

«AddressBlock»

«GreetingLine»

I want to take a moment to thank you for your continued support of Wide World Importers. Because loyal customers like you come back year after year, we are growing rapidly.

As you know, we will celebrate our 10th anniversary on March 15. In honor of that occasion, we are holding a special *March Madness* sale! Everything in the store will be 10% off throughout the month, and selected specials at higher discounts will be offered each day. Please pick up one of our promotional flyers the next time you visit the store for a complete schedule of these special offerings.

«FirstName», for even greater savings, be sure to bring this letter with you when you shop. Identify yourself as a VIP Customer by presenting the letter to your salesperson at the time of your purchase, and you will receive an additional 5% off your total bill.

Hello Andrea,

Thank you for your recent visit to our store. It was a pleasure to be able to answer your decorating questions and offer suggestions. As you requested, we have added your name to our online mailing list. You will be receiving our monthly newsletter, as well as advance notice of upcoming shipments and in-store events.

You can also visit our Web site at www.wideworldimporters.com for a schedule of events, links to online decorating resources, articles on furniture care, and more.

Contact us at customerservice@wideworldimport... (925) 555-0167.

Create and print labels, **page 274**

Send a personalized e-mail message to multiple recipients, **page 270**

Garth·Fort¶	Dan·Wilson¶
5678·Ford·Ave.¶	1234·Editorial·Way¶
Planter,·WA·10002¶	Harvest,·WA·10004¶
Mike·Tiano¶	Heidi·Steen¶
456·South·Rd.¶	678·Pine·St.¶
Harvest,·WA·10004¶	Agriculture,·WA·10003¶

9 Creating Form Letters, E-Mail Messages, and Labels

In this chapter, you will learn to:

- ✔ Understand mail merge.
- ✔ Prepare data for mail merge.
- ✔ Prepare a form letter.
- ✔ Merge a form letter with its data source.
- ✔ Send a personalized e-mail message to multiple recipients.
- ✔ Create and print labels.

Many businesses and other organizations communicate with their customers or members by means of letters, newsletters, and promotional pieces that are sent to everyone on a mailing list. The easiest way to generate a set of documents that are identical except for certain information—such as the name, address, and greeting of a letter—is to use a process called *mail merge*. If you have a list of potential recipients stored in a consistent format, you can use the mail merge process to easily produce a set of personalized documents and mailing labels.

In this chapter, you will use the Mail Merge wizard to guide you through the process of creating a form letter. You will select a data source, add a record to it, sort it, and filter it. You will then add merge fields for an address and greeting line to an existing form letter, preview the merged data, exclude recipients from the merge, merge the letters into a new document, and then save the merged file. You will also set up and send a merged e-mail message. Finally, you will create and print mailing labels.

See Also Do you need only a quick refresher on the topics in this chapter? See the Quick Reference entries on pages xxxix–lxiii.

> **Important** Before you can use the practice files in this chapter, you need to install them from the book's companion CD to their default location. See "Using the Book's CD" on page xxv for more information.

> **Troubleshooting** Graphics and operating system–related instructions in this book reflect the Windows Vista user interface. If your computer is running Microsoft Windows XP and you experience trouble following the instructions as written, please refer to the "Information for Readers Running Windows XP" section at the beginning of this book.

Understanding Mail Merge

The mail merge process combines the static information from one document with variable information from another document, as follows:

- *Main document.* This is a document, such as a letter or e-mail message, that contains the static text that will appear in all the merged documents, plus placeholders—called *merge fields*—that tell Word where to insert the variable information.

- *Data source.* This is a structured document, such as customer list stored in a Word table, a Microsoft Office Excel worksheet, or a Microsoft Office Access database table, or a Microsoft Office Outlook contacts list, that contains sets— called *records*—of information in a predictable format. You can use an existing data source, or you can create a new one as part of the mail merge process.

You can use the Mail Merge wizard in Word to merge a main document with a data source in easy steps. The first step is to select from a list of document types that includes letters, e-mail messages, envelopes, labels, and a directory. The type you select determines the subsequent steps. The end result is one copy of the merged document for every record in the data source.

You can merge the main document and data source into a new document, with each merged document separated from the next by a page break. You can then personalize the merged documents before printing, and you can save the document for later use. If you don't need to edit or save the merged documents, you can merge the main document and data source directly to the printer or to an e-mail message.

> **Tip** When you have some experience with mail merge, you might want to use the buttons on the Mailings tab to create and merge documents, instead of the Mail Merge wizard.

Preparing Data for Mail Merge

Before you can merge documents, you need to either specify an existing data source or create one. The data source consists of a matrix of rows and columns, with each row containing one record, such as the complete name and address of a customer, and each column containing a particular type of information—called a *field*—such as the first name of a customer. Each field is identified in the data source by the column heading—called a *field name*—in the first row of the data source.

> **Tip** Because the field names are also used as the merge fields in the main document, they cannot contain spaces. To make the field names readable with no spaces, capitalize each word, as in *PostalCode*, or replace the spaces with underscores, as in *Last_Name*.

	A	B	C	D	E	F	G
1	FirstName	LastName	Address1	City	State	PostalCode	
2	Linda	Martin	7899 38th St.	Tucker	NJ	90025	
3	Garth	Fort	5678 Ford Ave.	Planter	WA	10002	
4	Dan	Wilson	1234 Editorial Way	Harvest	WA	10004	
5	Mike	Tiano	456 South Rd.	Harvest	WA	10004	
6	John	Rodman	987 Hard Rock Way	Potential	DE	97540	
7							
8							

Field name (points to PostalCode in row 1)

Record (points to row 6)

Field (points to column C)

If the data source contains many records and it changes frequently, you might want to create it in a program designed for working with large amounts of data, such as Excel or Access. You can also use the contacts list from Outlook, Microsoft Windows Mail, or Microsoft Outlook Express (if your computer is running Microsoft Windows XP). If the data source contains only a few records and it won't be updated often, you can create it in Word, either as a table or as a list with each field separated by a tab. Or you can create it as part of the mail merge process.

What if you want to create merge documents for only a subset of the data in the data source? For example, you might have mail-order customers from all over the United States, but want to target a bulk mailing about a store sale to only customers with addresses in your state. After you specify the data source and create the main document, you can do the following:

- *Filter* the data source to create merged documents for only some of its data.
- Create a *query* (a set of selection criteria) to extract only the information you are interested in—for example, all the postal codes for your state.
- Sort the data source—for example, in postal code order for a bulk mailing.

When you use a filter or a query, all the data remains in the data source, but only the data that meets your specifications is used for the mail merge.

In this exercise, you will open a main document and use the Mail Merge Wizard to select the data source. You will then add a record to the data source, sort it, and filter it.

> **USE** the *02_PreparingData* document and *02_DataSource* workbook. These practice files are located in the *Chapter09* subfolder under *SBS_Word2007*.
>
> **BE SURE TO** start Word before beginning this exercise.
>
> **OPEN** the *02_PreparingData* document.

Start Mail Merge

1. On the **Mailings** tab, in the **Start Mail Merge** group, click the **Start Mail Merge** button, and then click **Step by Step Mail Merge Wizard**.

   The Mail Merge task pane opens, showing Step 1 of the wizard's six steps.

Mail Merge ▾ ✕
Select document type
What type of document are you working on?
◉ Letters
○ E-mail messages
○ Envelopes
○ Labels
○ Directory
Letters
Send letters to a group of people. You can personalize the letter that each person receives.
Click Next to continue.
Step 1 of 6
➡ Next: Starting document

2. In the **Mail Merge** task pane, with the **Letters** option selected, at the bottom of the pane, click **Next: Starting document**.

Step 2 appears in the Mail Merge task pane.

3. In the **Mail Merge** task pane, with the **Use the current document** option selected, click **Next: Select recipients**.

4. In the Step 3 pane, with the **Use an existing list** option selected, click **Browse**.

The Select Data Source dialog box opens so that you can navigate to and select the file in which your recipient information is stored.

5. In the **Favorite Links** list, click **Documents**, browse to the *MSP\SBS_Word2007\ Chapter09* folder, and double-click the *02_DataSource* workbook. Then click **OK** in the **Select Table** dialog box.

The Mail Merge Recipients dialog box opens, displaying the records contained in the data source.

6. Below the list of recipients in the top half of the dialog box, in the **Data Source** box, click *02_DataSource.xlsx*, and then click **Edit**.

The Edit Data Source dialog box opens.

7. Click **New Entry**, and then in the cell below *John*, type the following, pressing Tab to move from box to box:

FirstName   Heidi
LastName   Steen
Address1   678 Pine St.
City   Agriculture
State   WA
PostalCode   10003

> **Tip** You can add multiple records by clicking New Entry after you enter each record.

8. Click **OK**, and then click **Yes** to update the recipient list.

The new record appears at the bottom of the list of recipients in the Mail Merge Recipients dialog box.

9. Under **Refine recipient list**, click **Sort**.

The Filter And Sort dialog box opens, showing the Sort Records tab.

10. Click the **Sort by** arrow, click **PostalCode** in the list, and then click **OK**.

> **Tip** You can also sort data by clicking the arrow to the right of the field you want to sort on, and then clicking Sort Ascending or Sort Descending.

11. Scroll the recipient list to the right, and verify that the records are sorted in ascending order by the PostalCode field. Then under **Refine recipient list**, click **Filter**.

The Filter And Sort dialog box opens, showing the Filter Records tab.

> **Tip** You can also open the Filter And Sort dialog box by clicking the arrow to the right of any field name and then clicking Advanced.

12. Click the **Field** arrow, and then in the list, click **State**.

The Comparison box displays the default Equal To criterion.

13. In the **Compare to** box, type **WA**, and then click **OK**.

The Filter And Sort dialog box closes, and the Mail Merge Recipients dialog box is updated to show only Washington State residents in ascending PostalCode order. The other records are hidden and will be excluded from the merge process.

14. Click **OK** to close the Mail Merge Recipients dialog box.

> **CLOSE** the *02_PreparingData* document without saving your changes to the document or to the data source.

Using an Outlook Contacts List as a Data Source

Using information from an Outlook contacts list as the data source for the merge process requires a few extra steps in the Mail Merge Wizard.

To use Outlook information as the data source for a form letter:

1. On the **Mailings** tab, in the **Start Mail Merge** group, click **Start Mail Merge**, and then click **Step by Step Mail Merge Wizard**.

2. In the **Mail Merge** task pane, select the **Letters** option, and then click **Next: Starting document**.

3. In Step 2 of the wizard, select the **Use the current document** option, and then click **Next: Select recipients**.

4. In Step 3, select the **Select from Outlook contacts** option, and then click **Choose Contacts Folder**.

5. If you are prompted to select your Outlook profile, select the one you want to use, and then click **OK**.

   The Select Contacts dialog box opens.

6. Click a contacts list, and then click **OK**.

7. In the **Mail Merge Recipients** dialog box displaying your Outlook contacts, clear the check boxes of any contacts you want to exclude from the merge process. Then click **OK**.

8. In the **Mail Merge** task pane, click **Next: Write your letter**.

You can then continue with the next steps in the merge process, as explained in later topics in this chapter.

Preparing a Form Letter

One common type of main document used in the mail merge process is a form letter. This type of document typically contains merge fields for the name and address of each recipient along with text that is the same in all the letters. In the form letter, each merge field is enclosed in *guillemet characters*, also called *chevrons* (« and »)—for example, «AddressBlock».

February 18, 2007

«AddressBlock»

«GreetingLine»

I want to take a moment to thank you for your continued support of Wide World Importers. Because local customers like you come back year after year, we are growing rapidly.

Merge field

If you have already written the letter, you can insert the merge fields during the merge process; if you haven't written the letter, you can write it as part of the process. Either way, you first enter the text that will be common to all the letters and then insert the merge fields that will be replaced by the variable information from the data source.

> **Tip** If you need to stop before you finish the merge process, you can save the form letter to retain the work you have done so far. You can then open the form letter and resume from where you left off.

You can insert merge fields in two ways:

- From the Mail Merge task pane in Step 4 of the Mail Merge wizard.
- By clicking buttons in the Write & Insert Fields group on the Mailings tab.

Either way, clicking Address Block or Greeting Line opens a dialog box in which you can refine the fields' settings, whereas clicking individual fields inserts them with their default settings.

> **Tip** If you want to save the form letter without any mail merge information, you can click Start Mail Merge in the Start Mail Merge group on the Mailings tab, and then click Normal Word Document.

In this exercise, you will modify an existing form letter by adding merge fields for a standard inside address, an informal greeting line, and the recipient's first name.

> **USE** the *03_FormLetter* document and *03_DataSource* workbook. These practice files are located in the *Chapter09* subfolder under *SBS_Word2007*.
>
> **BE SURE TO** display non-printing characters before starting this exercise.

1. Open the *03_FormLetter* document.

2. In the Word message box prompting you to confirm that you want to run the command, click **Yes**.

   The Select Data source dialog box opens.

   > **Troubleshooting** You are prompted to attach the data source to the main document because the practice-file data source was not originally attached to the practice-file main document from your computer. When you are working with your own documents, you will not be prompted to attach the data source when you reopen your main document.

3. In the **Favorite Links** list, click **Documents**, and then browse to the *MSP\SBS_Word2007\Chapter09* folder. Double-click the *03_DataSource* workbook, and then in the **Select Table** dialog box, click **OK**.

   The main document opens with the *03_DataSource* workbook attached to it.

Start Mail Merge

4. On the **Mailings** tab, in the **Start Mail Merge** group, click the **Start Mail Merge** button, and then click **Step by Step Mail Merge Wizard**.

5. In the **Mail Merge** task pane, click **Next: Write your letter**.

6. In the document, position the insertion point in the second empty paragraph below the date, and then in the **Mail Merge** task pane, click **Address block**.

   > **Tip** You can easily position the insertion point without displaying non-printing characters by clicking at the right end of the date and then pressing the Down Arrow key twice.

The Insert Address Block dialog box opens. From this dialog box, you can refine the format of the fields that make up the Address Block merge field.

7. Click **OK** to accept the default settings.

   Word inserts the «AddressBlock» merge field into the document. When you merge the form letter with the data source, Word will substitute the component name and address information for this merge field.

8. Press the [Enter] key twice, and then in the **Mail Merge** task pane, click **Greeting line**.

   The Insert Greeting Line dialog box opens so that you can specify how the greeting line should appear in the merged letters.

Next

9. Under **Greeting line format**, click the arrow to the right of the second box, and then in the list, click **Joshua**.

10. Under **Preview**, click the **Next** button three times to view the greeting line for each of the recipients in the linked data source. Then click **OK** to close the Insert Greeting Line dialog box.

Word inserts the «GreetingLine» merge field into the document. When you merge the form letter with the data source, Word will replace this merge field with the word *Dear* and a space, followed by the information in the FirstName field, followed by a comma.

11. Position the insertion point at the beginning of the third paragraph of the letter (*For even greater savings...*).

12. In the **Mail Merge** task pane, click **More items**.

The Insert Merge Field dialog box opens.

```
Insert Merge Field                    ? ✕

  Insert:
        ○ Address Fields    ● Database Fields

  Fields:
  ┌──────────────────────────────────────┐
  │ FirstName                          ▲ │
  │ LastName                             │
  │ Address1                             │
  │ City                                 │
  │ State                                │
  │ PostalCode                           │
  │                                      │
  │                                      │
  │                                      │
  │                                    ▼ │
  └──────────────────────────────────────┘
  [ Match Fields... ]  [ Insert ]  [ Cancel ]
```

13. With the **Database Fields** option selected and **FirstName** highlighted in the **Fields** box, click **Insert**, and then click **Close**.

The «FirstName» merge field appears at the beginning of the third paragraph.

14. Without moving the insertion point, type a comma and press [Space]. Then change *For* to for.

The form letter is now ready for merging.

February 18, 2007

«AddressBlock»

«GreetingLine»

I want to take a moment to thank you for your continued support of Wide World Importers. Because loyal customers like you come back year after year, we are growing rapidly.

As you know, we will celebrate our 10th anniversary on March 15. In honor of that occasion, we are holding a special *March Madness* sale! Everything in the store will be 10% off throughout the month, and selected specials at higher discounts will be offered each day. Please pick up one of our promotional flyers the next time you visit the store for a complete schedule of these special offerings.

«FirstName», for even greater savings, be sure to bring this letter with you when you shop. Identify yourself as a VIP Customer by presenting the letter to your salesperson at the time of your purchase, and you will receive an additional 5% off your total bill.

Discounts and savings are our way of thanking you for your continued patronage of Wide World Importers. Remember, we are the one-stop design center for all of your home decor needs!

 CLOSE the *03_FormLetter* document without saving your changes.

Merging a Form Letter with Its Data Source

After you specify the data source you want to use and enter merge fields in the form letter, you can preview the merged letters before performing the actual merge. You can exclude recipients during this preview. When you are ready, you can either send the merged letters directly to the printer or you can merge them one after the other into a new document, separated by page breaks. If you merge to a new document, you have another chance to review and, if necessary, edit the merged letters before sending them to the printer.

In this exercise, you will preview merged letters, exclude recipients from the merge, merge the letters into a new document, and then save the merged file.

> **USE** the *04_MergingData* document and *04_DataSource* workbook. These practice files are located in the *Chapter09* subfolder under *SBS_Word2007*.
>
> **OPEN** the *04_MergingData* document. When Word asks you to confirm that you want to run a command that will attach data from the *04_DataSource* file to the document, click Yes, and then in the Select Data Source dialog box, browse to the *Chapter 09* folder, and double-click the *04_DataSource* file.

Start Mail Merge ▾

1. On the **Mailings** tab, in the **Start Mail Merge** group, click the **Start Mail Merge** button, and then click **Step by Step Mail Merge Wizard**.

2. At the bottom of the **Mail Merge** task pane, click **Next** twice to move to Step 5.

3. Scroll the letter until you can see the address block, the greeting line, and the third paragraph.

   Word displays a preview of how the first personalized letter will look when merged with the data source.

   February 18, 2007

   Linda Martin
   7899 38th St.
   Tucker, NJ 90025

   Dear Linda,

   I want to take a moment to thank you for your continued support of Wide World Importers. Because loyal customers like you come back year after year, we are growing rapidly.

   As you know, we will celebrate our 10th anniversary on March 15. In honor of that occasion, we are holding a special *March Madness* sale! Everything in the store will be 10% off throughout the month, and selected specials at higher discounts will be offered each day. Please pick up one of our promotional flyers the next time you visit the store for a complete schedule of these special offerings.

   Linda, for even greater savings, be sure to bring this letter with you when you shop. Identify yourself as a VIP Customer by presenting the letter to your salesperson at the time of your purchase, and you will receive an additional 5% off your total bill.

   Discounts and savings are our way of thanking you for your continued patronage of Wide World

4. Under **Preview your letters** in the **Mail Merge** task pane, click the **Next Record** button five times to preview all the letters.

>>
Next Record

> **Tip** You can also preview the next or previous documents by clicking the Next Record or Previous Record button in the Preview Results group on the Mailings tab.

First Record

5. On the **Mailings** tab, in the **Preview Results** group, click the **First Record** button.

6. To exclude this recipient (*Linda Martin*) from the merge, under **Make changes** in the **Mail Merge** task pane, click **Exclude this recipient**.

7. Preview the letters again. Then at the bottom of the **Mail Merge** task pane, click **Next: Complete the merge**.

8. In the **Mail Merge** task pane, click **Edit individual letters**.

   The Merge To New Document dialog box opens.

> Merge to New Document
>
> Merge records
> ⦿ All
> ○ Current record
> ○ From: [   ] To: [   ]
>
> [OK] [Cancel]

9. With the **All** option selected, click **OK**.

   Word creates a document called *Letters1* that contains a personalized copy of the form letter for each of the selected records.

10. On the **Quick Access Toolbar**, click the **Save** button.

    The Save As dialog box opens so that you can save the new document with a more specific name.

Save

11. With the contents of the *Chapter09* subfolder displayed, type My Merged Letters in the **File name** box, and then click **Save**.

    Word saves the new document in the specified folder with the name *My Merged Letters*.

CLOSE the *My Merged Letters* document, and then close the *04_MergingData* document without saving your changes.

Printing Envelopes

You can print an envelope based on an address in a document. To do this:

1. Select the lines of the address. (Do not select any blank lines above or below the address.)

2. On the **Mailings** tab, in the **Create** group, click the **Envelopes** button.

   The Envelopes And Labels dialog box opens. You can edit the address directly in the Delivery Address box, and you can enter a return address in the Return Address box. If you have electronic postage software installed on your computer, you can include electronic postage. You can click Options and then specify the envelope size and the font and font size of both the address and the return address.

   > **Tip** You can have Word supply the return address by clicking the Microsoft Office Button, clicking Word Options, and then in the Word Options window, clicking the Advanced tab. Toward the bottom of the page, under General, in the Mailing Address box, enter your address, and click OK. The address then appears by default as the Return Address in the Envelopes And Labels dialog box. If you want to use envelopes with a preprinted return address, you must select the Omit check box to avoid duplication.

3. Size 10 is the default envelope size. If you want to select a different envelope size, click **Options**, make your selection, and then click **OK**.

4. Insert an envelope in the printer, and then click **Print**.

Sending a Personalized E-Mail Message to Multiple Recipients

When you want to send the same information to all the people on a list—for example, all your customers, or all the members of a club or your family—you don't have to print letters and physically mail them. Instead, you can use mail merge to create a message that can be sent to a list of e-mail addresses. As with a form letter that will be printed, you can either use the Mail Merge wizard or use the buttons on the Mailings tab to insert merge fields into the document containing the text of the message, which we call the *form message*. These merge fields will be replaced with information from a data source such as a table or contacts list.

If you are using the wizard, be sure to select the E-Mail Messages option in Step 1. If you are not using the wizard, you can specify the list of e-mail addresses you want to send the message to by clicking the Select Recipients button in the Start Mail Merge group on the Mailings tab. You then have three options:

● Type an entirely new list of recipients.

● Use an existing list of recipients.

● Select recipients from an Outlook contacts list.

You can quickly add merge fields to a form message by using the buttons in the Write & Insert Fields group. Many e-mail messages need only a greeting line. Because e-mail messages tend to be less formal than printed letters, you might want to start the messages with something other than the predefined options (*Dear* and *To:*) by typing a custom greeting.

In this exercise, you will open an existing form message, use the buttons on the Mailings tab to create a short mailing list, add a custom greeting line merge field, and then complete the merge.

USE the *05_E-mail* document. This practice file is located in the *Chapter09* subfolder under *SBS_Word2007*.

OPEN the *05_E-mail* document.

1. On the **Mailings** tab, in the **Start Mail Merge** group, click the **Select Recipients** button, and then in the list, click **Type New List**.

   The New Address List dialog box opens.

2. Skipping over the Title field, type Andrea in the **First Name** field, type Dunker in the **Last Name** field, press the [Tab] key until you reach the **E-mail Address** field (the last field in the table), and then type andrea@consolidatedmessenger.com.

3. Click **New Entry**, and then add Judy Lew, whose e-mail address is judy@lucernepublishing.com.

> **Tip** If you have several e-mail addresses to add to the list, you can press Tab in the last field of the last entry, instead of clicking New Entry each time.

4. Repeat Step 3 to add Ben Miller, whose e-mail address is ben@wingtiptoys.com, and then click **OK**.

   The Save Address List dialog box opens, with the contents of your *My Data Sources* folder displayed. This dialog box is very similar to the Save As dialog box.

5. In the **Favorite Links** list, click **Documents**, navigate to the *MSP\SBS_Word2007* *\Chapter09* subfolder, type My E-Mail Data Source in the **File name** box, and then click **Save**.

   Word saves the data source in the specified location as an Access database.

> **Tip** If you look in the *Chapter09* folder at this point in the exercise, you will see two like-named database files. The smaller one is locking the database because Word is accessing it as the data source for this exercise. The locking file will disappear when you close the form message.

6. With the insertion point at the beginning of the document, press [Enter] twice, and then press the [↑] key twice.

7. On the **Mailings** tab, in the **Write & Insert Fields** group, click the **Greeting Line** button.

   The Insert Greeting Line dialog box opens.

8. In the first box under **Greeting line format**, replace *Dear* with Hello followed by a space. Then click the arrow to the right of the second box, and in the list, click **Joshua**.

9. In the **Preview** area, click the **Next** button twice to preview the greetings as they will appear in the e-mail messages.

10. Click the **First** button to return to the first record, and then click **OK**.

    Word inserts the «GreetingLine» merge field at the top of the form message.

«GreetingLine»

Thank you for your recent visit to our store. It was a pleasure to be able to answer your decorating questions and offer suggestions. As you requested, we have added your name to our online mailing list. You will be receiving our monthly newsletter, as well as advance notice of upcoming shipments and in-store events.

You can also visit our Web site at www.wideworldimporters.com for a schedule of events, links to online decorating resources, articles on furniture care, and more.

Contact us at customerservice@wideworldimporters.com with any of your decorating questions, or call (925) 555-0167.

11. On the **Mailings** tab, in the **Preview Results** group, click the **Preview Results** button.

Word shows a preview of the first message. You can click the Next Record button in the Preview Results group to preview the messages for other recipients. Clicking the Preview Results button again turns off the preview.

12. In the **Write & Insert Fields** group, click the **Highlight Merge Fields** button.

Word indicates the merge field with a gray highlight.

13. In the **Finish** group, click the **Finish & Merge** button, and then in the list, click **Send E-mail Messages**.

The Merge To E-Mail dialog box opens.

14. Under **Message options**, verify that **Email_Address** is selected in the **To** box, type Welcome to Wide World Importers! in the **Subject line** box, and verify that **HTML** is selected in the **Mail format** box.

15. With the **All** option selected under **Send records**, click **OK**.

Word converts the form message to an e-mail message and sends the message to each of the selected addresses in the data source.

> **Tip** A copy of each sent message appears in your Outlook *Sent Items* folder. If you plan on doing a large mailing, you might want to turn off the saving of sent messages.

> **CLOSE** the *05_E-mail* document without saving your changes.

Creating and Printing Labels

Most organizations keep information about their customers or clients in a worksheet or database that can be used for several purposes. For example, the address information might be used to send billing statements, form letters, and brochures. It might also be used to print sheets of mailing labels that can be attached to items such as packages and catalogs.

To create sheets of mailing labels, you first prepare the data source and then prepare the main document by selecting the brand and style of labels you plan to use. Word creates cells the size of the labels, set within a page the size of the label sheet, so that each record will print on one label in a sheet. You insert merge fields into one cell as a template for all the other cells. When you merge the main document and the data source, you can print the labels or create a new label document that you can use whenever you want to send something to the same set of recipients.

In this exercise, you will use the Mail Merge wizard to create mailing labels. You will then print the labels on standard paper to proofread them.

> **USE** the *06_DataSource* workbook. This practice file is located in the *Chapter09* subfolder under *SBS_Word2007*.
>
> **BE SURE TO** display non-printing characters and turn on the printer you will be using before starting this exercise. If you don't want to print the labels, you can proof them on-screen.

Microsoft Office
Button

1. Click the **Microsoft Office Button**, click **New**, and then in the **New Document** window, double-click **Blank document**.

A new blank document opens.

Start Mail
Merge ▾

2. On the **Mailings** tab, in the **Start Mail Merge** group, click the **Start Mail Merge** button, and then click **Step by Step Mail Merge Wizard**.

3. In the **Mail Merge** task pane, select the **Labels** option, and then click **Next: Starting document**.

4. With the **Change document layout** option selected, click **Label options**.

   The Label Options dialog box opens.

Label Options	? ✕
Printer information	

Printer information
  ○ Continuous-feed printers
  ● Page printers   Tray: Manual Paper Feed ▾

Label information
  Label vendors: Microsoft ▾

Product number:
  1/2 Letter
  1/2 Letter
  1/4 Letter
  1/4 Letter
  30 Per Page
  30 Per Page

Label information
  Type: 1/2 Letter Postcard
  Height: 8.5"
  Width: 5.5"
  Page size: 5.5" X 8.5"

[Details...] [New Label...] [Delete]   [OK] [Cancel]

5. Under **Label information**, click the **Label vendors** arrow, and in the list, click **Avery US Letter**.

6. In the **Product number** list, click **5159**, and then click **OK**.

   Word inserts a table that fills the first page of the main document.

7. At the bottom of the **Mail Merge** task pane, click **Next: Select recipients**.

8. With the **Use an existing list** option selected, click **Browse**, navigate to your *Documents\MSP\SBS_Word2007\Chapter09* folder, double-click the *06_DataSource* workbook, and then in the **Select Table** dialog box, click **OK**.

9. In the **Mail Merge Recipients** dialog box, clear the check boxes of the two recipients whose addresses are not in Washington State (WA), and then click **OK**.

   Word inserts a «Next Record» merge field in all the cells in the main document except the first.

10. At the bottom of the **Mail Merge** task pane, click **Next: Arrange your labels**, and then scroll the main document so that you can see its left edge.

11. With the insertion point positioned in the first cell, in the **Mail Merge** task pane, click **Address block**.

12. In the **Insert Address Block** dialog box, click **OK** to accept the default settings.

    Word inserts an «AddressBlock» merge field into the first cell.

«AddressBlock»¶   «Next·Record»¶
¤   ¤

«Next·Record»¶   «Next·Record»¶
¤   ¤

13. In the **Mail Merge** task pane, click **Update all labels**.

The «AddressBlock» merge field is copied to the other cells, after the «Next Record» merge field.

14. At the bottom of the **Mail Merge** task pane, click **Next: Preview your labels**.

Word displays the labels for the four recipients as they will appear after the merge.

Garth·Fort¶   Dan·Wilson¶
5678·Ford·Ave.¶   1234·Editorial·Way¶
Planter,·WA·10002¶   Harvest,·WA·10004¶
¤   ¤

Mike·Tiano¶   Heidi·Steen¶
456·South·Rd.¶   678·Pine·St.¶
Harvest,·WA·10004¶   Agriculture,·WA·10003¶
¤   ¤

Troubleshooting If you see only one label for the last record in the data source, under Preview Your Labels in the Mail Merge task pane, click the Previous Record button three times.

15. At the bottom of the **Mail Merge** task pane, click **Next: Complete the merge**. Then in the **Mail Merge** task pane, click **Print**.

The Merge To Printer dialog box opens.

16. With the **All** option selected, click **OK**.

17. In the **Print** dialog box, verify that the name of the printer you want to use appears in the **Name** box, and then click **OK** to print the labels.

    The labels are printed on regular paper on the printer you selected. If you want to print on label sheets, insert them in the printer's paper tray before clicking OK in the Print dialog box.

> **CLOSE** the label document without saving your changes.

Key Points

- To become familiar with the mail-merge process, you can use the Mail Merge wizard to create letters, e-mail messages, envelopes, labels, and directories. When you are comfortable with the process, you can use the individual buttons on the Mailings tab to create and modify mail-merge documents.

- The mail-merge process works by combining static information from one document with variable information from another document. The static information is stored in a main document, such as a form letter. You insert merge fields into this document to tell Word where to merge items of variable information. The variable information is stored in a data source. This file is organized into sets of information, called records, with each record containing the same items, called fields.

- You can use a structured file created in another program, such as an Excel worksheet, an Access database, or a contacts list from Outlook, Windows Mail, or Outlook Express, as a data source.

- You don't have to use all the records in a data source in the mail-merge process. You can filter the data and exclude specific records.

- You can merge the main document and the data source into a new document that can be edited and saved, or you can print the merged documents directly on your printer.

Chapter at a Glance

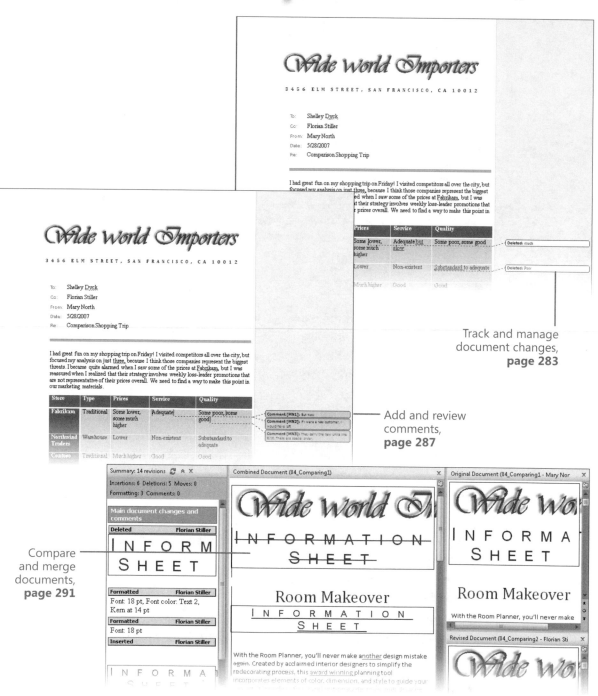

Track and manage document changes,
page 283

Add and review comments,
page 287

Compare and merge documents,
page 291

10 Collaborating with Others

In this chapter, you will learn to:

- ✔ Send a document directly from Word.
- ✔ Track and manage document changes.
- ✔ Add and review comments.
- ✔ Compare and merge documents.
- ✔ Password-protect a document.
- ✔ Prevent changes.
- ✔ Use document workspaces.

In today's workplace, many documents are developed collaboratively by a team of people. You might be the lead author of some documents that will be reviewed by your colleagues and managers, and you might be a reviewer of other documents. These days, most documents are reviewed on the screen rather than on printouts. In Microsoft Office Word 2007, it is easy to edit documents without losing track of the original test, make comments and ask questions, and accept or reject changes and respond to comments made by others.

Sometimes you will want other people to review a document but not change it. You can prevent other people from making changes to a document by assigning a password to it. You can also specify that only certain people are allowed to make changes, and what types of formatting and content changes are allowed.

If you send a document out for review and then receive several copies with changes and suggestions back from different people, you can merge the different versions into one file to simplify the process of reviewing and accepting or rejecting changes. If your organization uses a collaboration site built with Microsoft SharePoint products and technologies, you can store the document in a document workspace on the site so that only one person can actively work on the document at a time.

In this chapter, you will send documents for review by other people by attaching them to an e-mail message. You will track changes that you make to a document, and then accept and reject changes. You will review, add, delete, and hide comments, and merge three versions of the same document. Finally, after setting and removing a password and setting up editing and formatting restrictions, you will see how to create a document workspace on a SharePoint site.

See Also Do you need only a quick refresher on the topics in this chapter? See the Quick Reference entries on pages xxxix–lxiii.

Important Before you can use the practice files in this chapter, you need to install them from the book's companion CD to their default location. See "Using the Book's CD" on page xxv for more information.

Troubleshooting Graphics and operating system–related instructions in this book reflect the Windows Vista user interface. If your computer is running Microsoft Windows XP and you experience trouble following the instructions as written, please refer to the "Information for Readers Running Windows XP" section at the beginning of this book.

Sending a Document Directly from Word

After you create a document, you can quickly send it via e-mail from within Word, without starting your e-mail program. You simply point to Send on the Office menu, and click E-mail to display a message window. The current document is already attached to the message, so all you have to do is enter the e-mail addresses of anyone you want to receive the message and its attachment. If you want, you can modify the subject line, which contains the name of the document you are sending.

Tip If your organization uses SharePoint products and technologies to enhance collaboration and you have permission to create workspaces on a SharePoint site, you can create a document workspace when sending a document in e-mail by using Microsoft Office Outlook 2007. Before you send your message, in the message window, click the Attachment File button in the Include group on the Message tab, and then click Attachments Options. In the Attachment Options task pane, click the Shared Attachments option, and specify the URL for the site. For more information about document workspaces, see "Using Document Workspaces" later in this chapter.

In this exercise, you will attach three documents to an e-mail message so that you can send them for review.

USE the *01_Sending1*, *01_Sending2*, and *01_Sending3* documents. These practice files are located in the *Chapter10* subfolder under *SBS_Word2007*.

BE SURE TO have an e-mail program installed on your computer and an e-mail account set up before beginning this exercise. Microsoft Office Outlook 2007 is recommended. You can use another e-mail program, but the steps for attaching and sending a message might vary from those given in this exercise.

OPEN the *01_Sending1* document.

Microsoft Office
Button

1. Click the **Microsoft Office Button**, point to **Send**, and then click **E-mail**.

2. If the **Choose Profile** dialog box prompts you for a mail profile, select the profile you want, and then click **OK**.

   A message window opens with the name of the document in the Subject line and the document attached.

3. In the **To** box, type your own e-mail address.

Attach
File

4. On the **Insert** tab of the message window, in the **Include** group, click the **Attach File** button.

   The Insert File dialog box opens.

5. From your *Documents* folder, navigate to the *MSP\SBS_Word2007\Chapter10* folder.

6. Click *01_Sending2*, hold down the [Ctrl] key, click *01_Sending3*, and then click **Insert**.

   In the message window, the Attach box shows that three files are attached to the message.

7. On the **Message** tab of the message window, in the **Options** group, click the **High Importance** button.

   If the message recipient is using Outlook, the message header will display a red exclamation mark to indicate that it is important.

8. In the message content pane, type Please review the attached documents.

   You can format the text of the message in the same way you would the text of a document.

9. In the message header, click the **Send** button.

   Outlook sends the e-mail message with the attached documents. You will receive the e-mail message the next time you connect to your e-mail server.

CLOSE the *01_Sending1* document without saving your changes.

Faxing a Document

In addition to sending a document as an e-mail attachment from within Word, if you have signed up with an Internet fax service provider, you can send it as a fax. Although the exact terms vary from one provider to another, these services let you send and receive faxes from your computer without needing a fax machine or dedicated fax line.

After establishing Internet fax service, you can send the current document to the fax service by clicking the Microsoft Office Button, pointing to Send, and then clicking Internet Fax. You then follow the procedure specified by your fax service provider.

If you have not yet signed up with an Internet fax service provider, when you click Internet Fax, a message box appears. Clicking OK opens a Web page where you can choose a fax service provider.

Tracking and Managing Document Changes

When two or more people collaborate on a document, one person usually creates and "owns" the document and the others review it, adding or revising content to make it more accurate, logical, or readable. In Word, reviewers can turn on the Track Changes feature so that the revisions they make to the active document are recorded without the original text being lost. (Note that Track Changes affects only the active document, not any other documents that might also be open.) To turn on Track Changes, you click the Track Changes button in the Tracking group on the Review tab. You then edit the text as usual.

> **Tip** If you want to know whether Track Changes is turned on when you're working from a tab other than the Review tab, right-click the status bar and then click Track Changes on the Customize Status Bar menu. Word adds a Track Changes button to the status bar.

By default, your *revisions* appear in a different color from the original text, as follows:

● Insertions and deletions are inserted in the text in your assigned color and are underlined.

● In Print Layout view, you can display deletions in balloons rather than in the text. Simply click the Balloons button in the Tracking group on the Review tab, and then click Show Revisions In Balloons.

● In Print Layout view, formatting changes appear in *balloons* in the right margin.

● All changes are marked in the left margin by a vertical line.

> **Tip** The colors used for revisions are controlled by the settings in the Track Changes Options dialog box, which you can display by clicking the Track Changes arrow and then clicking Change Tracking Options.

You can display a ScreenTip identifying the name of the reviewer who made a specific change and when the change was made by pointing to a revision or balloon. The reviewer name is taken from the user information stored with the computer. If you are working on someone else's computer, you might want to change the name by clicking the Track Changes arrow, clicking Change User Name, typing the name and initials you want in the Word Options window, and then clicking OK.

You can work with revisions in the following ways by using the commands available from the Review tab:

- If you want to track changes without showing them on the screen, you can hide the revisions. You simply click the Display For Review arrow in the Tracking group and then in the list, click Final. To display the revisions again, you click the Display For Review arrow and click Final Showing Markup. You can also display the original version, with or without revisions.

- When revisions are visible in the document, you can select the types of revisions that are displayed, from the Show Markup list in the Tracking group—for example, you can display only comments or only insertions and deletions. You can also display or hide the revisions of specific reviewers from this list.

- You can move forward or backward from one revision mark or comment to another by clicking the Next or Previous button in the Changes group.

- You can incorporate a highlighted change into the document and move to the next change by clicking the Accept button in the Changes group. You can click the Reject button to remove the highlighted change, restore the original text, and move to the next change.

- You can accept all the changes at once by clicking the Accept arrow and then clicking Accept All Changes In Document. To reject all the changes at once, click the Reject arrow and then click Reject All Changes In Document.

> **Tip** To accept or reject a change, you can also right-click the change and then click Accept Change or Reject Change.

- You can accept or reject selected changes by highlighting the text containing changes you want to process and then clicking the Accept or Reject button.

● You can accept or reject only certain types of changes or changes from specific reviewers by displaying only the changes you want to accept or reject, clicking the Accept or Reject arrow, and then clicking All Changes Shown in the list.

In this exercise, you will open a document, turn on change tracking, make changes to the document, and accept and reject changes.

> **USE** the *02_TrackChanges* document. This practice file is located in the *Chapter10* subfolder under *SBS_Word2007*.
>
> **OPEN** the *02_TrackChanges* document in Print Layout view.

Track Changes ▾

1. On the **Review** tab, in the **Tracking** group, click the **Track Changes** button.

The active (orange) button indicates that Track Changes is turned on. Any changes that you make now will be indicated in the document in revisions.

2. In the table at the end of the document, in *Some much lower* in the third column, double-click **much**, and press the ⌈Del⌋ key.

Word changes the font color of the word *much* and indicates with strikethrough formatting that you deleted it. A vertical bar appears adjacent to the change in the left margin.

3. In the fourth column of the same row, position the insertion point at the right end of *Adequate*, press ⌈Space⌋, and then type but slow.

Word inserts the new text in the same color as the deletion, and indicates with an underline that you inserted it.

I had great fun on my shopping trip on Friday! I visited competitors all over the city, but focused my analysis on just three, because I think those companies represent the biggest threats. I became quite alarmed when I saw some of the prices at Fabrikam, but I was reassured when I realized that their strategy involves weekly loss-leader promotions that are not representative of their prices overall. We need to find a way to make this point in our marketing materials.

Store	Type	Prices	Service	Quality
Fabrikam	Traditional	Some ~~much~~ lower, some much higher	Adequate <u>but slow</u>	Some poor, some good
Northwind Traders	Warehouse	Lower	Non-existent	Poor to adequate
Contoso	Traditional	Much higher	Good	Good

Deleted text   Inserted text

4. In the fifth column of the *Northwind Traders* row, select the word **Poor**, and then type Substandard.

Word interprets this one change as both a deletion and an insertion.

5. Point to **Substandard**.

A ScreenTip displays your user name, the date and time you made the change, the type of change, and the affected text.

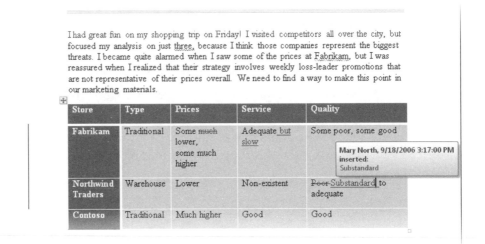

6. In the **Tracking** group, click the **Balloons** button, and then in the list, click **Show Revisions in Balloons**.

Word removes the deletions from the text and displays them in balloons in the right margin.

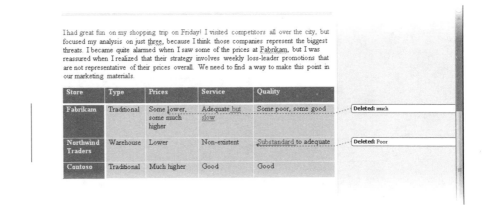

7. In the **Tracking** group, click the **Display for Review** arrow, and then in the list, click **Final**.

Display for Review

Word hides the revisions, displaying the document as it would appear if all the changes are accepted.

8. Click the **Display for Review** arrow, and in the list, click **Final Showing Markup** to make the revisions visible again.

9. Press Ctrl + Home to move to the beginning of the document.

10. In the **Changes** group, click the **Next** button.

Word selects the first change in the document—the deleted word *much*.

11. In the **Changes** group, click the **Accept** button.

Word accepts the change, removes the markup formatting and associated balloon, and moves to the next change (*but slow*).

12. In the **Changes** group, click the **Reject** button.

Word removes the inserted text, and because there are no more changes in this row of the table, it also removes the vertical bar from the left margin. It then moves to the next change (*Substandard*).

13. In the **Changes** group, click the **Accept** button to implement the deletion, and then click the same button again to implement the insertion.

A message box tells you that there are no more changes in the document.

14. Click OK to close the message box.

15. In the **Tracking** group, click the **Track Changes** button to stop tracking changes made to the active document.

CLOSE the *02_TrackChanges* document without saving your changes.

Adding and Reviewing Comments

In addition to tracking the changes made to a document, you can insert notes, or *comments*, to ask questions, make suggestions, or explain edits. To insert a comment, you select the text to which the comment refers, click the New Comment button in the Comments group on the Review tab, and type what you want to say in the balloon that appears. In Print Layout view, Word highlights the associated text in the document in the same color as the balloon and adds your initials and a sequential number to the balloon itself.

You can work with comments in the following ways:

● To display the reviewer's name and the date and time the comment was inserted, you point to either the commented text or the balloon.

- To review comments, you can scroll through the document, or in the case of long documents, you might want to click the Next or Previous button in the Comments group to jump from balloon to balloon.

- To edit a comment, you simply click the balloon and use normal editing techniques.

- To delete a comment, you click its balloon and then click the Delete button in the Comments group, or right-click the balloon and then click Delete Comment.

- To respond to a comment, you can add text to an existing balloon. You can also click the existing balloon and then click the New Comment button to attach a new balloon to the same text in the document.

- If the complete text of a comment isn't visible in its balloon, you can view it in its entirety by clicking the Reviewing Pane button in the Tracking group on the Review tab. (Clicking the Reviewing Pane arrow gives you the option of opening either a vertical or horizontal reviewing pane.) In addition to displaying comments, the reviewing pane displays all the editing and formatting changes you have made to a document, with the number of each type of change summarized at the top of the pane. To close the reviewing pane, click its Close button, or click the Reviewing Pane button again.

> **Tip** To change the size of the reviewing pane, point to its border, and when the pointer changes to a double-headed arrow, drag the border.

- You can turn off the display of comment balloons by clicking the Show Markup button in the Tracking group and then clicking Comments.

If multiple people have reviewed a document and you want to see only the comments of a specific person, you can click the Show Markup button, click Reviewers, and then click the check boxes of the reviewers whose comments you don't want to see.

In this exercise, you will show and review comments in a document, add a comment, delete one that is no longer needed, and then hide the remaining comments.

> **USE** the *03_Comments* document. This practice file is located in the *Chapter10* subfolder under *SBS_Word2007*.
>
> **OPEN** the *03_Comments* document in Print Layout view.

Display for
Review

1. If comments are not visible in the document, on the **Review** tab, in the **Tracking** group, click the **Display for Review** arrow, and then in the list, click **Final Showing Markup**.

2. On the **Review** tab, in the **Comments** group, click the **Next** button.

In the document, Word highlights in the first instance of commented text. It also positions the insertion point in the associated comment balloon.

> **Tip** If a document contains both comments and tracked changes, clicking the Next or Previous button moves sequentially among both elements.

3. In the **Comments** group, click the **Next** button.

Word moves to the next comment.

4. Point to **Adequate**.

A ScreenTip displays information about who inserted the comment and when.

5. In the fifth column of the same row, select the words **some good**, and then in the **Comments** group, click the **New Comment** button.

Word highlights the selection and displays a new balloon in the right margin.

6. In the comment balloon, type They carry the new Ultra line.

7. Click the comment balloon associated with the word *competitors*, and in the **Comments** group, click the **Delete** button.

Word deletes the comment and its balloon.

8. In the **Tracking** group, click the **Reviewing Pane** button.

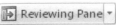

The reviewing pane opens to the left of the Word window, showing the two remaining comments.

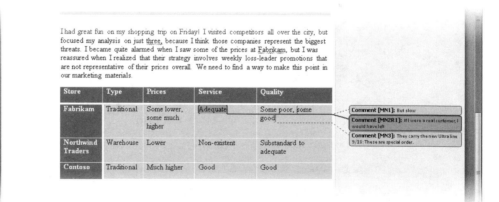

9. In the reviewing pane, click at the right end of the second comment, press [Enter], type the date and a colon (:), press [Space], and then type **These are special order.**

   The new text is added to the same comment in the reviewing pane.

10. In the **Tracking** group, click the **Reviewing Pane** button to close the pane, and then scroll the document so that you can see its text.

11. Click anywhere in the comment balloon associated with *Adequate*, and then in the **Comments** group, click the **New Comment** button.

   Word attaches a response comment to the same text in the document.

12. In the response comment balloon, type **If I were a real customer, I would have left.**

13. In the **Review** group, click the **Show Markup** arrow, and then click **Comments** to hide them.

CLOSE the *03_Comments* document without saving your changes.

Entering Handwritten Changes

With Word 2007 running on a computer or device with ink input capability, you can make handwritten changes to a document. You can make handwritten comments, circle words or paragraphs, cross things out, draw arrows, and sketch diagrams to make your point. To add a handwritten comment in Print Layout view:

1. Select the text to be commented. Then on the **Review** tab, in the **Comments** group, tap the **Ink Comment** button.

2. Write your comment.

   You can click the Eraser button in the Comments group to erase mistakes.

To annotate a document:

1. On the **Review** tab, in the **Ink** group, tap the **Start Inking** button.

   The Pens contextual tab is added to the Ribbon.

2. On the **Pens** tab, select the type of pen, color, and weight you want, and then make your annotations in the document.

   To remove individual annotations, use the Eraser tool. To remove all annotations, in the Select group, click the Delete All Ink button.

3. When you are done, in the Close group, click the **Close Ink Tools** button.

Other people don't need ink input capability to see your handwritten notes. Your annotations appear as objects in the Word document, where they can be moved and sized, or deleted when they are no longer necessary.

Comparing and Merging Documents

Sometimes you might want to compare several versions of the same document. For example, if you have sent a document out for review by colleagues, you might want to compare their edited versions with the original document.

Instead of comparing multiple open documents visually, you can tell Word to compare the documents and merge the changes into one document. Even if the changes were not made with Track Changes turned on, they are recorded in the merged document as revisions. From within that one document, you can view all the changes from all the reviewers or view only those from a specific reviewer.

In this exercise, you merge three versions of the same document and then evaluate and handle the revisions that indicate the differences between the versions.

> **USE** the *04_Comparing1*, *04_Comparing2*, and *04_Comparing3* documents. These practice files are located in the *Chapter10* subfolder under *SBS_Word2007*.
>
> **OPEN** the *04_Comparing1* document.

Compare

1. On the **Review** tab, in the **Compare** group, click the **Compare** button, and then click **Combine**.

> **Tip** Click Compare to compare two documents and display the differences between them in a third document. The documents being compared are not changed.

The Combine Documents dialog box opens.

Combine Documents	
Original document	Revised document
Label unmarked changes with:	Label unmarked changes with:
More >>	OK Cancel

2. Click the **Original document** arrow, and then in the list, click *04_Comparing1*.

3. Click the **Revised document** arrow, and then in the list, click *04_Comparing2*.

> **Troubleshooting** If you don't see the documents you want in the lists, click the Browse For Original or Browse For Revised button to the right of the corresponding box.

Under both documents, Word indicates to whom any revisions will be attributed.

4. In the lower-left corner of the dialog box, click **More**, and then under **Comparison settings**, verify that all the check boxes are selected.

5. Under **Show changes in**, click the **Original document** option, and then click **OK**.

> **Troubleshooting** If the documents contain conflicting formatting, you will see a message box asking you to confirm which document's formatting should be used.

Word compares the two documents and marks the differences in the document displayed in the center pane, *04_Comparing1*. To the left it displays the reviewing pane, and to the right, it displays the two documents being compared.

6. On the **Review** tab, in the **Compare** group, click the **Compare** button, and then click **Combine** to display the **Combine Documents** dialog box.

7. In the **Original document** list, click *04_Comparing 1*, and in the **Revised document** list, click *04_Comparing3*. Then click **OK**.

   The changes from the *04_Comparing3* version of the document are added to those of the other two versions.

8. Scroll through the document in the center pane to see all the revisions, and then scroll through the reviewing pane.

9. On the **Review** tab, in the **Tracking** group, click the **Show Markup** button, point to **Reviewers**, and then click **Florian Stiller**.

   ![Show Markup]

   The revisions made by Florian Stiller are hidden.

10. In the **Tracking** group, click the **Show Markup** button, point to **Reviewers**, and then click **All Reviewers** to redisplay all the revisions.

11. Press [Ctrl] + [Home] to move to the top of the document. Then in the **Changes** group, click the **Accept** arrow, and in the list, click **Accept All Changes in Document**.

   ![Accept]

   All the changes are accepted.

12. Close the reviewing pane, and close the two windows on the right side of the screen.

CLOSE the *04_Comparing1* document without saving your changes.

Password-Protecting a Document

Sometimes, you might want only certain people to be able to open and change a document. The easiest way to exercise this control is to assign a password to protect the document. Word then requires that the password be entered correctly before it will allow the document to be opened and changed. Anyone who doesn't know the password has no choice but to open a *read-only* version.

In this exercise, you will set a password for a document and then test the document's security by entering an incorrect password. You will open a read-only version of the document and then reopen it with the correct password. Finally, you'll remove the password-protection from the document.

USE the *05_Password* document. This practice file is located in the *Chapter10* subfolder under *SBS_Word2007*.

OPEN the *05_Password* document.

Microsoft Office Button

1. Click the **Microsoft Office Button**, and then click **Save As**.

2. With the *Chapter10* subfolder displayed in the **Save As** dialog box, type My Password in the **File name** box.

3. At the bottom of the dialog box, click **Tools**, and then in the list, click **General Options**.

The General Options dialog box opens.

General Options

General Options

File encryption options for this document

Password to open:

File sharing options for this document

Password to modify:

☐ Read-only recommended

Protect Document...

Macro security

Adjust the security level for opening files that might contain macro viruses and specify the names of trusted macro developers.

Macro Security...

OK   Cancel

> **Tip** If you want people to be able to read the document's contents but you don't expect them to change the document, you can select the Read-Only Recommended check box to tell Word to display a message suggesting that the document be opened as read-only. Then click OK to close the General Options dialog box without assigning a password.

4. In the **Password to modify** box, type P@ssword.

As you type the password, dots appear instead of the characters to keep the password confidential.

> **Important** Don't use common words or phrases as passwords, and don't use the same password for multiple documents. After assigning a password, make a note of it in a safe place. If you forget it, you will not be able to open the password-protected document.

5. Click **OK**.

The Confirm Password dialog box opens.

6. In the **Reenter password to modify** box, type P@ssword, and then click **OK** to set the password.

7. In the **Save As** dialog box, click **Save**.

Word protects the document by assigning the selected password, and then saves it in the *Chapter10* folder.

8. Close the *My Password* document.

9. Click the **Microsoft Office Button**, and then in the **Recent Documents** pane, click the **My Password** document.

Because this document is protected by the password you just set, the Password dialog box opens.

Password	? ✕
'My Password' is reserved by Mary North	
Enter password to modify, or open read only.	
Password:	
Read Only	OK	Cancel

10. In the **Password** box, type password, and click **OK**.

A message tells you that you typed an incorrect password.

11. In the message box, click **OK**.

12. In the **Password** dialog box, click **Read Only**.

The *My Password* document opens as a read-only document, as indicated by *(Read-Only)* in its title bar.

13. Close the document, and then reopen it.

A message reminds you that you previously opened this document as read-only and asks whether you want to do the same thing again.

14. In the message box, click **No**.

15. In the **Password** dialog box, type **P@ssword**, and then click **OK**.

Because you typed the correct password, the document opens.

16. Click the **Microsoft Office Button**, click **Save As**, click **Tools**, and then click **General Options**.

17. In the **General Options** dialog box, select the contents of the **Password to modify** box, press ⌷Del, click **OK**, and then click **Save**.

The document is no longer protected by a password.

> ✕ **CLOSE** the *My Password* document.

> **Tip** If you have signed up for the Microsoft Information Rights Management (IRM) Service, or if your organization is running its own rights management server, you can control who can see and work with your documents by granting permission to perform such tasks as opening, printing, saving, or copying a file to specific people. For more information, on the Review tab, in the Protect group, click the Protect Document button, and then click Restricted Access.

Preventing Changes

Sometimes you will want people to be able to open and view a document but not make changes to it. Sometimes you will want to allow changes, but only of certain types. For example, you can specify that other people can insert comments in the document but not make changes, or you can require that people track their changes. To prevent anyone from introducing inconsistent formatting into a document, you can limit the styles that can be applied. You can select the styles individually, or you can implement the recommended minimum set, which consists of all the styles needed by Word for features such as tables of contents. (The recommended minimum set doesn't necessarily include all the styles used in the document.)

To protect a document from unauthorized changes, you click the Protect Document button in the Protect group on the Review tab to display the Protect Document task pane, in which you specify the types of changes that are allowed.

In this exercise, you'll set editing and formatting restrictions to selectively allow modifications to a document.

> **USE** the *06_PreventingChanges* document. This practice file is located in the *Chapter10* subfolder under *SBS_Word2007*.
>
> **OPEN** the *06_PreventingChanges* document.

1. On the **Review** tab, in the **Protect** group, click the **Protect Document** button, and then in the list, click **Restrict Formatting and Editing**.

The Restrict Formatting And Editing task pane opens.

2. Under **Formatting restrictions** in the task pane, select the **Limit formatting to a selection of styles** check box, and then click **Settings**.

The Formatting Restrictions dialog box opens.

3. Scroll through the **Checked styles are currently allowed** list.

   The styles reflect those in the template attached to the open document, including styles that are available but not currently in use.

4. Click **Recommended Minimum**, and then scroll through the list again.

   All the selected styles are designated by the word *recommended*. The recommended set does not include some of the styles used in the document, so you need to add them.

5. In the list, select the **Address** check box. Then scroll the list, and select the **BulletList1**, **BulletList2**, **NumList1**, **NumList2**, and **Proch1** (meaning *Procedural heading*) check boxes.

6. Under **Formatting**, select the **Block Theme or Scheme switching** and the **Block Quick Style Set switching** check boxes.

7. Click **OK** to implement the restricted set of styles.

   Word displays a message stating that the document might contain formatting that has been applied directly rather than through styles and restricted styles, and asking if you want it removed.

8. In the message box, click **Yes**.

9. Under **Editing restrictions** in the task pane, select the **Allow only this type of editing in the document** check box. Then click the arrow to the right of the box below, and in the list, click **Tracked changes**.

10. Under **Start enforcement** in the task pane, click **Yes, Start Enforcing Protection**.

The Start Enforcing Protection dialog box opens.

You enter a password if you want only those people who know the password to be able to turn off document protection.

11. Without entering a password, click **OK**.

The Restrict Formatting And Editing task pane indicates that formatting and editing in this document is now restricted.

12. Close the task pane, and then display the **Home** tab.

The buttons in the Font and Paragraph groups are now unavailable.

13. Display the **Review** tab, and notice that the Track Changes button is not active.

14. In the document title, double-click the word **Office**, and type Operations.

Although Track Changes is not active, your change is marked as a revision.

> **CLOSE** the *06_PreventingChanges* document without saving your changes.

Using Document Workspaces

If your organization is running a collaboration site built with SharePoint products and technologies, you and your colleagues can develop documents from within a *document workspace*. The document workspace provides a forum in which multiple people in different locations can work on a single document. The document can be checked out by any member of the team. While the document is checked out, other people can view it but they cannot edit it. After the document is declared final, you can move it to a more permanent storage location and delete the document workspace.

To create and use a document workspace from within Word, you publish the document to the SharePoint site. The process of publishing creates the workspace and stores a copy of the document there so that other people can work on it. When you open the copy of the document stored on your computer, Word asks whether you want to download updates from the document workspace and provides a Document Management task pane with tools that enable you to keep your copy synchronized with the copy stored in the document workspace.

> **Tip** You don't have to publish a document to a document workspace to be able to work with it on a SharePoint site. If you upload the document to the site, you and your colleagues can work with it from there. Working with documents from within a SharePoint site is beyond the scope of this book. For information, refer to *Microsoft Windows SharePoint Services Step By Step* (ISBN 0-7356-2075-X) by Olga Londer, Todd Bleeker, Penelope Coventry, and James Edelen (Microsoft Press, 2005).

In this exercise, you will publish a document to a document workspace. You will explore the Document Management task pane, view the document workspace, and then delete it.

> **Important** The steps for this exercise assume that you have access to a site created with Microsoft Office SharePoint Server 2007. If you have access to a site created with a different version of SharePoint, the steps will be different.

> **USE** the *07_Workspace* document. This practice file is located in the *Chapter10* subfolder under *SBS_Word2007*.
> **BE SURE TO** have the user name and password for the SharePoint site available.
> **OPEN** the *07_Workspace* document.

1. Save the open document in the *Chapter10* subfolder with the name My Workspace.

Microsoft Office
Button

2. Click the **Microsoft Office Button**, point to **Publish**, and then click **Create Document Workspace**.

   The Document Management task pane opens, with the name of the current document entered in the Document Workspace Name box.

Document Management ▼ ✕

Document Workspace

Create a Document Workspace site if you want to share a copy of this document with others. Your local copy of the document will be synchronized with the server so that you can see your changes and work on the document with others. When you click Create, a new site is created automatically.

🔵 Tell me more…

Document Workspace name:

My Workspace

Location for new workspace:

(Type new URL)   ▼

Create

3. In the **Location for new workspace** box, type the URL of the site where you want to create the document workspace (or if you've previously connected to the site, select it from the list)

4. Click **Create**.

> **Troubleshooting** A message might appear saying that the URL you have typed is a restricted or non-trusted site. If you trust the site, open your Web browser and add the URL to your list of trusted sites. Then click Create again.

Word displays a couple of message boxes to let you know how the process is progressing.

5. If you are asked to supply your user name and password to connect to the site, provide your SharePoint site credentials in the **User name** and **Password** boxes, and then click **OK**.

When the document workspace is created and the document has been saved in the space, the Document Management task pane reappears with the name of the workspace at the top and five tabs that show information from the workspace.

You can download changes that have been made to a document stored in a workspace by clicking Get Updates. You can view or set options associated with the site by clicking Options.

6. In the task pane, click the **Members** tab.

   The task pane now shows the members of this workspace (currently just you). To add a new member, click Add New Members below the list box, and then complete the Add New Member dialog box. You can also send an e-mail message directly to members from the task pane.

7. In the task pane, click the **Tasks** tab.

   If there are any outstanding tasks associated with the document, they are listed on this tab. To add a new task, click Add New Task below the list box. If you click Alert Me About Tasks, you are taken to the New Alert page of the document workspace, where you can specify that you should be alerted when the tasks associated with the document change.

   > **Tip** If your organization uses workflow technology and a workflow has been set up for this document, you can click View Workflow Tasks to get information about your tasks.

8. In the task pane, click the **Documents** tab.

   The task pane now shows the names of any documents in this workspace (currently just *My Workspace*). To add a new document, click Add New Document below the list box. To create a new folder in which to store documents, click Add New Folder, and to be alerted when documents are added or changed, click Alert Me About Documents.

9. In the task pane, click the **Links** tab.

   If there are any links associated with the document, they are listed on this tab. To add a new link, click Add New Link below the list box, and to be alerted when links are added or changed, click Alert Me About Links.

10. Below the workspace name at the top of the **Document Management** task pane, click **Open site in browser**, and if necessary, enter your site credentials.

Your Web browser starts and opens the document workspace on the SharePoint site. You can add members, tasks, documents, and links in the workspace, and they will be reflected in the Document Management task pane in Word.

11. Close your Web browser without making any changes to the document workspace.

12. In the **Document Management** task pane, point to the name of the workspace, and click the arrow that appears.

A list of workspace commands appears.

13. In the list, click **Delete Workspace**, and then click **Yes** to confirm the deletion.

14. Close the **Document Management** task pane.

> **CLOSE** the *My Workspace* document without saving your changes, and if you are not continuing directly on to the next chapter, quit Word.

Key Points

- You can send a document for review via e-mail, and then when you receive the reviewed versions, you can merge them so that all the changes are recorded in one document.

- When you collaborate on a document, you can record the revisions you make to the document without losing the original text.

- You can insert comments in a document to ask questions or explain suggested edits. You can view comments individually in balloons in the right margin of the document or collectively in a reviewing pane.

- If you want only specific people to be able to work on a document, you can protect it with a password. If you want to allow only specific types of changes, you can restrict how people can edit and format the document.

- If you have access to a SharePoint site, creating a document workspace is a great way to collaborate with your colleagues on a document.

Chapter at a Glance

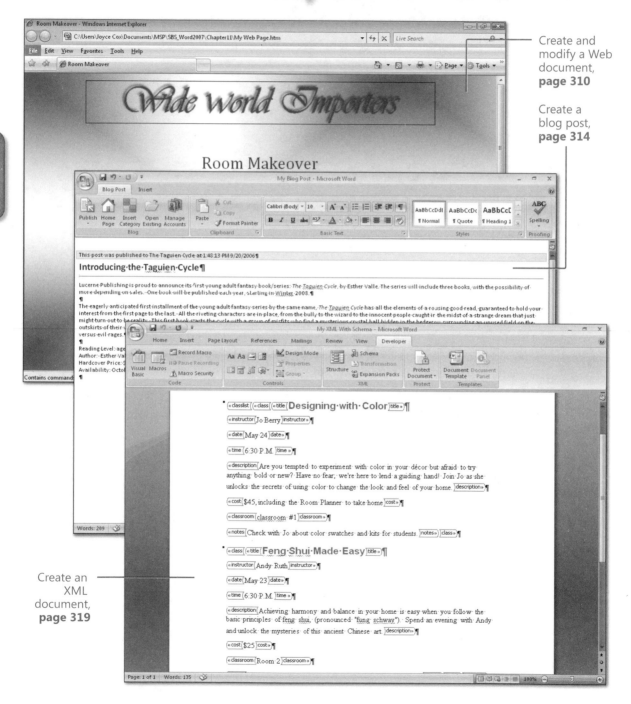

Create and modify a Web document, **page 310**

Create a blog post, **page 314**

Create an XML document, **page 319**

11 Creating Documents for Use Outside of Word

In this chapter, you will learn to:

✔ Save a file in a different format.

✔ Create and modify a Web document.

✔ Create a blog post.

✔ Create an XML document.

Sometimes you will create a document in Microsoft Office Word 2007 and then want to send it to someone who does not have Word 2007 installed on his or her computer. Word comes with several conversion utilities that you can use to save documents in other *file formats* so that you can distribute documents that your colleagues can read and use no matter what programs they work with.

One way of distributing the information in your documents is by converting them to *Web pages* so that people can read them on the Web. The Web has become a major part of our everyday lives. We use it to shop, check the news, find out how our favorite sports team is doing, and research topics. It's also a great publishing tool if you are trying to reach a broad audience. For example, your organization might want to publish a Web newsletter to provide information while advertising its goods or services. Or you might want to use built-in Word tools to create and post articles to a *blog* (short for *Web log*) about a particular topic.

In addition to converting documents into Web pages, you can convert them into *Extensible Markup Language (XML)* documents. The XML format distinguishes different parts of a document, giving it a structure that enables you to identify and extract items of information. For example, if you write a training document including procedures whose numbered steps are uniquely identified with a Procedure style, and then convert the document to XML format, all the procedures can be extracted into a different file for a different purpose—perhaps as a frequently asked questions (FAQ) page for your organization's Web site.

In this chapter, you will first learn about saving documents in other file formats. You will then preview a document in Web Layout view, save the document as a Web page, and make adjustments necessary for optimum presentation on the Web. You will create a blog post, register an existing blog account, and then publish the blog post. Finally, you will save a document as an XML file and view its XML tags, and then attach a schema containing custom tags to it.

See Also Do you need only a quick refresher on the topics in this chapter? See the Quick Reference entries on pages xxxix–lxiii.

> **Important** Before you can use the practice files in this chapter, you need to install them from the book's companion CD to their default location. See "Using the Book's CD" on page xxv for more information.

> **Troubleshooting** Graphics and operating system–related instructions in this book reflect the Windows Vista user interface. If your computer is running Microsoft Windows XP and you experience trouble following the instructions as written, please refer to the "Information for Readers Running Windows XP" section at the beginning of this book.

Saving a File in a Different Format

When you save a Word document, the default file save format is the Microsoft Office Word 2007 DOCX format. If you want to be able to use the file with an earlier version of Word or with a different program, you can save it in a different file format.

See Also For information about the DOCX format, see the sidebar "The DOCX Format" later in this chapter.

To save a document in a different file format, display the Save As dialog box, and then change the Save As Type setting to the format you want to use. If you want to save a

Word document in a format that can be opened by the widest variety of programs, use one of the following formats:

- **Rich Text Format (*.rtf).** Save the document in this format if you want to preserve its formatting.

- **Text Only (*.txt).** Save the document in this format if you want to preserve only its text.

If you want someone to be able to view a document but not change it, you can save the document as a Portable Document Format (PDF) file. In recent years, PDF has become a common standard for distributing information. The text and graphics in a PDF file are essentially static, and because a PDF file breaks a document into discrete pages, it mimics the way information appears on a printed page. Unlike a printed document, however, a PDF file can be sent by e-mail to many recipients, or it can be made available on a Web page for download to anyone who wants it. Using a PDF file can also help guarantee the quality of your document when you print it because it sets exact page breaks, which ensures that the pages are printed as you intended them to be.

You can open and read PDF files by using a PDF reader such as Adobe Acrobat Reader, which is available as a free download from the Adobe Web site as well as from many Web sites that distribute PDF files. You can create PDF files from Word documents by purchasing the full version of Adobe Acrobat.

> **Important** The PDF file is no longer a Word document, and it cannot be opened, viewed, and edited in Word. To view the document, you must have a PDF reader installed on your computer.

Saving a PDF File

You might want to check the Microsoft Downloads Web site for a free add-in that converts Word documents to PDF files. After you successfully install the add-in, you can save a document in PDF format by following these steps:

1. Click the **Microsoft Office Button**, point to **Save As**, and then click **PDF or XPS**.

   The Publish As PDF Or XPS dialog box opens.

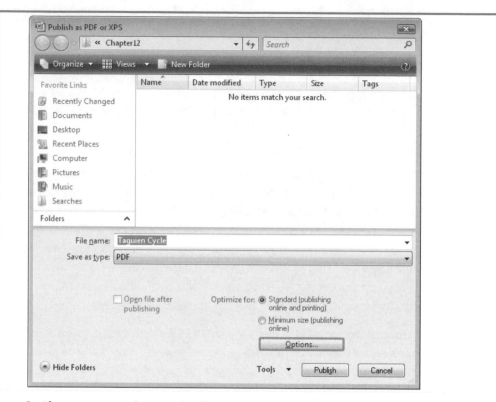

2. If you want to change the file name, in the **File name** box, type a new name for the converted document.

3. If you will be distributing the PDF file online, select the **Minimum size (publishing online)** option.

> **Tip** Whether you will distribute the PDF file in print or online, you can click Options to fine-tune the PDF output by selecting only certain pages of the document, including or excluding any existing comments and tracked changes, creating bookmarks in the PDF to the document headings or Word bookmarks, and so on.

4. In the **Publish as PDF or XPS** dialog box, click **Publish**.

> **Tip** With the same add-in, you can save documents in the XML Paper Specification (XPS) format, which is the new Microsoft XML-based format for delivering documents as electronic representations of the way they look when printed. You can also download separate SaveAsPDF and SaveAsXPS add-ins.

Using Add-Ins

Add-ins are utilities that add specialized functionality to a program (but aren't full-fledged programs themselves). There are several sources of add-ins:

- You can purchase add-ins from third-party vendors—for example, you can purchase an add-in that tracks the entire print history of a document.

- You can download free add-ins from the Microsoft Web site or other Web sites.

- When installing a third-party program, you might install an add-in to allow it to interface with a 2007 Microsoft Office system program. For example, you can install an add-in to capture screens from within an Office document.

> **Important** Be careful when downloading add-ins from Web sites other than those you trust. Add-ins are executable files that can easily be used to spread viruses and otherwise wreak havoc on your computer. For this reason, default settings in the Trust Center intervene when you attempt to download or run add-ins.

To use some add-ins, you must first install them on your computer and then load them into your computer's memory, as follows:

1. Click the **Microsoft Office Button**, and then in the lower-right corner, click **Word Options**.

2. In the page list in the left pane of the **Word Options** window, click **Add-Ins**.

3. At the bottom of the page, click the **Manage** arrow, and in the list, click the type of add-in you want to install. Then click **Go**.

   A dialog box corresponding to the type of add-in you selected opens. For example, if you select COM Add-Ins, the COM Add-Ins dialog box opens; if you select Templates, the Templates And Add-Ins dialog box opens.

4. In the dialog box, click **Add**.

5. In the **Add** dialog box, navigate to the folder where the add-in you want to install is stored, and double-click its name.

   The new add-in appears in the list of those that are available for use.

6. In the **Checked items are currently loaded** list, select the check box of the new add-in, and then click **OK**.

   The add-in is now available for use in Word.

To unload an add-in, display the Add-Ins dialog box and clear the add-in's check box to remove the add-in from memory but keep its name in the list. To remove the add-in from the list entirely, click the add-in name, and then click Remove.

Creating and Modifying a Web Document

You don't need to be a Web designer to create a Web page. From within Word 2007, you can view a document in Web Layout view, make any necessary adjustments in Word, and then save the document as a Web page, as easily as you would save it in any other format.

When you save a document as a Web page, Word converts the styles and formatting in the document to *Hypertext Markup Language (HTML)* codes, which are called *tags*. These tags tell your Web browser how to display the document. During the conversion, some of the formatting might be changed or ignored because it is not supported by all Web browsers. If that is the case, Word alerts you and gives you the option of stopping the conversion process so that you can make adjustments to the formatting to make it more compatible.

> **Tip** In the Web Options dialog box, you can specify which browsers you anticipate will be used to view your Web pages. You can also have Word disable any features that are incompatible with the specified browsers.

After you save a document as a Web page, it is no longer a Word document. It is saved in HTML format with the *.htm* or *.html* file name extension. However, you can still open, view, and edit the Web page in Word, just as you would a normal document. (You can also open and edit HTML-format Web pages created in other programs.) Making changes can be as basic as replacing text and adjusting alignment, or as advanced as moving and inserting graphics. When you finish modifying the Web page, you can resave it as a Web page, or save it as a regular Word document.

In this exercise, you will check that your computer is optimized for displaying documents as Web pages as they will appear in Microsoft Internet Explorer 6 or later. You will then preview a document in Web Layout view and make any adjustments necessary for this medium. Finally, you will save the document as a Web page, open the Web page in Word to make some modifications, and then save and view your changes.

USE the *02_Web* document. This practice file is located in the *Chapter11* subfolder under *SBS_Word2007*.

BE SURE TO install a Web browser on your computer before beginning this exercise. Windows Internet Explorer 7 or later is recommended; the steps might be different for other browsers and versions.

OPEN the *02_Web* document.

Microsoft Office
Button

1. Click the **Microsoft Office Button**, and then click **Word Options**.

   The Word Options window opens.

2. In the page list in the left pane, click **Advanced**. Then at the bottom of the **Advanced** page, in the **General** section, click **Web Options**.

   The Web Options dialog box opens.

> **Web Options**
>
> Browsers | Files | Pictures | Encoding | Fonts
>
> Target Browsers
>
> People who view this Web page will be using:
>
> Microsoft® Internet Explorer® 6 or later
>
> Each choice above gives smaller Web pages than the choice before
>
> Options
>
> ☑ Allow PNG as a graphics format
> ☑ Disable features not supported by these browsers
> ☑ Rely on CSS for font formatting
> ☐ Rely on VML for displaying graphics in browsers
> ☑ Save new Web pages as Single File Web Pages
>
> OK | Cancel

3. On the **Browsers** tab, verify that the **People who view this Web page will be using** option is set to **Microsoft Internet Explorer 6 or later**.

4. Under **Options**, select all five check boxes, and then click **OK** in each of the open dialog boxes.

Web Layout

5. On the **View** toolbar, click the **Web Layout** button, and then if the **Zoom** level is not set to **100%**, use the slider to adjust the magnification to that percentage.

   Word displays the page as it will appear in your Web browser. As you can see, you need to increase the page margins and adjust the size of the quote box.

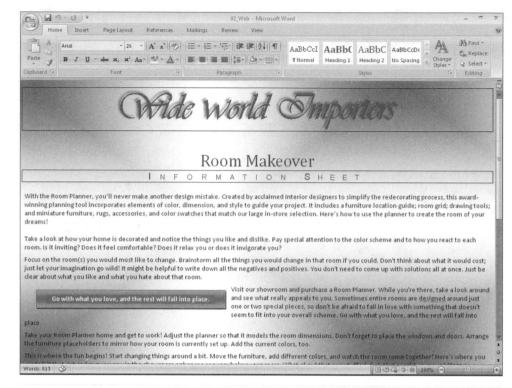

 Select ▾

6. On the **Home** tab, in the **Editing** group, click the **Select** button, and then in the list, click **Select All**.

Dialog Box
Launcher

7. With all the text of the document selected, click the **Paragraph** Dialog Box Launcher.

8. In the **Paragraph** dialog box, under **Indentation**, change the **Left** and **Right** settings to **1.25"**, and then click **OK**.

The text is now indented from the left and right edges of the window.

9. Click the quote box to select it, drag its middle-right handle to the left until its box is half its original width and the quote wraps to two lines.

The Web document is now more readable.

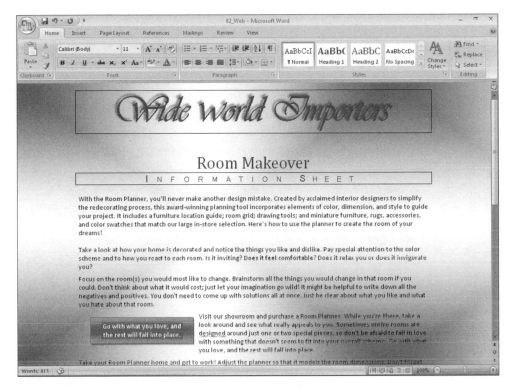

10. Click the **Microsoft Office Button**, and then click **Save As**.

11. With the contents of the *Chapter 11* subfolder displayed in the **Save As** dialog box, type My Web Page in the **File name** box.

12. Click the **Save as type** arrow, and then in the list, click **Web Page**.

13. Click **Change Title**. Then in the **Set Page Title** dialog box, type Room Makeover in the **Page title** box, and click **OK**.

    This title will appear in the title bar of the Web browser window.

14. In the **Save As** dialog box, click **Save**.

    The Microsoft Office Word Compatibility Checker tells you that the Small Caps effect used for the *Information Sheet* subtitle is not supported by Web browsers and will be changed to all capital letters.

15. In the **Compatibility Checker**, click **Continue**.

    Word saves the document as an HTML file called *My Web Page*.

16. Press Ctrl + End to move to the end of the document, and then type Looking for free advice? Check our schedule of decorating mini-seminars!

17. If you want, format the text to make it stand out. Then save the Web page.

18. Click the **Start** button, and in the right pane, click **Documents**. Then in the **Documents** window, navigate to the *MSP\SBS_Word2007\Chapter11* folder.

The *Chapter11* folder contains *My Web Page* and a folder named *My Web Page_files*, which contains supporting files for the Web page.

19. Double-click **My Web Page**.

Your Web browser starts, and the Web page opens. You can scroll to the bottom of the page to see the changes you made to the HTML file in Word.

> **CLOSE** your Web browser, the Documents window, and the *My Web Page* HTML file.

Creating a Blog Post

A blog is a personal Web site. It might be a personal online diary, or it might provide commentary, news, or information about a specific subject, such as a genre of music, a political point of view, a medical condition, or local news. A blog consists of *posts* that can include text, images, and links to related blogs, Web pages, and other media.

Word 2007 makes it easy to create posts that you can upload to your blog. If you have already set up a blog space with a blog service provider, you can register your blog space with Word the first time you create a blog post. If you haven't yet set up the blog space, you will need to register with a service provider before you can publish your first post. Thereafter, Word uses your registered blog account information when you create or publish a post.

Setting Up a Blog Account

To set up a blog, you must first decide which blog service provider you want to use. Many service providers, such as Windows Live Spaces (*spaces.live.com*) and Blogger (*www.blogger.com*), offer blog space free of charge. If your organization is running Microsoft Office SharePoint Server 2007, the site manager can set up a blog space for you.

To open a Windows Live Spaces account and create a blog space:

1. Start your Web browser, and then in the **Address** bar, type http://spaces.live.com.

2. On the **Windows Live Spaces** home page, click **Create your space**.

3. On the **Sign in** page, type your Windows Live ID and password, and click **Sign In**.

> **Tip** You can use MSN Hotmail, MSN Messenger, or Microsoft Passport account credentials as your Windows Live ID and password.

4. On the **Create your Windows Live Space** page, type a title for your space and the Web address you want, and then click **Check availability**.

5. If Windows Live Spaces reports that the Web address is available, click **Create**; if it is not available, repeat Step 4 with another name.

6. On the **You've created your space** page, click **Go to your space**.

7. In the upper-right corner of your blog page header, click **Options**.

8. On the left side of the page, in the **Options** pane, click **E-mail publishing**.

9. On the **E-mail Publishing** page, select the **Turn on e-mail publishing** check box, type up to three e-mail addresses you will use to publish blog posts, type a secret word (the password you will use to register your blog account in Word), and then click **Save**.

You can then enter information about yourself (your profile), give access to friends, and add content directly on your blog's home page.

> **Tip** You can register multiple blog accounts, and then choose the account you want to use for each blog post you create.

In this exercise, you will register your existing blog space in Word, create a blog post, publish it to your blog, and then view the published blog post.

> **USE** the *03_Blog* document. This practice file is located in the *Chapter11* subfolder under *SBS_Word2007*.
>
> **BE SURE TO** set up an account with Windows Live Spaces or another blog service provider before starting this exercise.

Microsoft Office
Button

1. Click the **Microsoft Office Button**, and then click **New**.

2. In the **Blank and recent** pane of the **New Document** window, click **New blog post**. Then click **Create**.

   Word creates a document and the Register A Blog Account dialog box opens. If you already have a blog account, you can click Register Now, and follow the instructions to register your existing account. If you don't have a blog account, you can click the Office Online link for information about getting an account.

Register a Blog Account
To start blogging, register your blog account. If you skip this step now, you will be prompted for this information the first time you post.
If you don't have a blog yet, visit Microsoft Office Online to learn about blog providers that work with Microsoft Office Word.
Office Online
Register Now   Register Later

> **Important** It's not essential to have a blog account before creating a blog post. You can click Register Later and skip to Step 8. Word will prompt you again to register your account the first time you publish a blog post or the next time you create a blog post.

   The following steps are for registering a blog account created on Windows Live Spaces.

3. Click **Register Now**.

   The New Blog Account dialog box opens.

New Blog Account

Welcome to the blog registration wizard. This wizard will help you configure Microsoft Office Word to post to your blog. To get started, choose your blog provider:

Blog [Choose your blog provider ▾]   📄 Refresh List

My provider isn't listed
I don't have a blog yet

[Next]   [Cancel]

4. Click the **Blog** arrow, click **Windows Live Spaces**, and then click **Next**.

The New Windows Live Spaces Account dialog box opens.

New Windows Live Spaces Account

Enter the information below to register your Windows Live Spaces account. Click OK to contact your provider and configure your account settings.

Step 1: Set up e-mail publishing

To publish to your Windows Live Spaces account, you must first set up e-mail publishing for your space.
Show me how!

Step 2: Enter account information

Space Name [   ]
Secret Word [   ]
☐ Remember Secret Word

[Picture Options]   [OK]   [Cancel]

5. Enter your space name and secret word, and then click **OK**.

> **Tip** With Windows Live Spaces, your space name is part of your space address. For example, if your space address is *http://lucernepublishing.spaces.live.com/*, the space name is *lucernepublishing*.

The Picture Options dialog box opens.

6. In the **Picture Options** dialog box, verify that **None – Don't upload pictures** is selected in the **Picture provider** box, and then click **OK**.

> **Tip** If you want to be able to upload pictures, you can get information about setting up a provider by clicking the links in the Picture Options dialog box.

A message appears when your account has been successfully registered.

7. In the message box, click **OK**.

Word displays a blank blog post with a title placeholder at the top. The Ribbon includes only the Blog Post and Insert tabs.

8. Click the title placeholder, and type *Introducing the Taguien Cycle*.

9. Click the **Microsoft Office Button**, and click **Open**. Then in the **Open** dialog box, browse to the *Documents\MSP\SBS_Word2007\Chapter11* folder, and double-click the *03_Blog* document.

10. Select all the paragraphs below the heading, and on the **Home** tab, in the **Clipboard** group, click the **Copy** button. Then close the *03_Blog* document.

11. In the blog post, click below the line, and then on the **Blog Post** tab, in the **Clipboard** group, click the **Paste** button.

You can use the buttons in the Basic Text group on the Blog Post tab to format the title and text so that it looks the way you want.

12. On the **Quick Access Toolbar**, click the **Save** button.

13. With the contents of the *Chapter 11* folder displayed in the **Save As** dialog box, type *My Blog Post* in the **File name** box, and then click **Save**.

14. On the **Blog Post** tab, in the **Blog** group, click the **Publish** arrow, and then in the list, click **Publish as Draft**.

15. If the **Connect to Your Space** dialog box opens, enter your space name and secret word, and then click **OK**.

A message appears when the blog post has been published to your blog.

This post was published to The Taguien Cycle at 1:48:13 PM 9/20/2006

Introducing the Taguien Cycle

Lucerne Publishing is proud to announce its first young adult fantasy book/series: *The Taguien Cycle*, by Esther Valle. The series will include three books, with the possibility of more depending on sales. One book will be published each year, starting in Winter 2008.

The eagerly anticipated first installment of the young adult fantasy series by the same name, *The Taguien Cycle* has all the elements of a rousing good read, guaranteed to hold your interest from the first page to the last. All the riveting characters are in place, from the bully to the wizard to the innocent people caught in the midst of a strange dream that just might turn out to be reality. This first book starts the cycle with a group of misfits who find a mysterious crystal ball hidden in the hedgerow surrounding an unused field on the outskirts of their village. After they accidently unlock the power of the crystal, their lives will never be the same again, as they become lost in a world where the battle of good versus evil rages.

Reading Level: ages 12 and up
Author: Esther Valle
Hardcover Price: $24.99
Availability: October 2008

16. In the **Blog** group, click the **Home Page** button.

Your default Web browser opens, displaying the home page of your registered blog space.

17. At the right end of the toolbar, click **Edit your space**, scroll to the bottom of the page, and under **Recent Entries**, click **Introducing the Taguien Cycle**.

Word displays the draft of the blog post. You can edit the post in your Windows Live Spaces blog just as you would edit it in Word, and you can make formatting changes such as changing the font, size, color, or paragraph alignment.

18. After making any necessary changes, click the **Publish Entry** button.

Word publishes the post to your blog.

CLOSE the *My Blog Post* document.

Creating an XML Document

As we mentioned earlier, basic Web pages are coded in HTML so that they can be displayed in a Web browser. HTML is a small, fixed subset of *Standard Generalized Markup Language (SGML)*, a comprehensive system for coding the structure of text documents and other forms of data so that they can be used in a variety of environments. *Extensible Markup Language (XML)* is another subset of SGML. However, instead of being fixed like HTML, XML can be customized (extended) to store data so that it can be used in many ways in many environments—for example, as text, in a database or spreadsheet, or as a Web page.

Creating sophisticated, multi-purpose XML files can involve highly technical processes that are designed by experienced systems analysts and application developers. However, with Word 2007, anyone can participate in these processes by creating a Word document and then saving it as an XML file. During conversion, Word tags the file based on its styles and other formatting and saves it with an *.xml* extension.

You can open and edit an XML file in Word, in the same way you can an HTML file. You can also open it in an XML editor such as XMetal, or as a plain text file in a text editor such as Notepad.

If you want more control over the tagging of a document, you can attach an *XML schema* to it. The schema is an additional file that describes the structure allowed in the document, including the names of structural elements and what elements can contain what other elements. For example, a book might be divided into parts that can each contain chapters, which in turn can contain topics, which in turn can contain a heading, paragraphs, numbered and bulleted lists, tables, and other elements. The schema might also define formatting attributes that you can apply to text within speci-fied elements. Word uses the schema to validate the document content and prompts you when content has been incorrectly tagged. Generally, companies employ a spe-cialist with in-depth knowledge of XML to create custom schemas, but anyone can use an existing schema to tag a Word document and save it as an XML file.

In this exercise, you will first save a document in XML format. Then you will attach a schema to a document, tag document elements to create valid structure, and save that file as an XML file.

USE the *04_XML* document and the *04_XMLSchema* document schema. These practice files are located in the *Chapter11* subfolder under *SBS_Word2007*.

OPEN the *04_XML* document.

Microsoft Office
Button

1. Click the **Microsoft Office Button**, and then click **Save As**.

2. In the **Save As** dialog box, type My XML in the **File name** box, click **Word XML Document** in the **Save as type** list, and then click **Save**.

   Nothing appears to change, except that the title bar now displays *My XML*.

3. Close the document.

Start

4. Click the **Start** button, click **Documents**, and then in the **Documents** window, navigate to the *MSP\SBS_Word2007\Chapter11* folder.

5. Right-click the **My XML** file, point to **Open With**, and then click **Notepad**.

The Notepad plain text editor opens, displaying the contents of the XML file.

This "simple" method of creating XML files turns out to be not so simple after all! Hundreds of tags enclosed in greater than (>) and less than (<) signs make it possible for this plain text document to be displayed exactly as it appears in Word.

6. Close Notepad, and then in the **Chapter11** window, double-click the *04_XML* document to reopen it in Word.

7. Click the **Microsoft Office Button**, and click **Word Options**. Then on the **Popular** page of the **Word Options** window, under **Top options for working with Word**, select the **Show Developer tab in the Ribbon** check box, and click **OK**.

The Developer tab appears on the Ribbon.

8. On the **Developer** tab, in the **XML** group, click the **Schema** button.

The Templates And Add-Ins dialog box opens.

9. On the **XML Schema** tab of the dialog box, click **Add Schema**.

10. In the **Add Schema** dialog box, navigate to the *Documents\MSP\SBS_Word2007\ Chapter11* folder, and then double-click *04_XMLSchema*.

    The Schema Settings dialog box opens.

11. In the **Alias** box, type *04_XMLSchema*, and then click **OK**.

    Word adds the schema to the list of available schemas and attaches it to the document.

12. In the **Templates and Add-ins** dialog box, click **XML Options**.

    The XML Options dialog box opens.

XML Options

XML save options
- ☐ Save data only
- ☐ Apply custom transform
- Custom transform: [ ]   Browse...

Schema validation options
- ☑ Validate document against attached schemas
- ☐ Hide schema violations in this document
- ☐ Ignore mixed content
- ☐ Allow saving as XML even if not valid

XML view options
- ☐ Hide namespace alias in XML Structure task pane
- ☐ Show advanced XML error messages
- ☐ Show placeholder text for all empty elements

Schema Library...   OK   Cancel

13. Under **Schema validation options**, verify that the **Validate document against attached schemas** check box is selected and the **Hide schema violations in this document** check box is cleared.

14. Under **XML view options**, verify that the **Hide namespace alias in XML Structure task pane** check box is cleared, and then select the **Show advanced XML error messages** check box.

15. Click **OK** to close the **XML Options** dialog box, and then close the **Templates and Add-ins** dialog box.

The XML Structure task pane opens.

16. In the **XML Structure** task pane, verify that the **Show XML tags in the document** check box is selected.

> **Tip** When you don't need to see XML tags in a document, you can hide them by clearing the Show XML Tags In The Document check box.

17. Click anywhere in the document window. Then at the bottom of the **XML Structure** task pane, in the **Choose an element to apply to your current selection** list, click **classlist {04_XMLSchema}**.

18. In the message box asking how you want to apply the selected element, click **Apply to Entire Document**.

Word selects all the text in the document, adds an opening XML tag and a closing XML tag at either end of the document to indicate that the entire document is now a classlist element, and lists the element in the Elements In The Document box in the XML Structure task pane.

19. Select all the text from *Designing with Color* down through *Check with Jo about color swatches and kits for students*. Then in the **Choose an element to apply to your current selection** box, click **class**.

Word tags the selection as a class element. All the information between the two class tags belongs to one particular class.

> **Tip** By default, the List Only Child Elements Of Current Element check box is selected. This simplifies the list of elements by showing only the ones that are valid in the current location. If you want to see a complete list of elements allowed in this schema, clear this check box. Invalid elements are then flagged with a slash inside a circle (the "not allowed" symbol).

20. Select the *Designing with Color* heading, and tag it as **title**. Then select each of the next six paragraphs one at a time, and tag them in turn as **instructor**, **date**, **time**, **description**, **cost**, and **classroom**.

> **Tip** It is helpful to have non-printing characters displayed when you are selecting paragraphs for tagging.

As you tag each element, it appears in the Elements In The Document box. An X next to the classlist and class elements indicates that the structure is not valid according to the schema rules, and three dots under the classroom element and at the end of the class element tell you that an element is missing.

21. Point to the **X** beside *class*.

A ScreenTip tells you that untagged text is not allowed in the class element; all text must be enclosed in valid start and end element tags.

22. Select the sentence that begins *Check with Jo* (the only remaining untagged text in the class element). Then in the **Choose an element to apply to your current selection** list, click **notes**.

Word tags the element, and the X next to *class* disappears.

23. Select all the text from *Feng Shui Made Easy* down to *Andy will need the screen set up for his PowerPoint slides*. In the **Choose an element to apply to your current selection** box, click **class**.

Word tags the element and the X next to *classlist* disappears.

24. Select each of the paragraphs in this class in turn, and tag them as **title**, **instructor**, **date**, **time**, **description**, **cost**, and **notes**.

In the Elements In The Document box, a question mark appears next to the second class element, and a wavy purple line appears in the left margin of the document to show you the section with invalid structure.

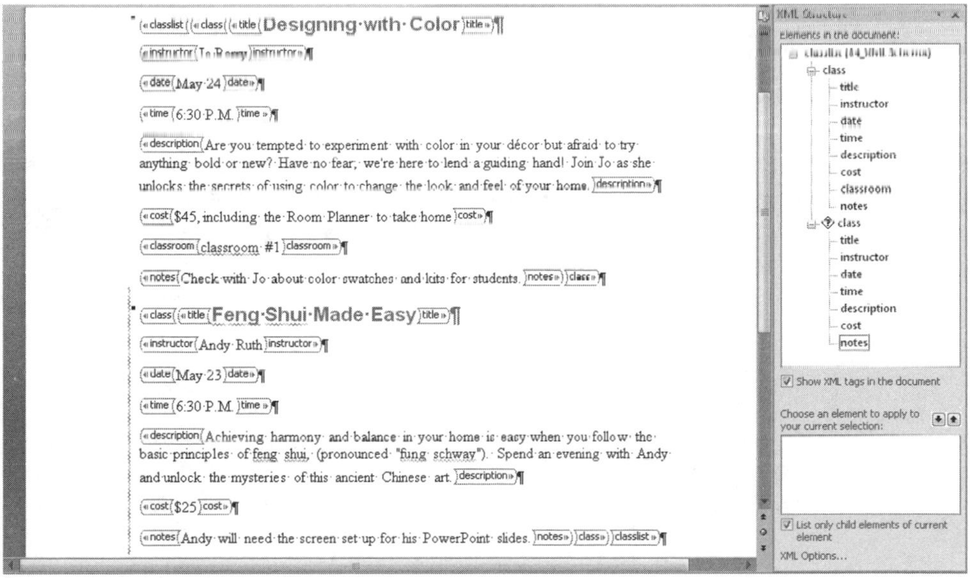

25. Point to the question mark.

Word tells you that according to the rules laid out by the schema, the class element is incomplete.

26. In the *Feng Shui Made Easy* class in the document, click to the right of the **cost** end tag, press the [Enter] key, type Room 2, select the text, and tag it as **classroom**.

The document's structure is now fully valid, and you're ready to save the document as an XML file.

> **Troubleshooting** If the Allow Saving As XML Even If Not Valid check box is cleared in the XML Options dialog box, Word will not allow you to save a document as XML unless the structure is valid. If Word tells you that it cannot save your document as XML because its structure violates the rules set by the schema, you have three choices: save the file as a Word document; click Cancel and change the option in the XML Options dialog box; or click Cancel and go back to the Elements In The Document box of the XML Structure task pane to correct the structure of marked elements.

27. Click the **Microsoft Office Button**, click **Save As**, name the file My XML With Schema, change the **Save as type** setting to **Word XML Document**, and then click **Save**.

28. Close the **XML Structure** task pane, and then close the **My XML With Schema** document.

29. Click the **Microsoft Office Button**, and then in the **Recent Documents** pane, click **My XML With Schema**.

The XML file opens in Word, where you can edit it like a normal document.

> **BE SURE TO** hide the Developer tab by displaying the Word Options window and clearing the Show Developer Tab In The Ribbon check box.
>
> **CLOSE** the *My XML With Schema* file, and if you are not continuing directly on to the next chapter, quit Word.

> **Tip** The power of XML lies in its flexibility. After you create an XML file, you can apply a *transform* (also called a *translation*) to it to pull only the data you need and put it in the format you want. For example, you could apply one transform to the list of classes that extracts the title, description, instructor, cost, date, and time of the class and then formats that information as a Web page for customers. You could also apply a different transform that extracts the date, classroom, and notes and then formats that information as a memo for setup staff. The subject of transforms is beyond the scope of this book. For more information, see *Microsoft Office Word 2007 Inside Out*, by Katherine Murray and Mary Millhollon (Microsoft Press, 2007).

The DOCX Format

The Microsoft Office 2007 system introduces a new file format based on XML, called Microsoft Office Open XML Formats. By default, Word 2007 files are saved in the DOCX format, which is the Word variation of this new file format.

The DOCX format provides the following benefits:

- File size is smaller because files are compressed when saved, decreasing the amount of disk space needed to store the file, and the amount of bandwidth needed to send files in e-mail, over a network, or across the Internet.

- Recovering at least some of the content of damaged files is possible because XML files can be opened in a text program such as Notepad.

- Security is greater because DOCX files cannot contain macros, and personal data can be detected and removed from the file. (Word 2007 provides a different file format—DOCM—for files that contain macros.)

Key Points

- If you want to send a document to people who might not have Word installed on their computers, you can save the document in a more universal file format so that it can be opened in other programs.

- Word documents can easily be converted to Web pages. In Web Layout view, you can see how a document will look in a Web browser, and you can make adjustments to the layout from within Word.

- The XML format stores information in such a way that it can be extracted and manipulated in a variety of ways in a variety of programs. With Word, you can convert a document to XML with a straightforward save process, or you can use a schema to ensure the validity of the document's structure before saving it as an XML file.

Chapter at a Glance

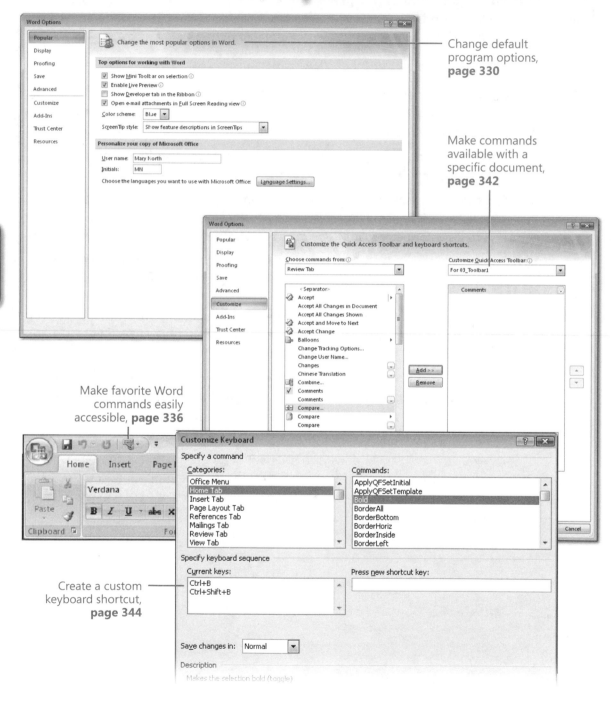

Change default program options, **page 330**

Make commands available with a specific document, **page 342**

Make favorite Word commands easily accessible, **page 336**

Create a custom keyboard shortcut, **page 344**

12 Customizing Word

In this chapter, you will learn to:

✔ Change default program options.

✔ Make favorite Word commands easily accessible.

✔ Make commands available with a specific document.

✔ Create a custom keyboard shortcut.

If you use Microsoft Office Word 2007 only occasionally, you might be perfectly happy with the default environment options and behind-the-scenes settings. However, if you create a lot of documents, you might find yourself wishing that you could change aspects of the program to customize it for the kinds of documents you create.

In this chapter, you will explore the pages of the Word Options window to understand the ways in which you can customize the program. Then you will add buttons to the Word 2007 Quick Access Toolbar, and to a document's custom toolbar. Finally, you will create a keyboard shortcut for a command so that you can invoke it without using your mouse.

See Also Do you need only a quick refresher on the topics in this chapter? See the Quick Reference entries on pages xxxix–lxiii.

Important Before you can use the practice files in this chapter, you need to install them from the book's companion CD to their default location. See "Using the Book's CD" on page xxv for more information.

Troubleshooting Graphics and operating system–related instructions in this book reflect the Windows Vista user interface. If your computer is running Microsoft Windows XP and you experience trouble following the instructions as written, please refer to the "Information for Readers Running Windows XP" section at the beginning of this book.

Changing Default Program Options

In earlier chapters, we mentioned that you can change settings in the Word Options window to customize the Word environment in various ways. For example, you can create new AutoCorrect entries, adjust the save period for AutoRecover information, and determine the Print setting to use. Knowing which settings are where in the Word Options window will make the customizing process more efficient.

In this exercise, you will open the Word Options window and explore several of the available pages. There are no practice files for this exercise.

BE SURE TO start Word before beginning this exercise.

Bold

1. On the **Home** tab, in the **Font** group, point to the **Bold** button.

   Word displays a ScreenTip that includes the button name, its keyboard shortcut, and a description of its purpose.

   See Also For information about keyboard shortcuts, see "Creating a Custom Keyboard Shortcut" later in this chapter.

Microsoft Office
Button

2. Click the **Microsoft Office Button**, and then at the bottom of the Office menu, click **Word Options**.

   The Word Options window opens, displaying the Popular page.

Word Options	
Popular	Change the most popular options in Word.
Display	
Proofing	**Top options for working with Word**
Save	☑ Show Mini Toolbar on selection
Advanced	☑ Enable Live Preview
	☐ Show Developer tab in the Ribbon
Customize	☑ Open e-mail attachments in Full Screen Reading view
Add-Ins	Color scheme: Blue ▾
Trust Center	ScreenTip style: Show feature descriptions in ScreenTips ▾
Resources	**Personalize your copy of Microsoft Office**
	User name: Mary North
	Initials: MN
	Choose the languages you want to use with Microsoft Office: [Language Settings...]
	OK Cancel

3. Under **Top options for working with Word**, click the **Color scheme** arrow, and then in the list, click **Silver**.

> **Tip** If having the Mini toolbar appear when you select text is more of a hindrance than a help, you can disable that feature by clearing the Show Mini Toolbar On Selection check box. Similarly, you could disable the live preview of styles and formatting by clearing the Enable Live Preview check box. If you create documents for international audiences, you can make additional editing languages available by clicking Language Settings, choosing the languages you want to have available, and then clicking OK.

4. Click the **ScreenTip style** arrow, and then in the list, click **Don't show feature descriptions in ScreenTips**.

5. Under **Personalize your copy of Microsoft Office**, verify that the **User Name** and **Initials** are correct, or change them to the way you want them to appear.

6. Click **OK** to close the Word Options window.

   The program window elements are now silver.

7. In the **Font** group, point to the **Bold** button.

   The ScreenTip now includes only the button name and its keyboard shortcut.

8. Display the **Word Options** window, and in the page list in the left pane, click **Display**.

   On this page, you can adjust how documents look on the screen and when printed

9. In the page list, click **Proofing**.

This page provides options for adjusting the AutoCorrect settings and for refining the spell-checking process.

See Also For information about AutoCorrect and checking spelling, see "Correcting Spelling and Grammatical Errors" in Chapter 2, "Editing and Proofreading Documents."

10. Display the **Save** page.

On this page, you can change the default document format; the AutoRecover file save rate and location; the default location to which Word saves new files you create; and the default location for files you check out from document management servers (such as Microsoft Office SharePoint Server 2007) and drafts of those files saved while you are working offline. You can also specify whether you want the fonts used within the current document to be embedded in the document, in the event that someone who opens the document doesn't have those fonts on his or her computer.

11. Under **Save documents**, click the **Save files in this format** arrow.

In the list, notice the many formats in which you can save files. One of these is the Word 97-2003 Document format that creates .doc files compatible with earlier versions of Word. If you have upgraded to Word 2007 but your colleagues are still working in an earlier version of the program, you might want to select this option so that they will be able to view and work with any document you create.

> **Tip** If you want to save just one document in a format that is compatible with earlier versions of the program, you can point to the Save As arrow on the Office menu, and then click Word 97-2003 to display the Save As dialog box with this format already selected as the Save As Type setting.

12. Click away from the list to close it, and then display the **Advanced** page.

This page includes options related to editing document content; displaying documents on-screen; printing, saving, and sharing documents; and a variety of other options.

13. Take a few minutes to explore all the options on this page.

Although these options are labeled advanced, they are the ones you are most likely to want to adjust to fit the way you work. At the bottom of the page are the following buttons:

- File Locations, which you click to change the default locations of various types of files associated with Word and its documents.

- Web Options, which you click to adjust settings for converting a document to a Web page.

- Service Options, which you click to adjust settings related to working with documents stored on SharePoint sites.

See Also For information about converting a Word document to a Web page, see "Creating and Modifying a Web Document" in Chapter 11, "Creating Documents for Use Outside of Word." For information about storing documents on SharePoint sites, see "Using Document Workspaces" in Chapter 10, "Collaborating with Others."

14. Display the **Trust Center** page.

This page provides links to information about privacy and security. It also provides links to the Trust Center settings that control the actions Word takes in response to documents that are provided by certain people or companies, that are saved in certain locations, or that contain ActiveX controls or macros.

15. Under **Microsoft Office Word Trust Center**, click **Trust Center Settings**, and then in the page list in the left pane of the Trust Center window, click **Trusted Locations**.

On this page, you can specify the locations from which Word will not block content.

16. Explore the other pages of the Trust Center window, and then click **Cancel** to return to the Word Options window.

17. In the **Word Options** window, display the **Resources** page.

On this page are links for activating, updating, and maintaining your Office programs. Most of these links require that you have Internet access.

BE SURE TO reverse any changes you don't want to keep before moving on.

CLOSE the Word Options window.

See Also For information about using the settings available on the Customize page, see the topics that follow. For information about working with add-ins, see the sidebar "Using Add-Ins" in Chapter 11, "Creating Documents for Use Outside of Word."

Making Favorite Word Commands Easily Accessible

If Word 2007 is the first version of the program you have ever worked with, you will by now have become accustomed to working with commands represented as buttons on the Ribbon. However, if you have upgraded from an earlier version, you might have identified a few commands that no longer seem to be available.

> **Tip** You can find out where a favorite Word 2003 command appears on the Office menu or Ribbon by searching Word Help for *2003 commands*, and then displaying the *Reference: Locations Of Word 2003 Commands In Word 2007* topic. Scroll to the bottom of the topic and click the Word Ribbon Mapping Workbook link under New Locations Of Familiar Commands.
>
> You can find a list of all the commands that do not appear on the Ribbon but are still available in Word by displaying the Customize page of the Word Options window and then clicking Commands Not In The Ribbon in the Choose Commands From list.

For the 2007 Microsoft Office release, Microsoft conducted extensive research to find out how people actually use the programs in the Office suite. As a result, a few Word features that seemed superfluous have been abandoned, and a few others that were used very rarely have been pushed off to one side. If you sorely miss one of these side-lined features, you can make it a part of your Word environment by adding it to the Quick Access Toolbar.

You might also want to customize the Quick Access Toolbar if you regularly use buttons that are scattered on various tabs of the Ribbon and don't want to switch between tabs to access the buttons. If you use only a few buttons, you can add them to the Quick Access Toolbar and then hide the Ribbon by double-clicking the active tab—the Quick Access Toolbar and tab names remain visible. (You can temporarily redisplay the Ribbon by clicking the tab you want to view, or permanently redisplay it by double-clicking any tab.)

> **Tip** As you add buttons to the Quick Access Toolbar, it expands to accommodate them. If you add many buttons, it might become difficult to view the text in the title bar, or all the buttons might not be visible. To resolve this problem, you can move the Quick Access Toolbar below the Ribbon by clicking the Customize Quick Access Toolbar button and then clicking Show Below The Ribbon.

In this exercise, you will add a button to the Word 2007 Quick Access Toolbar.

USE the *02_Commands* document. This practice file is located in the *Chapter12* subfolder under *SBS_Word2007*.

OPEN the *02_Commands* document.

Customize Quick
Access Toolbar

1. At the right end of the **Quick Access Toolbar**, click the **Customize Quick Access Toolbar** button.

   By default, the Save, Undo, and Repeat buttons appear on the Quick Access Toolbar.

You can add a button to the toolbar for any of the common commands that appear in the Customize Quick Access Toolbar list by clicking the command in the list.

Clicking an inactive command displays its button on the toolbar.

2. In the **Customize Quick Access Toolbar** list, click **More Commands**.

The Word Options window opens, displaying the Customize page.

You can add a less common command to the Quick Access Toolbar by selecting it in the list of available commands on the left side of the page, and then clicking Add (or double-clicking the command) to copy it to the list of toolbar commands on the right side of the page.

3. Click the **Choose commands from** arrow, and then in the list, click **Commands Not in the Ribbon**.

The available commands list changes to include only the commands that are available in Word 2007 but do not appear on any tab of the Ribbon.

4. In the available commands list, click **AutoText**, and then click **Add** to add the command to the global Quick Access Toolbar.

The arrow to the right of the command indicates that clicking the AutoText button will display a list of options. In this case, clicking the AutoText button will display a gallery from which you can insert a saved text item in a document.

5. At the top of the available commands list, click **<Separator>**, and then click **Add**.

The separator—a horizontal line indicating the beginning or end of a group of commands—appears at the bottom of the toolbar commands list.

Move Up

6. In the toolbar commands list, click **<Separator>**, and then click the **Move Up** button.

The separator moves up one position to separate the three default commands from the AutoText command. Buttons appear from left to right on the Quick Access Toolbar in the same order that they appear from top to bottom in the toolbar commands list.

7. In the **Word Options** window, click **OK**.

   The Quick Access Toolbar expands to accommodate the separator bar and button you added.

   Separator ⌐ ⌐AutoText
   bar │ │ button

8. On the first page of the document, position the insertion point to the right of *For general deliveries* and to the left of the colon, press ⎡Space⎤, and then type to Consolidated Messenger.

9. Select the words **Consolidated Messenger**, and on the **Quick Access Toolbar**, click the **AutoText** button.

   AutoText

10. In the **AutoText** gallery, click **Save Selection to AutoText Gallery**.

    The Create New Building Block dialog box opens.

    See Also For information about building blocks, see "Inserting Saved Text" in Chapter 2, "Editing and Proofreading Documents," and "Inserting Ready-Made Document Parts" in Chapter 8, "Working with Longer Documents."

11. Type cm in the **Name** box, and then click **OK**.

12. Position the insertion point at the left end of the *Phone numbers* paragraph, press ⎡Enter⎤, press the ⎡↑⎤ key, type Urgent deliveries should be taken directly to the and then press ⎡Space⎤.

13. On the **Quick Access Toolbar**, click the **AutoText** button.

    The AutoText gallery now includes the *Consolidated Messenger* entry you just added.

General

cm

Consolidated Messenger

JC

JC

Joyce Cox

Joyce Cox

[icon] Save Selection to AutoText Gallery

14. In the **AutoText** gallery, click **cm** to insert the saved text in the document.

> **Tip** You can also replace an AutoText name with its corresponding entry by typing the name and then pressing the F3 key.

15. Press [Space], and then type employee to whom they are addressed.

16. At the right end of the **Quick Access Toolbar**, click the **Customize Quick Access Toolbar** button, and then in the list, click **More Commands**.

17. In the **Word Options** window, click **Reset**. Then in the message box asking you to confirm that you want to restore the Quick Access Toolbar to its default command set, click **Yes**.

18. Close the **Word Options** window.

The AutoText button and separator no longer appear on the Quick Access Toolbar.

CLOSE the *02_Commands* document without saving your changes.

> **Important** When you quit Word, you will be asked whether you want to save the Building Blocks template, which is where AutoText entries are saved. To discard the AutoText entry you created in this exercise, click No.

Making Commands Available with a Specific Document

In addition to customizing the global Quick Access Toolbar to make a set of buttons available for all documents, you can customize the Quick Access Toolbar for a specific document. For example, to work with a document that contains a complex table-based layout, you might want to increase your efficiency by providing one-click access to commands that allow you to turn the rulers and gridlines on or off without switching to the View tab.

See Also   For information about table-based layouts, see "Using a Table to Control Page Layout" in Chapter 5, "Presenting Information in Columns and Tables."

In this exercise, you will add a button to a document-specific Quick Access Toolbar. Then after testing the button, you will remove it from the toolbar.

> **USE** the *03_Toolbar1* and *03_Toolbar2* documents. These practice files are located in the *Chapter12* subfolder under *SBS_Word2007*.
> **OPEN** the *03_Toolbar1* document.

Customize Quick
Access Toolbar

1. At the right end of the **Quick Access Toolbar**, click the **Customize Quick Access Toolbar** button, and then in the list, click **More Commands**.

   The Word Options window opens, displaying the Customize page. A list of available commands appears on the left side of the page, and a list of the commands available from the global Quick Access Toolbar appears on the right.

2. Click the **Customize Quick Access Toolbar** arrow, and then in the list, click **For 03_Toolbar1**.

   > **Troubleshooting**   If the current document is read-only, the only option available in the list is For All Documents (Default). You cannot customize the Quick Access Toolbar for a read-only document.

   The toolbar command list is now empty, ready for you to specify which commands should appear on this document-specific toolbar.

3. Click the **Choose commands from** arrow, and then in the list, click **Review Tab**.

   The available commands list now contains all the commands that are available from the Review tab on the Ribbon, including several that are related to adding, editing, and deleting comments.

4. In the available commands list, click the second **Comments** command (the one with the arrow button to its right). Then click **Add**.

The Comments command appears in the toolbar commands list. The arrow button to the right of the command indicates that clicking this button on the Quick Access Toolbar will display a menu of options.

Arrow button

5. Click **OK**.

The Quick Access Toolbar now includes the Save, Undo, and Repeat buttons from the default toolbar and the Comments button from the custom toolbar. The custom toolbar appears within a separate box on the Quick Access Toolbar.

6. Open the *03_Toolbar2* document from the *Chapter12* subfolder, notice that the custom toolbar is not available for this document, and then close it.

7. Scroll the *03_Toolbar1* document, and at the end of the paragraph below the numbered list, select **thirsting for more**.

8. On the **Quick Access Toolbar**, click the **Comments** button.

Although no arrow appears next to the button, a group of comment options appears.

Comments

Comments group

9. In the **Comments** group, click **New Comment**, and in the comment balloon, type *Paolini now says he is "finally making good headway" on the third book.* Then click anywhere in the text of the document (not the balloon).

10. Click the **Customize Quick Access Toolbar** button, and then click **More Commands**.

11. On the **Customize** page of the Word Options window, click **For 03_Toolbar1** in the **Customize Quick Access Toolbar** list to display the list of buttons on the custom toolbar. Then click **Reset**.

12. In the **Reset Customizations** message box, click **Yes** to return the document-specific toolbar to its default contents (empty). Then click **OK**.

Now only the buttons assigned to the default Quick Access Toolbar are visible.

CLOSE the *03_Toolbar1* document without saving your changes.

> **Tip** If you send a document for which you have created a custom toolbar to someone else, or if you make the document available for collaborative development in a document work-space, the custom toolbar is available to anyone who opens the document in Word 2007.

Creating a Custom Keyboard Shortcut

Another way to access commands quickly is to use *keyboard shortcuts*—combinations of two or more keys that invoke a command. Keyboard shortcuts are particularly efficient if your hands are already on the keyboard typing document text. Word has a large variety of built-in keyboard shortcuts. For example, to format text as bold, you can simply select it and then press Ctrl+B.

If a command you use frequently doesn't have a built-in keyboard shortcut, you can create one from the Customize page of the Word Options window. Clicking Customize at the bottom of this page opens the Customize Keyboard dialog box, where you can choose the categories and commands you want and assign keyboard shortcuts.

In this exercise, you will assign keyboard shortcuts to two commands, and then test the keyboard shortcuts. There are no practice files for this exercise.

> **OPEN** a new blank document.

Customize Quick
Access Toolbar

1. At the right end of the **Quick Access Toolbar**, click the **Customize Quick Access Toolbar** button, and then in the list, click **More Commands**.

   The Word Options window opens, displaying the Customize page.

2. At the bottom of the window, to the right of **Keyboard shortcuts**, click **Customize**.

   The Customize Keyboard dialog box opens. The Ribbon tabs are listed in the Categories box on the left, and the commands available for the selected category are listed in the Commands box on the right.

3. In the **Categories** list, click **Home Tab**, and then in the **Commands** list, click **Bold**.

   In the Current Keys box, Word displays the keyboard shortcuts already assigned to the Bold command.

Customize Keyboard	? ✕

Specify a command

Categories:

- Office Menu
- Home Tab
- Insert Tab
- Page Layout Tab
- References Tab
- Mailings Tab
- Review Tab
- View Tab

Commands:

- ApplyQFSetInitial
- ApplyQFSetTemplate
- Bold
- BorderAll
- BorderBottom
- BorderHoriz
- BorderInside
- BorderLeft

Specify keyboard sequence

Current keys:

- Ctrl+B
- Ctrl+Shift+B

Press new shortcut key:

Save changes in: Normal

Description

Makes the selection bold (toggle)

[Assign] [Remove] [Reset All...]   [Close]

> **Tip** To delete an existing keyboard shortcut to make it available for reassignment, select it in the Current Keys box, and then click Remove.

4. In the **Commands** list, click **DecreaseIndent**.

5. Click to position the insertion point in the **Press new shortcut key** box, and then press Ctrl+D.

   Under the Current Keys box, Word tells you that this keyboard shortcut is already assigned to the FormatFont command.

6. Press the Backspace key (not Del) to clear the **Press new shortcut key** box, and then press Alt+D.

   Under the Current Keys box, Word tells you that this keyboard shortcut is currently unassigned (unless you have already assigned it to a different command).

7. Click **Assign**.

8. Repeat Steps 4, 5, and 7 to assign the keyboard combination Alt+I to the **IncreaseIndent** command.

9. Close the **Customize Keyboard** dialog box and the **Word Options** window.

> **Tip** Using the options in the Save Changes In list, you can save new keyboard shortcuts either in a template to make them available to all documents using that template, or in a specific document to make them available only within that document.

   Now let's test the new keyboard shortcut.

10. On the **View** tab, in the **Show/Hide** group, select the **Ruler** check box to display the horizontal and vertical rulers.

11. Press Alt+I twice to indent the paragraph, and then press Alt+D once to decrease the indent.

   On the ruler, the indent markers jump to the 1-inch mark and then jump back to the 0.5-inch mark.

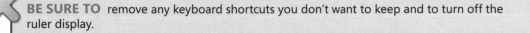

BE SURE TO remove any keyboard shortcuts you don't want to keep and to turn off the ruler display.

Tracking Down Built-In Keyboard Shortcuts

The list of built-in Word keyboard shortcuts is extensive and too long to reproduce here. To print a list of these shortcuts:

1. At the right end of the Ribbon, click the **Help** button.
2. In the **Search** box, type keyboard shortcuts, and then click **Search**.
3. In the results list, click **Keyboard shortcuts for Microsoft Office Word**.
4. Click the **Show All** link at the beginning of the topic to display all the text, and then on the toolbar, click the **Print** button.

Key Points

- The Word environment is flexible and can be customized to meet your needs.
- Most of the environment settings are gathered on the pages of the Word Options window.
- You can provide one-click access to any Word 2007 command by adding a button for it to the Quick Access Toolbar, either for all documents or for a single document.
- When the major work in a document involves typing, you can increase efficiency by using keyboard shortcuts, because you don't have to take your hands off the keyboard to use your mouse.
- It's worth taking the time to memorize common built-in keyboard shortcuts and to create custom shortcuts for favorite commands that don't already have them.

Glossary

add-in A utility that adds specialized functionality to a program.

attribute Individual items of character formatting, such as style or color, which determine how text looks.

balloon A box containing a comment, deletion, or formatting change that appears to the right of a document when Track Changes is turned on.

bar chart A chart in which data is plotted in rows to illustrate comparisons among individual items.

blog A personal Web site.

bookmark A location in a document that marks text so that it can be found quickly.

building blocks Frequently used text saved in a gallery, from which it can be inserted quickly into a document.

bullet A small graphic to the left of each item in a bulleted list.

caption A description of a graphic or figure.

cell A box at the intersection of a column and row in a table or worksheet.

cell address The location of a cell, expressed as its column letter and row number, as in A1.

character formatting The collection of attributes applied to text.

character spacing The space between characters, which can be expanded or contracted so that characters are pushed apart or pulled together.

character style A variation of a font, such as bold or italic.

chart A visual representation of numeric data.

chart area The entire area occupied by a chart, including the legend and any titles.

chevron The « or » characters that surround each merge field in a main document; also known as *guillemet* characters.

Click and Type A feature that allows you to double-click a blank area of a document to position the insertion point in that location, with the appropriate paragraph alignment already in place.

Clipboard A storage area shared by all Office programs where cut or copied items are stored.

column In a chart, a vertical representation of plotted data from a table or worksheet. In page layout, the area between margins where text is allowed to flow. (Pages can have a single column or multiple columns.)

column break A break inserted in the text of a column to force the text below it to move to the next column.

column chart A chart in which data is plotted in columns to illustrate comparisons among individual items or changes over time.

column headings The gray boxes at the top of the columns in a worksheet. See also *row headings*.

comment A note inserted in a document and displayed either in a balloon or the reviewing pane.

cross-reference entry An entry in an index that refers readers to a related entry.

cycle diagram A type of diagram used to represent a circular sequence of steps, tasks, or events; or the relationship of a set of steps, tasks, or events to a central, core element.

data marker A graphic representation of a plotted value, such as a bar or column.

data point A plotted value in a table or worksheet.

data series A set of related data points in a table or worksheet.

data source A file that provides the variable information used in the mail-merge process.

demote In an outline, the process of changing a heading to a lower-level heading or body text.

desktop publishing A process that creates pages by combining text and objects such as tables and graphics in a visually appealing way.

destination file A file into which you insert an object created in another program.

diagram A visual representation of information, such as a process or a relationship.

Dialog Box Launcher A button that launches a dialog box containing options for refining a command.

digital signature A security mechanism used on the Internet that relies on two keys, one public and one private, that are used to encrypt messages before transmission and to decrypt them on receipt.

Document Map A pane that displays a linked outline of a document's headings and allows you to jump to a heading in the document by clicking it in the Document Map.

document window The window that provides a workspace for an open document.

document workspace A space on a SharePoint site, created to facilitate the collaborative development of a single document.

Draft view A view that displays the content of a document with a simplified layout.

drag-and-drop editing A way of moving or copying selected text by dragging it with the mouse pointer.

dragging A way of moving objects by pointing to them, holding down the mouse button, moving the mouse pointer to the desired location, and releasing the button.

drawing canvas A graphical object on which you can draw shapes and objects to create a compound graphic, which moves and changes size with the canvas.

drawing object An object created with Word, such as a shape, a diagram, or WordArt text.

drop cap An enlarged, decorative capital letter that appears at the beginning of a paragraph.

embedded object An object that is created in a different program but that is incorporated into a Word document.

endnote A note that appears at the end of a section or the document to add tangential information to a discussion or report. See also *footnote*.

Extensible Markup Language (XML) A system for coding the structure of text documents and other forms of data so that they can be used in a variety of environments.

field A placeholder that tells Word to supply the specified information in the specified way. Also, the set of information of a specific type in a data source, such as all the last names in a contacts list.

field name A first-row cell in a data source that identifies data in the column below.

file A named set of information, such as a program or data created with that program.

file format The system used to code a file so that the program that created it, or other programs, can open and work with it.

filter To extract records from a data source, excluding records that don't match the filtering criteria.

flow The way text continues from the bottom of one column to the top of the next column.

font A complete set of characters that all have the same design.

font color One of a range of colors that can be applied to text.

font effect An attribute, such as superscript, small capital letters, or shadow, that can be applied to a font.

font size The size of the characters in a font, in points.

font style An attribute that changes the look of text. The most common font styles are regular (or plain), italic, bold, and bold italic.

footer A region at the bottom of a page whose text can be applied to all or some of the pages in a document.

footnote A note or citation that appears at the bottom of a page to explain, comment on, or provide references for text in a document. See also *endnote*.

formula A mathematical equation that performs a calculation, such as addition.

Full Screen Reading view A view that displays as much of the content of the document as will fit in the screen at a size that is comfortable for reading.

gallery A grouping of thumbnails that display options visually.

graphic Any piece of art used to illustrate or convey information or to add visual interest to a document.

gridlines Lines that visually clarify the information in a chart.

group A category of buttons on a tab.

grouping Assembling several objects, such as graphics, into a single unit so they act as one object and can easily be moved and sized.

guillemet characters The « and » characters that surround each merge field in a main document; also known as *chevrons*.

header A region at the top of a page whose text can be repeated on all or some of the pages in a document.

hierarchy diagram A diagram that illustrates the structure of an organization or entity.

hover To pause the pointer over an object, such as a menu name or button, for a second or two to display more information, such as a submenu or ScreenTip.

Hypertext Markup Language (HTML) A tagging system used to code documents so that they can be viewed as pages in a Web browser.

indent marker A marker on the horizontal ruler that controls the indentation of text from the left or right side of a document.

index An alphabetical list of concepts and terms and the page numbers where they are found.

index entry An entry in the body of a document that tags terms to be included in Word's automated construction of an index.

index entry field The XE field, including the braces ({}), that defines an index entry.

justify To make all lines of text in a paragraph or column fit the width of the document or column, with even margins on each side.

keyboard shortcut A combination of two or more keys that perform an action when pressed together.

landscape The orientation of a horizontal page whose width is larger that its height.

legend A key that identifies the series in a chart.

line break A manual break that forces the text that follows it to the next line. Also called a *text wrapping break*.

line graph A graph in which lines are used to show changes in values over time.

linked object An object that exists in a source file and that is inserted in a document with a link to that source file.

list diagram A diagram in which lists of related or independent information are visually represented.

live preview A feature of a thumbnail that displays what an option will look like if applied to a document.

mail merge A process used to personalize individual documents based on information in a data source.

main document The mail merge document that contains the information that doesn't change.

manual page break A page break inserted to force subsequent information to appear on the next page.

margin Blank space around the column in which text can flow on the page.

matrix diagram A diagram used to show the relationship of components to a whole.

merge field Fields in a main document that tell Word where to insert corresponding information from a data source.

Microsoft Clip Organizer A tool that lets you arrange clip art images, pictures, sounds, and movie clips into collections.

Microsoft Office Button A button that provides access to a menu with commands that manage Word and Word documents as a whole (rather than document content).

Microsoft Office Word Help button A button with a question mark (?) at the right end of the Ribbon that can be clicked to open the Word Help window.

nested table A table that is positioned inside another table.

note separator A line that separates footnotes or endnotes from regular text.

object An item, such as a graphic, video clip, sound file, or worksheet, that can be inserted in a Word document and then selected and modified.

Office menu A menu that contains commands related to managing documents (such as creating, saving, and printing). This menu takes the place of the File menu that appeared in previous versions of Word.

orientation The direction—horizontal or vertical—in which a page is laid out.

orphan At the bottom of a page, a single line of a paragraph that continues on the next page.

Outline view A view that shows headings and body text and can be used to evaluate and reorganize the structure of a document.

paragraph In word processing, a block of text of any length that ends when you press the Enter key.

paragraph formatting Collectively, the settings used to vary the look of paragraphs.

paragraph style A set of formatting that can be applied to the paragraph containing the insertion point by selecting the style from a list.

parent folder The folder in which another folder is contained.

permissions Authorization that allows access to designated documents or programs.

picture A scanned photograph, clip art, or another type of image created with a program other than Word.

pie chart A chart used to show how parts relate to the whole.

plot area The area bordered by the category (x) and value (y) axes in a chart.

point The unit of measure for expressing the size of characters in a font, where 72 points equals 1 inch.

portrait The orientation of a vertical page whose width is smaller that its height.

post Content published to a blog.

Print Layout view A view that shows how a document will look when printed.

process diagram A diagram used to visually represent the ordered set of steps required to complete a task.

promote In an outline, to change body text to a heading, or to change a heading to a higher-level heading.

pyramid diagram A diagram used to illustrate proportional or interconnected relationships.

query Selection criteria for extracting information from a data source for use in the mail merge process.

Quick Access Toolbar A toolbar that displays the Save, Undo, and Repeat buttons by default, but can be customized to show other commands.

quick table A table with sample data that you can customize.

read-only Available for viewing but protected from alterations.

record A set of fields of information about a single item in a data source, often structured in a row.

reference mark An indicator in the text of a document that further information is available in a corresponding footnote or endnote.

relationship diagram A diagram used to show convergent, divergent, overlapping, merging, or containment elements.

revision marks Underlines, strike-through marks, and colored text that distinguishes revised text from original text.

revisions Changes in a document that are marked with revision marks when Word's Track Changes feature is turned on.

Ribbon An area across the top of the screen that makes almost all the capabilities of Word available in a single area.

row headings The gray boxes at the left end of the rows in a worksheet. See also *column headings*.

ScreenTip Information displayed in a small window when you rest the pointer over a button or window element.

section break A break inserted so that subsequent information can have different page formatting (such as different orientation) than preceding information.

select To highlight an item in preparation for making some change to it.

selection area An area in a document's left margin in which you can click and drag to select blocks of text.

sizing handle Small circles, squares, or sets of dots that appear at the corners and sides of a selected object. These handles can be dragged to change the shape of an object.

smart tag A flag that identifies information of a certain type, such as an address. Click the button associated with the tag to quickly perform common tasks related to that type of information.

SmartArt graphic A predefined set of formatting for creating and formatting a diagram.

soft page break A page break that Word inserts when the text reaches the bottom margin of a page.

source file A file containing an object that is inserted in a destination file.

stacked graphics Graphics that overlap each other.

Standard Generalized Markup Language (SGML) A system for coding the structure of text and other data so that it can be used in a variety of environments.

status bar An area across the bottom of the program window that gives information about the current document.

Styles A gallery of text formatting that can be applied quickly to paragraphs and characters.

subentry In an index, a subordinate entry.

tab An area on the Ribbon that contains buttons organized in groups.

tab leader A repeating character (usually a dot or dash) that separates text before the tab from text or a number after it.

tab stop A location in the text column where text will align after you press the Tab key to insert a tab character.

table of authorities A table used in legal papers and other types of official documents that lists statutes, citations, case numbers, and similar information.

table of contents A sequential list of the headings in a document and the page numbers where they are found.

table of figures A list of graphics, pictures, or figures and their corresponding captions.

tabular list A list that arranges text in simple columns separated by left, right, centered, or decimal tab stops.

tag A command inserted in a document that specifies how the document, or a portion of the document, should be formatted.

template A predefined set of text, formatting, and graphics, stored in a special type of document that can be used as the basis for other documents.

text wrapping break A manual break that forces the text that follows it to the next line. Also called a *line break*.

theme A predefined set of font and color specifications that can be applied to any document.

Thesaurus A tool that supplies synonyms for a selected word.

thumbnail A picture representation of choices available in a gallery; or of pages in a document.

tick-mark label The labels along each axis in a chart, identifying the data.

title bar An area at the top of the program window that displays the name of the active document.

transform A command that extracts specified information from an XML file.

View toolbar A toolbar on the right end of the status bar that contains tools for adjusting the view of document content.

watermark Faint text or a graphic that appears in the background of all the pages of a document.

Web Layout view A view that shows how a document will look when viewed in a Web browser.

Web page An HTML document that can be viewed in a Web browser.

widow At the top of a page, a single line of a paragraph that continues from the previous page.

wildcard characters When using the Find and Replace dialog box, characters that serve as placeholders for a single character, such as *?ffect* for *affect* and *effect*, or for multiple characters.

word processing The writing, editing, and formatting of documents in a word processor.

word wrap The automatic breaking of a line of text when it reaches the page margin.

WordArt A gallery of text styles that you can use to create text with special effects.

x-axis Also called a *category axis*, the vertical aspect of a chart, representing the categories of the data.

XML schema A description of a document's structure.

y-axis Also called a *value axis*, the horizontal aspect of a chart, showing the values of the data.

z-axis Also called a *series axis*, the depth aspect of a 3-D chart, showing a series of data.

Index

C

What do you think of this book?

We want to hear from you!

Do you have a few minutes to participate in a brief online survey?

Microsoft is interested in hearing your feedback so we can continually improve our books and learning resources for you.

To participate in our survey, please visit:

www.microsoft.com/learning/booksurvey/

...and enter this book's ISBN-10 number (appears above barcode on back cover*). As a thank-you to survey participants in the United States and Canada, each month we'll randomly select five respondents to win one of five $100 gift certificates from a leading online merchant. At the conclusion of the survey, you can enter the drawing by providing your e-mail address, which will be used for prize notification only.

Thanks in advance for your input. Your opinion counts!

* Where to find the ISBN-10 on back cover

ISBN-13: 000-0-0000-00000-0
ISBN-10: 0-0000-00000-0

00000

0 000000 000000

Example only. Each book has unique ISBN.

Microsoft Press

No purchase necessary. Void where prohibited. Open only to residents of the 50 United States (includes District of Columbia) and Canada (void in Quebec). For official rules and entry dates see:

www.microsoft.com/learning/booksurvey/